Redemption, Rehabilitation and Risk Management

D1602554

Redemption, Rehabilitation and Risk Management provides the most accessible and up-to-date account of the origins and development of the probation service in England and Wales.

The book explores and explains the changes that have taken place in the service, the pressures and tensions that have shaped change, and the role played by government, research, Napo and key individuals from its origins in the nineteenth century up to the plans for the service outlined by the Conservative/Liberal Democrat government.

The probation service is a key agency in dealing with offenders; providing reports for the courts that assist sentencing decisions; supervising released prisoners in the community and working with the victims of crime. Yet despite dealing with more offenders than the prison service, at lower cost and with reconviction rates that are lower than those associated with prisons, the probation service has been ignored, misrepresented, taken for granted and marginalised, and probation staff have been sneered at as 'do-gooders'. The service as a whole is currently under serious threat as a result of budget cuts, organisational restructuring, changes in training and increasingly punitive policies. This book details how probation has come to such a pass.

By tracing the evolution of the probation service, *Redemption, Rehabilitation and Risk Management* not only sheds invaluable light on a much misunderstood criminal justice agency, but offers a unique examination of twentieth-century criminal justice policy. It will be essential reading for students and academics in criminal justice and criminology.

George Mair has been Professor of Criminal Justice in the School of Law, Liverpool John Moores University since 1995. Previously, he was Principal Research Officer in the Home Office Research and Planning Unit. He is a leading authority on community penalties and has published widely on this topic. He was a member of the Merseyside Probation Board, 2001–7.

Lol Burke is Senior Lecturer in Criminal Justice, Liverpool John Moores University. He has worked as a Probation Officer and a Senior Probation Officer. He was involved in the delivery of probation training prior to his appointment at LJMU. He is editor of the *Probation Journal*.

'This is an important, timely, and hugely engaging and challenging book. The esteemed authors offer a sophisticated account of the changes within the probation service over the past hundred years and critical reflection on what has happened since. Essential reading for students and academics in criminal justice and criminology, of course, but every politician and policy maker should be required to read the book too, and to reflect and act upon its key messages.'

Professor Loraine Gelsthorpe, Institute of Criminology,
University of Cambridge

'*Redemption, Rehabilitation and Risk Management* is a comprehensive, engaging and timely history of the probation service in England and Wales which will be an essential resource for students and academics alike. Drawing on their considerable experience in research and practice contexts, George Mair and Lol Burke have produced an extremely valuable contribution to the literature on probation which charts the fascinating evolution, over more than a century, of a key player in the criminal justice system.'

Dr Gwen Robinson, Reader in Criminal Justice, Sheffield University

Redemption, Rehabilitation and Risk Management

A history of probation

George Mair and Lol Burke

 Routledge
Taylor & Francis Group

LONDON AND NEW YORK

First published 2012
by Routledge
2 Park Square, Milton Park, Abingdon, Oxon, OX14 4RN

Simultaneously published in the USA and Canada
by Routledge
711 Third Avenue, New York, NY 10017

Routledge is an imprint of the Taylor & Francis Group, an informa business

British Library Cataloguing in Publication Data
A catalogue record for this book is available from the British Library

Library of Congress Cataloguing in Publication Data
  Mair, George.
  Redemption, rehabilitation and risk management : a history
of probation / George Mair and Lol Burke.
     p. cm.
  1. Probation–Great Britain. 2. Rehabilitation–Great Britain. I. Burke,
Lol. II. Title.
  HV9345.A5M35 2011
  364.6'30941–dc22   2011006344

ISBN 13: 978-1-84392-250-6 hbk
ISBN 13: 978-1-84392-249-0 pbk
ISBN 13: 978-0-20380-596-1 ebk

Typeset in Times New Roman
by Glyph International

MIX
Paper from
responsible sources
FSC   FSC® C004839
www.fsc.org

Printed and bound in Great Britain by
TJ International Ltd, Padstow, Cornwall

Contents

List of tables

Acknowledgements

For a number of reasons, this book took rather longer to complete than we had planned and we are grateful to Brian Willan for his patience (little did we realise that he would have retired before we finished writing). That virtue seems to have been inherited by his daughter Julia who has waited without complaint.

Our thanks are also due to Judith Rumgay, who read and commented astutely on the opening chapters, and our colleague Matthew Millings who read the whole manuscript.

Part of Chapter 7 is based on George Mair's article 'Developments in Probation in England and Wales 1984–93', contained in a 1996 collection of essays edited by Gill McIvor, entitled *Working With Offenders* (London: Jessica Kingsley).

Finally, of course, we owe our families a serious debt of gratitude for all their understanding and support while we worked on the book. George would like to thank Carmel for her unfailing love and patience, as well as his children Ruth and Ethan. Lol would like to acknowledge the debt of thanks he owes his parents – Morgan and Veronica – who passed away before this book was completed. The love and support they gave throughout their lives continues in the memories of their family.

Introduction

In 2007 the probation service in England and Wales was 100 years old. Its birthday was celebrated by several major conferences as well as booklets providing an overview of the history of the service (National Probation Service 2007; Napo 2007). Understandably, there was a great deal of satisfaction in what the service had achieved in its 100 years and how far it had come, but it was notable that in the respective booklets both the Director of Probation in the Home Office and the National Association of Probation Officers (Napo) representing probation staff spoke of uncertainty about the future of the service, thereby tempering the celebratory mood. And there was a lot to be anxious about. Probation had been under persistent attack by Conservative and Labour governments since the early 1990s. It had been subject to fundamental structural change as it was reorganised into a National Probation Service under direct government control in 2001, and then had become a part of the National Offender Management Service (NOMS) in 2004 alongside the prison service (although in 2007 it was still unclear exactly what form NOMS would take). The Offender Management Bill, which had been presented to Parliament in November 2006, contained provisions to end the monopoly of Probation Boards on providing probation services and to replace Boards with Trusts. The promise of the Effective Practice Initiative had remained unfulfilled. New sentences – the community order and the suspended sentence order – had recently replaced the probation order, the community service order and the various other community sentences run by the service. And the pressure to meet externally imposed targets was unrelenting. For probation service staff, then, celebration might not have been the most appropriate response to the centenary; a more considered response would have been to ask how it had come to this.

With this book we set out to answer such a question. A centenary is, of course, a timely moment to look back and reflect upon the contributions of any organisation, but it was more the uniquely difficult circumstances confronting the probation service that provided the impetus for the book. Probation had always been a Cinderella service – except it had never actually arrived at the ball. Its Ugly Sisters – perhaps the police and the prison service – have treated it for most of its existence with condescension. It has been misrepresented, unfairly attacked, sneered at, caricatured, marginalised, even ignored by politicians and public.

Yet despite all of this, its staff have carried on for 100 years with the thankless task of trying to effect change in offenders in the community, and have always proved amenable (perhaps too much so) to take on extra tasks. It is difficult to imagine the last 100 years without the probation service, even though probation officers have never achieved – and probably never desired – the symbolic status we give to police or prison officers.

The aim of the book is, quite simply, to offer an accessible yet rigorous account of the origins and development of probation in England and Wales (probation has had a different history in the other countries that make up the UK; for a succinct accounts of its development in Scotland see McIvor and McNeill 2007, and for Northern Ireland O'Mahony and Chapman 2007). We try to explain why developments have occurred in the form that they have taken; the pressures and tensions that have shaped change; the critical role played by the Home Office, Napo and a number of key individuals; the missed opportunities. Too many studies of probation tend to view it as a stand-alone agency, but it has always been a part of the criminal justice system – although, until recently, perhaps not a fully engaged part. It is also deeply embedded in the social, cultural, political and economic conditions within which it operates. An awareness of the context, then, is necessary to understanding the emergence and development of probation. We have briefly sketched in some of this context whenever most relevant, although we are aware that this represents a light-touch approach. To fully situate probation in the conditions in which it has operated would necessitate a very different, and much longer, book.

As criminologists we foreground crime, law and order in our work, yet it is a chastening experience to read general historical accounts of post-war Britain and note just how rarely criminal justice is mentioned. Neither Peter Hennessy (2006, 2007), Dominic Sandbrook (2006, 2007, 2010), nor David Kynaston (2007, 2009) in their histories covering (so far) the period 1945–74 have much to say about crime. They do, of course, say a great deal about the conditions which can lead to crime and responses to it – housing, unemployment, affluence, divorce, alcohol consumption, education and the like – but in books of 500–600 pages criminal justice issues are lucky if they get half a dozen pages of discussion, and probation none at all. Similarly, in the personal accounts of their time in power of Margaret Thatcher, John Major and Tony Blair, when criminal justice was at its height as a policy issue, there is surprisingly little about the subject (Thatcher 1993; Major 1999; Blair 2010). So probation needs to be contextualised in a balanced way; on the one hand we must recognise its significance, but also acknowledge that from a wider perspective it is a relatively small player.

Indeed the size of the probation service, in terms of its numbers compared to the other traditional criminal justice agencies (police, courts, prisons) may have a part to play in explaining its history. Given the small number of probation officers, the service has always been easy to marginalise and also easy to change. In addition, probation is invisible; unlike the police or the prison service, probation officers do not (yet?) wear uniforms or work in a closed institution. Yet the size and the invisibility of the service do not explain how it has reached its present position. *Redemption, Rehabilitation and Risk Management* shows how the key issues that are often assumed to be behind the problems facing the service have – for the most part – been around since its beginnings. There has been no carefully plotted and co-ordinated conspiracy by government to take over and centralise – and perhaps thereby destroy – the service; this happened gradually and only became inevitable due to a process of reaching a 'tipping point' that fitted with wider governmental aims.

There are, of course, other historical accounts of the probation service available and it is worth noting how these differ from this one. First, in chronological terms, is Dorothy Bochel's (1976) *Probation and After-Care*, which covers the history of the service from its beginnings up to the Criminal Justice Act of 1972, which introduced the community service order, the suspended sentence supervision order, and four experimental day training centres. This is an invaluable study of the first 70 years of the service but suffers from two limitations. First, it is now 30 years old and while – with the benefit of hindsight – 1972 is an appropriate date to end a historical study of probation as the new sentences introduced by the Act changed probation profoundly, there have been many developments since then that are not covered. Second, the book reads like an authorised, official history; it does not capture fully the tensions and struggles that went on, it rarely makes use of statistics or research to illuminate its arguments and it does not touch upon the ways in which probation officers went about their tasks. Despite these limitations, *Probation and After-Care* remains an indispensable volume for anyone interested in the history of probation.

Next is the famous quartet of essays written during the mid-80s by Bill McWilliams (1983, 1985, 1986, 1987) which explore 'the history of ideas sustaining the English probation service since its beginnings in the late nineteenth century' (McWilliams 1987: 97). Taken together the essays offer a detailed explanation of how the original missionary ideal gave way to the diagnostic era which in turn was replaced by pragmatism. Their major limitation lies in the failure to provide adequate evidence to show how these three phases were actually practised by probation officers. McWilliams relies on a variety of academic, religious and governmental writings for his argument but at no point confronts the crucial question of how far probation officers utilised these texts in their work. In the third essay, four social enquiry reports – one each from the 1930s, 1940s, 1950s and 1960s – are used to make his case although, to his credit, McWilliams (1986: 259) does note that 'it obviously cannot be demonstrated that they are representative of practice in general at the time'. Like Bochel's book, simply because of the passage of time, the essays are now somewhat dated but they are a key source for the history of probation.

The third account is a study of the London probation service. *Crimefighters of London* (Page 1992), as the title might suggest, is more tabloid than broadsheet, but this is not meant to diminish its achievements. It is an immensely readable, straightforward history of the development of probation in London until, as a result of legislative changes, the Inner London Probation and After-Care Service came into being on 1 April 1965. Page uses a great deal of archival material to forward his argument and the book is particularly notable for highlighting the contributions of individual officers. However, it ends in 1965 and it is – given the nature of its subject-matter – a local study.

In 2004 Maurice Vanstone's *Supervising Offenders in the Community* was published. This is a highly original study building on the work of McWilliams, and exploring the history of the supervision of offenders in the community up to 2000 by examining what the author calls 'practice and practice discourses' (Vanstone 2004a: viii). This is done by analysing a wide range of documentary sources as well as interviews with serving and retired probation officers. The book is a hugely stimulating and influential study, but, as Vanstone acknowledges, it faces the same problem as McWilliams' essays: it is impossible to know how far the discourses discussed were put into practice; even when practitioners are writing about their practice there may be various reasons why this does not reflect fully what they did. They may be justifying their practice, they may be highlighting or obscuring certain aspects of their work, they may fail to recall exactly what they did (and, of course, there is the further issue of how the offender perceives what the probation officer has been doing). Because Vanstone's focus is the supervision of offenders there is no discussion of community service or the organisational development of probation, but as a study of the history of ideas behind offender supervision this book is likely to prove the definitive account.

Finally, and most recently, there is Philip Whitehead and Roger Statham's *The History of Probation* with its intriguing sub-title *Politics, Power and Cultural Change 1876–2005*. The authors offer a general account of the history of the service which updates the work of Dorothy Bochel, but the book is somewhat unbalanced and rather idiosyncratic. It is really a study of the 1979–2005 period rather than a full historical survey; slightly more than 10 per cent of the book covers the first 70 years or so of the service, while the remaining 90 per cent discusses the past 25 years. Despite its claim to examine politics, power and cultural change there is relatively little on these issues and how they relate to each other. While the personal experiences and knowledge of the authors is instructive and informative when it is used, it sits oddly with the more macro approach that is its normal style. Whitehead and Statham were long-serving members of the probation service, a point which they rightly acknowledge gives strength to their book as well as weakness.

Redemption, Risk and Rehabilitation provides the most up-to-date and balanced account of the history of probation in England and Wales. A history which has international resonance due to the influence the service has had throughout the world – most recently in helping to shape the emergence and development of probation services in eastern Europe following the collapse of communism. Our credentials as authors are based on extensive knowledge of the probation service from a number of perspectives. For George this involves more than 25 years researching and writing about the probation service from within government (as a member of the Home Office Research and Planning Unit) and as an academic, as well as a period of 10 years as a member first of a local probation committees and then Probation Board. With regard to Lol, it has meant a similar period of experience, first spent working in a probation service as a Probation Officer then a Senior Probation Officer, subsequently training newly recruited officers as part of a university training consortium, before becoming a full-time academic.

This is very much an inclusive and synthesising history. We have relied upon a wide range of written material and have used our judgement about how much weight to give it. All documentary evidence is partial and written with a specific audience or audiences in mind. Our readers can always go to the originals and decide for themselves whether we have used them accurately or not. All statistics are taken from Home Office or, after 2007, Ministry of Justice statistical publications (*Criminal Statistics*, *Probation Statistics*, *Prison Statistics*, *Offender Management Statistics*, *Sentencing Statistics*) unless otherwise stated.

Chapter 1 explores the origins of probation in England and Wales. These are messy, contingent and various, and cover social, political, cultural and economic factors. The second half of the nineteenth century can be seen as a lengthy gestation period leading up to the 1907 Probation of Offenders Act. Chapter 2 covers the first decade of probation. It discusses the Act and its limitations as well as the Departmental Committee that was set up to examine the workings of the Act, and draws attention to the achievements of that period as well as the tensions that emerged. The 1920s, as Chapter 3 explains, was a key period for the development of probation despite the decade beginning with swingeing cuts in government expenditure. Various government reports meant that the local autonomy of probation services was slowly constrained, probation officers became more professional and the service grew in size. By the early 1930s, probation was the default disposal in the lower courts, and was extending its responsibilities. Chapter 4 discusses the various departmental committees relevant to probation that reported during this decade, noting especially the Committee on Social Services in courts of summary jurisdiction, which made the case for a wholly public service and more training. The regulation of probation work was also attempted by Napo with the publication in 1935 of *A Handbook of Probation*. The war years led to more punitive sentencing and a decline in the use of probation, but the 1948 Criminal Justice Act acknowledged its importance although the close working relationship with the Home Office was beginning to show signs of wear and tear. With Chapter 5, we enter the post-war period when, initially, we might see a golden age for probation as it expanded its responsibilities and its staff became the experts on casework with offenders. But research failed to prove that probation was unequivocally effective, and prison numbers and crime began rising, factors that were to prove significant in the future. Chapter 6 covers the 1960s and the first half of the 1970s, a key time of change for the service. It changed its name (to the Probation and After-Care Service) following the introduction of parole; it began the process of losing responsibility for juveniles who had been the core client-group for the service since its beginnings; and it was redefined as an alternative to custody following the criticisms of Martinson (1974) and the introduction of community service and day training centres. The loss of certainty about what it was for can be seen by the number of attempts to redefine probation at the end of the 1970s, which are discussed in Chapter 7. The chapter also examines the many developments in probation during the 1980s, the growing pressure placed on the service by government, and the momentary optimism offered by the 1991 Criminal Justice Act. In Chapter 8 we take the story up to the present day. Since the arrival of Michael Howard as Home Secretary in 1993, probation seems to have been under sustained attack in an increasingly punitive penal climate. The Effective Practice Initiative was introduced but, like IMPACT in the early 1970s, ended with a whimper; a national service was introduced but scarcely given time to settle down before more radical changes were made with the arrival of NOMS; the names of orders were changed, new orders were introduced culminating (for now) with the community order and the suspended sentence order in the 2003 Criminal Justice Act. The combination of being marginalised in NOMS, becoming just another provider of services as a result of contestability, and the harsh cuts required by the current economic situation do not hold out much promise for the service. In the concluding chapter we attempt to sum up some of the key factors behind the 100 years of probation.

'The past', as L P Hartley noted in the opening of his 1953 novel *The Go-Between*, 'is a foreign country: they do things differently there.' But, whether or not things are done differently in the past, what is done continues to reverberate in the present as Hartley's novel memorably shows. Probation's current situation is not simply a result of what has been going on in the last few years; it is tied inextricably to the choices, tensions and initiatives that have marked out its history since 1907 and which we discuss in this book. By exploring its past this book helps to illuminate the present of a vital – and all too often misunderstood and under-appreciated – part of the criminal justice system in England and Wales. Our hope is that this study does not prove to be an epitaph for the service.

1 Origins

An Act of Parliament represents not only a beginning, but also a culmination. On the one hand, an Act sets out new legislation that will take effect from a specified date – it may be new forms of practice, new modes of allocation of services, new forms of control, new agencies – but the implication is that the Act is a starting point. But an Act is also the summation of activity that may have taken considerable time and energy to pull together and formulate. In this chapter, we will discuss the various ideas, individuals, initiatives and organisations that lie behind the 1907 Probation of Offenders Act. It is difficult enough today to try to elucidate the origins of recent Acts of Parliament; these tend to be complex, convoluted and all too often bathed in degrees of political spin. Looking back more than 100 years there is probably rather less spin to worry about (although it would be naive to claim that spin did not exist), but also less information in general. We do, of course, have the benefit of hindsight, which permits a more objective assessment of the factors that influenced the Act, but we do not have any real feel for what was considered at the time to be important.

It would be an artificial task – as well as an impossible one – to try to pinpoint a precise moment when the idea of probation began. As David Garland has consistently argued, there is very little evidence for concerted, carefully planned policy making in criminal justice; instead it is 'a matter of fragmentary lines of development crossing and intersecting, or else being lost as they go off on implausible tangents' (Garland 1985: 208). Probation emerges from a number of disparate ideas, developments and initiatives that can be found in the nineteenth century; a variety of factors that were not necessarily related to each other in any clear way at the time, although it is now possible to discern linkages. All of the factors examined in this chapter played a part in the emergence of probation, but it is important to emphasise that we do not list them in a simple chronological fashion or classify them according to their significance. The order in which they are discussed tends to move from the more general to the more specific. The key point to bear in mind is that while the various factors are discussed separately here, they certainly did not exist in separate silos. We have attempted to examine them individually only in order to simplify the analysis.

Religion

It is difficult today to appreciate fully the significance of religion in Victorian Britain. We now live in what is, essentially, a secular society, whereas mainstream Victorian culture was deeply embedded in a world view founded upon religion. And not just any religion: the Church of England or some of the sects that had broken away from it (Methodists or Baptists, for example) dominated the lives of the English. The works of the great Victorian novelists and poets – Charles Dickens, Robert Browning, George Eliot, Alfred Tennyson, Anthony Trollope – are profoundly concerned, either directly or indirectly, with issues of religious import. Politics, too, seems to have been driven to a considerable degree by religious impulses and the Evangelical movement in particular was especially influential.

> Evangelical propaganda led to the suppression of duels and blood sports, evangelical drives to protect children in factories enjoyed some success, evangelicals played an important role in prison reform, and in their most impressive accomplishment by 1807 they had succeeded in abolishing the slave trade … They played a dominant role in education: 55 per cent of children between 5 and 15 were enrolled in church-run Sunday schools. Every major figure in British political life from 1830 to 1870 with the exception of Palmerston was touched by evangelicalism … The intellectual, moral and political cultures of Victorian Britain were based on evangelical Christian foundations.
>
> (Allard 2005: 2–3)

William Wilberforce, one of the key individuals in the fight to abolish slavery, was an Evangelical Quaker; the Earl of Shaftesbury, who led the battle for factory reform and child labour, was proud to be an Evangelical (and was also involved in penal reform):

> I think a man's religion, if it is worth anything, should enter into every sphere of life, and rule his conduct in every relation. I have always been – and, please God, always shall be – an Evangelical.
>
> (www.spartacus.schoolnet.co.uk/IRashley.htm)

John Howard and Elizabeth Fry, both significant figures in prison reform, were closely associated with Evangelicals (Ignatieff 1978), as was Mary Carpenter (Radzinowicz and Hood 1986). And the importance of the Evangelical movement in penal reform generally throughout the nineteenth century is demonstrated by Martin Wiener (1990).

The Evangelical movement was religion in action. Evangelicals were not content simply to sit in church on Sundays and worship God; they were concerned with going out and grappling with social problems in an attempt to ameliorate them. They had a profound concern for the souls and well-being of the poor and oppressed, and encouraged rescue work for those who deserved redemption. Salvation – the saving of souls – was central to their beliefs and this involved missionary work with sinners. But the redemption of sin, and, therefore, mercy 'could not be extended to all' (McWilliams 1983: 138); only those who were deserving of help could be saved. Thus, it was important to classify sinners into those who could be saved (or reformed) and those who could not, and mercy would be extended to the former group. It is somewhat ironic to consider that classification (admittedly based on clinical judgement rather than actuarial assessment) is so deeply rooted in the early days of missionary work with offenders and yet its most recent incarnations – the Offender Group Reconviction Scale (OGRS) and the Offender Assessment System (OASys) – were initially met with considerable unease by probation staff (Mair 2001).

This is not the place for a detailed analysis of the theology of the Evangelical movement and how it provided a powerful basis for dealing with what we might now call social problems (see Ignatieff 1978; McWilliams 1983; Vanstone 2004a; and Wiener 1990 for more detail), but the significance of Evangelicalism for penal reform generally in the nineteenth century, and for the development of the probation service specifically, cannot be underestimated. As McWilliams (1983) has shown, the religious impulse behind probation was superseded within 30–40 years of the introduction of probation in 1907, although its shadow lingered on until the introduction of the National Probation Service in 2001.

Philanthropy

The charitable impulse in Victorian life was just as significant as – and, indeed, intimately related to – the importance of religion. Christianity enjoined its adherents to practise charity towards those who were in need; this would not only save the soul of the giver, but also help the needy, and this injunction was deeply engrained amongst Victorians even of limited means. Victorian philanthropy indeed may have been

> ... little less than a golden age of Christian social service that yielded benefits far beyond the provision of welfare services. It provided the foundation of civil society. It humanized urban industrial life and relations between rich and poor. It introduced a higher moral tone to working-class life. It contributed to social cohesion. It gave skills and status to disadvantaged groups and, as such, has been described as a nursery school for democracy.
>
> (Bowpitt 2007: 106)

Charitable ventures aimed at young delinquents, such as the Marine Society and the Philanthropic Society, had been established by the beginning of the nineteenth century, and soon after the Society for the Improvement of Prison Discipline and for the Reformation of Juvenile Offenders was formed, which advocated segregating young offenders from adult criminals (Pinchbeck and Hewitt 1969; 1973). That there was a considerable need for philanthropic endeavours was made clear by the work of Henry Mayhew with his *London Labour and the London Poor* first published in 1851 (and interestingly followed up in 1862 by *The Criminal Prisons of London*), which showed graphically the extent of poverty in the metropolis. Mayhew's work was followed up in the 1860s by Joseph Rowntree's studies of poverty (the first of which examined the links between crime and poverty), and towards the end of the century by Charles Booth's massive survey *Life and Labour of the People in London*. These studies not only demonstrated empirically the existence of poverty, they also classified different kinds of poverty and – by implication – suggested that as there was so much poverty difficult choices would have to be made about who should be helped given the limited resources available.

With no state apparatus to support or direct it, charity had, for more than half of the nineteenth century, been ad hoc, localised, loosely organised – and thus increasingly seen as inefficient. In 1869 the Charity Organisation Society (COS) was formed with the aim of improving charitable work by organising it, regulating it, and scientifically classifying those who might be its objects into the deserving and the undeserving. Only the former would receive assistance; helping the latter would be wasteful. But how was it possible to differentiate between those who genuinely deserved help and those who did not? The answer was by careful inquiry into those who applied for help – one of the principles of the COS:

> Careful investigation of applications for charitable aid, by competent officers, each case being duly considered after inquiry, by a Committee of experienced volunteers, including representatives of the principal local charities and religious denominations.
>
> (Mowat, quoted in Garland 1985: 116)

Charitable activity, however, in addition to its philanthropic aims, can also be seen as having a political objective. Peter Young has argued that

> ... charitable activity, including probation, operated as a mechanism which politically incorporated a possibly oppositional working-class culture into an institutional and cultural structure based on middle-class values and ideologies. Thus social work should not be seen as a gradual liberalisation and democratisation of society, but as a directed attempt to circumscribe the scope of legitimate action and life styles available to working-class people.
>
> (Young 1976: 55)

While the close relationship between religion and charity slowly began to unravel towards the end of the century, for much of the second half of the nineteenth century the links between the two were inescapable. Charity was one of the distinguishing features of the religious individual. Charity was meant to save sinners. Charity was putting Christian beliefs into practice and thus was especially suited to Evangelicals. Not all could be saved or helped and thus the need to differentiate between sheep and goats was the same for religion and philanthropy.

It would be difficult to over-emphasise how many of the great philanthropists were driven by their religious beliefs: Wilberforce, Shaftesbury, Fry, Carpenter, Rowntree, Barnardo, to name but a few.

But this is not to suggest that charity and religion always proceeded smoothly hand-in-hand. Garland (1985) has demonstrated that there were real tensions between groups in the charity movement. And given the levels of need found by the likes of Rowntree, Booth and Mayhew it slowly became evident that charity alone – no matter how well organised or efficient – was not enough. The state began to move into the sphere of social work as the century ended.

Crime

While crude data on the numbers committed for trial for indictable offences began to be collected in 1805, it took a further 50 years before anything that might be termed a useful data set began to appear in 1857. It is, therefore, difficult to be precise about trends in crime during the nineteenth century. Radzinowicz and Hood (1986: 113–15) argue for three discernible periods: for the first 40 years of the century they see 'unrelieved pessimism' with crime steadily increasing, followed by 30 years of 'qualified optimism' and then a final 30 years of 'unfaltering optimism [when] [t]he war against crime seemed to be won'. Wiener (1990: 15) argues that there was considerable anxiety about crime in the early Victorian period with 'contemporaries almost unanimous in perceiving an ever-rising amount of criminality of all kinds, and particularly offences committed by juveniles'. Perhaps somewhat surprisingly, the flogging of adults was abolished in 1861, only to be reintroduced almost immediately in 1863 with the Security against Violence Act (the Garotter's Act) of that year, which was a result of the panic engendered by the garotting outrages of 1862.

Perceptions of crime changed, however, as the second half of the century developed.

Although non-indictable offences increased during the last 30 years of the century the more serious indictable offences fell, so much so that Wiener (1990: 258) can talk of the 'success of Victorian criminal policy'. It is possible to discern two very general responses to crime that would seem to be related respectively to the first half of the century when crime was seen to be increasing and therefore a problem, and the second when crime was increasingly seen as being under control and less of a problem. Because of the perception of crime as a problem, there were various responses to try to deal with it – one of these being the establishment of police forces first in London, then in the counties and boroughs (and this, of course, had an impact upon levels of crime). There were also a variety of charitable endeavours focusing particularly on juveniles as they were seen as being heavily involved in crime. As early as 1815 the Society for Investigating the Causes of the Alarming Increase of Juvenile Delinquency in the Metropolis had been established. In a report the following year the Society argued against the imprisonment of young offenders because of the effects of contamination by adult prisoners (Pinchbeck and Hewitt 1973). In 1817 the Society for the

Improvement of Prison Discipline and the Reformation of Juvenile Offenders was formed, and it too argued for the separation of juvenile from adult criminals. The Children's Friend Society appeared in 1830 (Radzinowicz and Hood 1986). The reformatory movement ultimately succeeded with the Reformatory Schools Act of 1854 and the Industrial Schools Act of 1857 (see below).

As a result of the perception that crime was becoming much less of a problem, during the second half of the century there were more concerted moves to punish less harshly and more constructively, the beginnings of what we would now refer to as the rehabilitation of the criminal. Perhaps the most significant moment in this trend was the *Report of the Departmental Committee on Prisons* in 1895 (the Gladstone Report) which advocated introducing a more reform-minded approach to dealing with prisoners who were to be seen as reclaimable and no longer as hopeless cases.

It is ironic that we think that it is only since around 1980 that crime has been a serious problem in England and Wales. Even a brief examination of a handful of the various nineteenth-century studies would suggest that for much of the century crime was a topic of considerable significance for government (e.g. Garland 1985; Radzinowicz and Hood 1986; Rawlings 1999; Wiener 1990). And this in an era when there were no mass media, few developed rapid transport links in the country, no mass communications and little feel for what we now call public opinion.

Exceptional cases

As the discussion of both religion and philanthropy has noted, classification was a vital aspect of the workings of both. Theologically speaking, not all could be saved; and for practical purposes not all of the poor could be helped. Singling out the exceptional types, therefore, who were redeemable or reclaimable became a key task and various groups were defined as requiring special treatment because of their circumstances. The most significant of these was children.

During the preceding centuries, children had been simply treated as small adults but as the nineteenth century began there were increasingly significant developments in dealing with juveniles who were either criminals or who seemed to be on the verge of becoming so. Some of the most important charitable ventures in this direction have already been mentioned, but even before these had been established the Marine Society had been founded in 1756 and the Philanthropic Society in 1788. The former aimed to divert boys of 12–16 from the criminal justice system by sending them to sea, while the latter seems to have focused (at least initially) more upon children at risk (see Radzinowicz and Hood 1986: 133–8). In 1825 the principle of segregating young offenders from adults was put into practice when one of the prison hulks[1] was specifically set aside for young convicts; it was closed down within 20 years as 'an unredeemed failure' (Radzinowicz and Hood 1986: 144). But the principle remained and in 1838 a penitentiary for boys was opened at Parkhurst on the Isle of Wight (it too closed as a failure, in 1864). The next steps were the introduction of reformatory schools (inspired by Mary Carpenter and supported by Shaftesbury – both Evangelicals) in 1854, which were to be used for offenders under the age of 16 following a prison sentence of at least two weeks. These were quickly followed by industrial schools in 1857 for those aged between 7 and 14 who had not been convicted but were considered to be in moral danger. In 1873 Benjamin Waugh's book *The Gaol Cradle: Who Rocks It?* angrily attacked the way in which juveniles were dealt with by the criminal justice system, demanding at one point 'May not the time have come to abandon altogether the practice of juvenile imprisonment?' (Waugh 1873: 89).

But it was not simply humanitarian concerns for the welfare of children and young offenders that drove such developments. Crime was perceived to be – to a considerable degree – a problem associated with juveniles, so focusing upon them would confront the problem effectively. Even more so, by targeting juveniles, crime in general would be tackled:

> Notions about juvenile crime and habitual criminals dovetailed in the theory that the criminal class was constantly regenerated by the transmission through upbringing of criminal dispositions. If juveniles could be reached before they became firm in the mould the vicious process might be stayed and the criminal class would diminish.
>
> (McConville 1981: 329)

While crime was a juvenile problem, it was also seen as being closely associated with drunkenness. By the middle of the century 'drink became perhaps the leading explanation for crime' (Wiener 1990: 79) and around the same time habitual drunkenness increasingly became accepted as a disease. Thus in 1879, by which time prosecutions for drunkenness had begun to decline, the Habitual Drunkards Act created a category of diminished responsibility for those defined by magistrates as habitual drunkards. While this was initially restricted to 'gentlemen', over the next ten years or so the punishment of drunkenness began to be questioned by both politicians and police officers (Wiener 1990). In what follows, the significance of both juvenile and drunk offenders for the early probation service will be noted.

During the course of the century, then, certain categories of offender became accepted as necessitating special treatment, so that by the time of the Gladstone Committee in 1895 it was officially acknowledged that

> Habitual criminals, habitual drunkards, mentally disordered offenders, first offenders, young prisoners, women, women with infants, remand prisoners and debtors were all believed to require distinct methods of treatment in special institutions.
>
> (Rawlings 1999: 120)

Sentencing

Some of the developments in sentencing that are relevant to the origins of probation have already been noted, for example the introduction of reformatory schools for juvenile offenders. If a case could be made for differentiating between offenders, then different methods of dealing with these special cases was the logical next step. One of the most significant series of moves during the second half of the century was the increasing extension of summary punishment. One of the main justifications for this was that young offenders (as exceptional cases) would be treated less harshly, but costs and the ability to convict for less serious offences also played a part. These steps led inevitably to the considerable extension of the criminal law, but they also led to a huge increase in sentences other than imprisonment – primarily fines and recognisances.

The first significant legislation was the Juvenile Offenders Act of 1847 which permitted magistrates to try children up to the age of 14 for offences of simple larceny. Three years later the age limit was extended to 16. The Criminal Justice Act of 1855 not only extended the kinds of offence that could be dealt with summarily, but also covered adults. A further Act in 1879 again widened the number of offences that could be dealt with for juveniles and adults. Obviously, this 'vast extension of summary powers' (Radzinowicz and Hood 1986: 622) led to a considerably increased workload in the magistrates' courts, less punitive sentences and perhaps also some recognition amongst magistrates that, given their increased workload, an increased range of penalties might be helpful.

The use of recognisance is particularly important for the origins of probation. Its own origins would seem to be somewhat vague (see Vanstone 2004a) but it seems clear that the principle of withholding punishment is rooted in common law. Bochel (1976: 3) describes recognisance as 'an undertaking by the person before the court, with or without sureties, to reappear when called upon, and to observe conditions set by the court'. Because of the lack of statistical data it is difficult to tell how often recognisance was used by sentencers in the first half of the nineteenth century but one of the founding narratives of probation is that some Warwickshire magistrates were using it in the 1820s to commit a young offender to the care of a suitable employer. The main source for this information is Matthew Davenport Hill, who had practiced as a lawyer in Warwickshire and as Recorder of Birmingham from 1841 followed the scheme and tried to improve it by relying on 'guardians' rather than employers (who might not always be available or willing) and by

> keeping a register of those released and by arranging, with the help of the Chief Superintendent of Police, for 'a confidential officer' to visit the guardian, inquire about the conduct of the offender, and record his findings. Hill thus had some check on the outcome of his decisions.
>
> (Bochel 1976: 5)

Hill's efforts seem to have been followed up in Portsmouth and Middlesex by Edward Cox who appears to have made some further improvements to Hill's scheme:

> as well as calling upon parents or friends to enter into recognizances to bring a person up for judgement, with sureties, as an alternative to imprisonment,

[Cox] is said to have experimented with supervision during the period of suspension by appointing a special 'inquiry officer' to supervise the behaviour of probationers in Middlesex. It has been pointed out that Cox's method of employing recognizances to come up for judgement, with sureties, and a special officer for the supervision of offenders, represented a considerable advance towards to-day's essential elements of probation, compared with Hill's token punishment, rudimentary supervision and follow-up enquiries.

(Bochel 1976: 5–6)

The key points to bear in mind are that recognisances seem to have been used very inconsistently by the courts, there were no statutory powers of supervision, and it might be all too easy to see such a sentence as being equivalent to being 'let off'.

Disenchantment with prison

Even during the first half of the century, there were signs of disenchantment with prison with the reformatory movement providing a crucial step in the case of juveniles. Ignatieff (1978: 186) argues that 'Magistrates were particularly concerned about the "criminalizing" effects of small imprisonments on juveniles.' As noted previously, exceptional cases logically required exceptional treatment, and while this might mean more punitive forms of custody it could also mean punishing some exceptional cases in ways which did not involve imprisonment. The spread of summary jurisdiction also led to the downgrading. of imprisonment as a punishment. Indeed, between 1880 and 1894 the average length of a custodial sentence fell from 48.3 days to 34.4, which, as Wiener (1990) argues, is a measure of success for the Victorian criminal justice system but can equally be seen as an indicator of disillusion with prison. These developments, however, while providing an important foundation, did not lead inevitably to the much more concerted changes in attitude towards the prison in the final decade of the century.

In 1869, Sir Edmund Du Cane was appointed Chairman of the Directors of Convict Prisons and in 1877 he became Chairman of the Prison Commissioners, combining both posts until 1895 when he retired. Du Cane was, therefore, the single most important individual for the organisation and operation of prisons in England and Wales for a quarter of a century. He has been judged fairly harshly:

his was a closed mind, intolerant of critics. He was honourable and just but tough, at times even heartless. He was autocratic, a disciplinarian, a lover of orderly arrangements of all sorts of things, including human beings.

(Radzinowicz and Hood 1986: 527)

It is, thus, easy to blame Du Cane for the increasing punitiveness of prison regimes and the increased severity of prison discipline during his period in control.

However, it is worth remembering that the above description could be applied to many so-called eminent Victorians, and Forsythe (1991: 28–9) reminds us that Du Cane was 'a determined fighter for healthier conditions in prisons as well as an advocate of more efficient prisoner aid societies'.

From 1890, criticism of Du Cane almost amounted to a concerted attack upon his methods. Forsythe (1991) notes Home Office concerns, adverse comments from some fellow members of the Prison Commission, attacks by prisoners who had recorded their experiences (especially Irish nationalist prisoners), criticism from pressure groups such as the Howard Association and the Humanitarian League, and a series of press articles almost certainly the work of W.D. Morrison, a chaplain at Wandsworth prison and a well-known commentator on penal issues. Ironically, Morrison criticised prisons for one of the reasons it was claimed to be a success – deterrence – by arguing that the number of recidivists in custody proved otherwise. The government's response to such a major assault on Du Cane was to set up the Gladstone Committee in 1894.

The significance of the Gladstone Committee is generally agreed to be difficult to over-estimate: Harding et al. (1985: 187) note that it could be seen as 'the single most important influence on the way in which the prison system was to develop during the twentieth century'. Sean McConville (1995: 144), on the other hand, talks of 'the absurdly overvenerated Gladstone Committee of 1894–95'. Essentially, the report of the Committee introduced reformation as an aim of imprisonment, alongside – not replacing – deterrence; individualisation of treatment and classification of prisoners into different categories were further recommendations. The Prison Act of 1898 introduced legislation to implement such recommendations, thereby ensuring official acknowledgement that considerable changes were needed in the organisation and operation of the prison system.

The new sciences

There is little doubt that the emergence and development during the nineteenth century of four 'new sciences' – psychology, criminology, eugenics and statistics – had implications for the origins of probation. And it is important to emphasise that each of these sciences had significant points of overlap with each other.

The development of criminal statistics, for example, could hardly help but lead to much improved knowledge about trends in crime and sentencing. But the science of statistics more generally led to a decreasing emphasis on free will as an explanation for offending as regular patterns of crime were discovered; as Wiener (1990: 163) notes 'the order it [statistics] uncovered seemed to dispense with individual free will'. This de-emphasis on the freedom of the individual slowly influenced state intervention (amongst other things), so that the idea of minimal state interference in the lives of its citizens began to regress. This, in turn, had implications for the way in which offenders were dealt with so that what had been a reliance upon deterrence began to shift towards ideas about reform and rehabilitation – which involved intervening in the lives of criminals.

Interestingly, two of the key individuals in the development of statistics as a science, Francis Galton and Karl Pearson, were eugenicists. The former is credited with coining the term eugenics, while the latter 'developed and championed perhaps the most coherent form of eugenic ideology, integrating it into a framework of social Darwinism, Fabianism and positivism' (MacKenzie 1979: 42), in other words, aligning it with some of the most modern thinking of the time. Eugenics, with its rather unsavoury connections with ideas about racial purity and its aim to improve the physical and mental qualities of future generations, 'appears to modern eyes as a marginal and disreputable concern, associated more with the methods of European fascism than the formation and strategies of the British Welfare State' (Garland 1985: 142). Despite this, eugenics was taken seriously by many.

As Radzinowicz and Hood (1986) demonstrate, by the last decade of the century many offenders were thought to be 'feeble-minded' and this was commonly viewed as an inherited condition. Such offenders required different treatment from imprisonment and eugenics offered this by arguing for segregation or sterilisation. Indeed, Garland (1985: 144) suggests that eugenicists were opposed to short terms of imprisonment. Assessment and classification were key aspects of the work of eugenicists – and these were to become equally important tools for the probation officer. While it may not fit with the foundation narrative of the origins of probation with its emphasis on benevolence and humanitarianism, there is little doubt that eugenics played a part in the beginnings of the service.

In *Punishment and Welfare*, David Garland (1985) unravels the hidden connections between eugenics and criminology and points to the relationship between the two (some individuals combined both in their work). He also traces the rise of criminology, and shows how this fitted in with other ideological and cultural movements. Criminology not only meant much more knowledge about offenders and their differences, but also encouraged an interest in the environmental and social conditions that led to offending, new ideas about treating offenders, an emphasis upon assessment and classification, and a search for the causes of crime. The ambitions of criminology were considerable; its aim was, simply, the elimination of crime:

> either by prevention, reformation or extinction. This triple strategy required not only procedures of assessment and classification, which could identify offenders as corrigible or incorrigible, but also a *diversity of dispositions, sanctions and techniques* to implement these objectives. Thus we find that a major demand of the criminologists was for an extended repertoire of penal sanctions and institutions, including juvenile reformatories, preventive detention institutions, institutions for inebriates, for the feeble-minded, a variety of prison regimes, forms of supervision, conditional liberation, indeterminate sentences and 'pre-delinquent interventions'.
>
> (Garland 1985: 96, emphasis in original)

If Garland is correct, the significance of criminology as a background factor in the origins of probation would seem to be considerable.

Finally, and briefly – though this is certainly not meant to underestimate its significance – there is the influence of psychology, again almost impossible to disentangle from eugenics and criminology. Psychology, crucially, played a significant role in moving arguments about the reasons for offending away from those which emphasised the deliberate choice of wickedness, towards more deterministic reasons (the offender could not help himself). Two recent studies of the origins of probation – both written by authors who have spent considerable parts of their working lives as probation officers – are keen to acknowledge the importance of psychology:

> It is a core argument of this history that probation theory and practice are an integral part of the story of psychology's dominance in the processes of social control.
>
> (Vanstone 2004a: 27)

> The history of probation has been closely associated with an emphasis on the psychology of the individual, which means that explanations for offending have, on the whole, been conceptualised within a framework of faulty and maladjusted individuals rather than the wider social structure.
>
> (Whitehead and Statham 2006:17)

The Massachusetts example

Up to now we have been discussing, for the most part, ideas and developments of various kinds that are background factors for the origins of probation. They may well have been necessary for the emergence of probation but they were by no means sufficient; if there were only the factors already discussed there is no guarantee that probation would have happened. Something more was necessary and – somewhat ironically, considering that we tend to consider probation as such a British phenomenon – that something was the example of a functioning and effective probation movement in the USA, especially in Massachusetts.

Another key part of the foundation narrative of probation is the story of John Augustus, the Boston cobbler, who from 1841 until his death in 1859 'stood bail for offenders brought before the Boston courts, and undertook their supervision between suspension of sentence on bail and recall for judgement which the courts made nominal on evidence of reformation' (Bochel 1976: 7). Vanstone (2004a) has demonstrated that Augustus did not work alone (the myth suggests that his was an heroic solitary struggle) and that he was involved in the temperance movement (as was the early probation movement in England). It should also be emphasised that he worked voluntarily – he was not an agent of the court. His work must have been perceived as successful as it was carried on after his death by other volunteers until State Agents were formally appointed by the State legislature in 1869, to carry out investigations of cases (of offenders under 17 years of age) before they came to court and to supervise them on conviction. In 1878 the practice was extended to adults.

It is only very recently that policy transfer has been recognised as a factor in the movement and development of policies; Jones and Newburn (2007:1) note 'a growing perception that, over the past two decades, social policy in the UK has increasingly involved the importation of ideas from abroad, particularly from the United States'. But policy transfer would certainly seem to have taken place with regard to probation in the later nineteenth century, despite the lack of the kind of transport and communication systems we now have available. The Massachusetts probation scheme did not make its way across the Atlantic on its own, and a surprising number of key individuals from England seem to have visited Boston and its probation system and made their views known to the authorities on their return.

William Tallack, Secretary of the Howard Association, visited the USA and enthused about probation when he returned to England; indeed, the Howard Association became a supporter of the idea. Rose (1961: 141) points out that 'the information brought back from the United States by Tallack about the progress of probation there was instrumental in popularising the idea in the 1880s'. That the government was interested in what was going on in other countries is evident in the request by the then Home Secretary, William Harcourt, for the Foreign Office to collect information from other countries about their methods of dealing with young offenders. In 1881, the Association sent their information about the Massachusetts system to the Home Secretary. Another member of the Association, Joseph Sturge, a Birmingham magistrate, had also visited Boston and had been impressed by what he saw. Perhaps most significantly, yet another impressed visitor to Boston was Howard Vincent, who was responsible for introducing the Probation of First Offenders Bill to Parliament (and who later worked closely with the Howard Association). Between the Probation of First Offenders Act in 1887 and the Probation of Offenders Act in 1907, the American influence continued to be brought to bear on the authorities.

W.D. Morrison in *Juvenile Offenders* discussed various examples of probation-type systems from across the world, but noted particularly the US system: 'The probation system, as it is practised in the United States, is much more economical as well as more natural than the system which exists in England' (Morrison 1896: 191). It is worth noting that the cost is emphasised, but this is because Morrison is comparing probation to industrial schools. Morrison worked as a chaplain in Wandsworth prison in London and it is likely that his book was noted by the Home Office. Indeed, at the same time as Morrison's book was published, Evelyn Ruggles-Brise, Chairman of the Prison Commissioners, visited America to examine its penal systems and submitted a report to the Home Secretary which considered probation favourably. Ruggles-Brise, however, pointed out that there was a need for supervision and pre-trial enquiries. He considered there was potential for unnecessary competition between probation officers and police officers, and he was uneasy about the costs of a probation scheme. In the arguments that were to take place about who should be appointed as probation officers, he was a strong supporter of the police (Bochel 1976).

Edward Grubb, Tallack's successor as Secretary of the Howard Association, visited the US in 1904 and pushed for the adoption of probation along American lines on his return. And Howard Vincent returned to the US in 1904 and again made much of probation when he came back to England. Shortly before the 1907 Act, a study of young offenders was published which advocated much greater help for this group on the grounds that prison made them worse and that if they were successfully treated then criminality would fall (Russell and Rigby 1906). The authors described schemes from a variety of countries but saw most benefit in the American system of probation. And, before legislating, the Home Office specifically requested 'HM Representative in Washington to procure and forward to this country as much information as possible respecting the latest develop-ments of the system of probation of offenders in the United States of America', resulting in a 25-page document setting out the organisation and operation of probation in various American states (Home Office 1907: 3).

Pressure groups

While pressure groups are much more ubiquitous today, it should not be assumed that they either did not exist or played little part in penal reform in the nineteenth century. As the preceding section has noted, the Howard Association (which originated in 1866) was a consistent and formidable supporter of probation, pressing its claims on government regularly. And Howard Vincent's relationship with the Association has also been mentioned. The first Secretary of the Association, William Tallack, who held the post for 35 years, was a Quaker (note the Evangelical connection) who became a well-known writer on penological matters. The Association campaigned on a wide range of penal issues, but not always on what we might expect to be the 'right' side; for example, they tended to be in favour of corporal punishment even for juveniles, although it should be emphasised that they were not alone in this and their argument was that whipping was preferable to imprisonment (Radzinowicz and Hood 1986: 689–719).

The Howard Association may have been the most important of the pressure groups concentrating on penal reform, but was by no means the only one. Indeed, other charities too got involved in this subject:

> there was no shortage of associations, organisations and pressure groups that concerned themselves with criminal justice and penal reform. The Howard Association, the Penal Reform League, the Reformatory and Refuge Union and the Humanitarian League were all directed towards objectives similar to those proposed by criminology. These groups, along with various social work organisations, the State Children's Association, the Committee on Wage Earning Children and the Association for the Feeble-Minded gave important and consistent support to the criminological programme, as did the writings of their individual members.
>
> (Garland 1985: 108–9)

Garland (1985) unpicks the various tensions, contradictions and inconsistencies that characterised the programmes of the pressure groups, but he also shows how their separate programmes overlapped at key points. In a sense, the various factors already discussed as contributing to the emergence of probation can be seen to come together in the work of penal reform groups, especially the Howard Association. The religious impulse and philanthropic motives were the foundation of the Association. Its objectives were penal reform so it focused upon crime, exceptional cases such as juveniles, the failings of prison. It had close links with the various 'scientific' developments we have discussed, and it kept abreast of developments abroad so that it could utilise the example of probation in Massachusetts to help persuade the government.

With the US example and, crucially, the support of the Howard Association as well as other groups, probation now had a firm platform from which to develop. The possibility of probation – or something like it – had been becoming more solid as the second half of the century moved on. However, despite the fact that we might prefer to see policies initiated as a result of careful planning and design, the key sparks that ignited probation were a result of fortuitous circumstances rather than any grand design.

The prototype

In 1862 the Church of England Total Abstinence Society was founded in response to a perceived problem with excessive drinking. Within a few years, it had changed its objectives and its name and became the Church of England Temperance Society (CETS). In the course of their work, the Society's missionaries visited 'cabstands, railway stations and lodging houses' (Vanstone 2004a: 7) in order to help those who were prone to drunkenness, exhorting them to mend their ways. In 1876, in response to a letter from a Hertfordshire printer, Frederic Rainer, to the Chairman of the CETS, a CETS missionary was appointed to cover Southwark Police Court to work primarily with those who were brought before the court on drunkenness offences. Hinde (1951: 193) suggests that temperance work was a 'good and necessary thing' particularly for young people as he quotes figures to suggest that in 1877 in Liverpool alone a total of 5,371 individuals under the age of 21 were found guilty of being drunk and incapable.

Despite there being no legal basis for such court missionary work, the appointment seems to have been judged successful, and partly because of this and partly due to the Summary Jurisdiction Act of 1879 encouraging greater use of recognisances, the number of full-time missionaries working in courts grew to eight by 1880. It seems that from the start missionary work was not confined to the courts, but also involved meeting prisoners on release and even 'acting in family and neighbours' quarrels, interviewing children who were beyond their parents' control, assessing applicants for the poor box, and so on' (Wiener 1990: 306). Indeed, it is probable that the missionaries began to be used for the purposes of inquiring into circumstances before sentence before the 1887 Probation of First Offenders Act. Without wishing to labour the point too much, it could be argued that key aspects of what became probation were in place prior to legislation: supervision of offenders (albeit rudimentary), work with released prisoners, crime prevention, reports for the court, welfare work. These tasks did not form a fully worked-out set of coherent practices but their presence is significant.

In 1886, Howard Vincent, MP, who had been Director of Criminal Investigation at Scotland Yard, introduced the Probation of First Offenders Bill to Parliament. Vincent was opposed to imprisonment wherever possible. To some extent, he had been inspired by the example of the Massachusetts system, but in his time with the Metropolitan Police he had also been very aware of police practice under the Prevention of Crime Acts of 1871 and 1879, whereby the police were responsible for the supervision of ex-convicts, as he had been responsible for setting up the Convict Supervision Office which carried out this work. He seems to have been 'greatly impressed' (Bochel 1976: 10) by how the police dealt with this responsibility and, as a result, in his Bill he suggested that those placed on probation should be supervised by police officers. Supervision was a vital part of Vincent's vision of probation, but to rely on the police for this was not welcomed. As Radzinowicz and Hood (1986: 637) argue:

> This led to bitter controversy, bred confusion, encouraged ambivalence, and without doubt played an important part in delaying the introduction of probation for two decades.

Vincent's Bill was to apply to first offenders only and to subject such individuals to police supervision, thereby associating them with released convicts; it was, therefore, viewed with some revulsion by members of the judiciary and the Home Office. The Bill ran into trouble in the House of Lords and proceeded no further.

Vincent was not about to give up, however, and kept pressing the Home Office for support. A revised Bill had its first reading in January 1887 and during its course through the House various changes were made to the supervision aspect. First, police supervision would only be applied at the court's discretion; then police supervision was amended to supervision by some unspecified authority, possibly officers of Discharged Prisoners' Aid Societies, clergymen or priests, or police superintendents (Bochel 1976: 13–14). Despite the unsatisfactory nature of the supervision clause, the Bill made it through the Commons but again ran into trouble in the Lords where, as a result of government insistence that amendments were needed, the clause proposing supervision by an authority was dropped so that the Bill might pass through the Lords, which it duly did. The price of success, however, was that there was to be no systematic supervision, even though the supporters of probation all acknowledged that this was the key to success.

The key points of the Probation of First Offenders Act 1887 were:

- It applied only to those with no previous convictions.
- The offender had to be convicted of an offence punishable by no more than two years imprisonment.
- Consideration had to be given to the youth, character and antecedents of the offender, and the nature of the offence.

- Where these conditions applied the offender could, instead of being sentenced, be released on 'entering into recognisance, with or without sureties and during such period as the Court may direct, to appear and receive judgement when called upon, and in the meantime to keep the peace and be of good conduct' (Section 1 of the Act).
- A fixed abode was necessary.

Despite the obvious need for the Act – one-third of those in prison at the time were first offenders convicted of trivial offences, almost one in five were under 20 years old, and almost three-quarters had been sentenced to less than 12 months – it was not used often in the years that followed (Radzinowicz and Hood 1986).

There were a number of reasons for this lack of use. First, as there was no statutory form of supervision, courts were reluctant to use the Act to release offenders when there was no way of keeping a check on offenders' behaviour. Second, no resources were made available to carry out the kinds of inquiry needed into the character of the offender, so a significant aspect of assessment for suitability was lacking. Third, there was no Home Office encouragement of the courts to make use of the Act for five years. Only in 1892, as a result of promptings by the Howard Association, was a Home Office Circular issued to magistrates encouraging them to use the provisions of the Act. A fourth problem lay in the fact that the Act required a conviction to be recorded, something that magistrates were unhappy about, as W.D. Morrison pointed out:

> a serious objection to the Probation of First Offenders Act, passed in 1887, is that its application necessarily involves a conviction, which, in the case of persons charged for the first time with offences of a trifling nature, is the very thing it seems so desirable to avoid, inasmuch as a conviction, especially for an offence imputing dishonesty, inflicts an indelible stain upon the accused person, and may be a serious obstacle to future success in life.
>
> (Morrison 1896: 189)

Fifth, and almost certainly as a result of the word 'youth' being used to describe one of the factors that should be considered before using probation, it is likely that magistrates may have interpreted the Act as applying only to young people. Sixth, the Act applied only to first offenders, a further restriction on its use. And, finally, there was another option at hand with the Summary Jurisdiction Act of 1879, which may indeed have been preferable to magistrates as recording a conviction was not required under this legislation.

Slowly, the new Act began to be used more often: it 'was being used four times more frequently in 1896 than it had been in 1888' (not surprisingly perhaps given that 1888 was only the first year of its operation) and 'it began to be resorted to more frequently than was the Summary Jurisdiction Act for indictable offences tried summarily' (Radzinowicz and Hood 1986: 639). At the same time, the number of CETS missionaries working in the courts grew so that by 1900 there were a hundred men and at least a dozen women missionaries. All the evidence suggests that the work carried out by the missionaries was held in high regard by magistrates. The Howard Association regularly pressed the case for probation: it was a more humane alternative to imprisonment (especially for young offenders); it was more effective in reducing crime than imprisonment; and it was cheaper than imprisonment. Howard Vincent continued to argue for probation, and the Home Office began to show some interest.[2]

Perhaps the final, crucial step was the Liberal victory in the general election of 1906 after which Herbert Gladstone, who had chaired the Gladstone Committee, became Home Secretary. Gladstone, therefore, had a strong interest in penal reform; indeed, the Committee had urged that

> at a minimum, first offenders, juveniles, habitual criminals, habitual drunkards, the weak-minded, female prisoners with infants, and unconvicted prisoners be systematically separated and treated by means appropriate to their situations and natures.

> (Wiener 1990: 378)

His Under-Secretary, Herbert Samuel, was also keen on penal reform and the Permanent Under-Secretary, C.E. Troup, too, seems to have been a supporter. Thus, the individuals who could make a difference were all in place in 1906. In 1905, 1906 and 1907 Howard Vincent had again been involved in presenting Bills to develop probation but nothing came of these. Late in 1906, however, the government presented their Probation of Offenders Bill to the House of Commons although there was not enough time in the Parliamentary session to get the Bill through. It was reintroduced in March 1907 and received Royal Assent in August 1907.

The path to probation as we know it – assuming that the 1907 Act is the defining legislation – was neither simple nor swift. On the contrary, it was complicated, convoluted, contested and contingent. A variety of background factors – ideological, cultural, legal, charitable, academic – were necessary to provide an adequate foundation for ideas about 'probation', but without concrete examples and powerful support these background factors might never have resulted in the 1907 Act. It was fortunate that the CETS missionaries moved into the courts when they did, and equally fortunate that their efforts were appreciated by magistrates. The significance of the efforts of Howard Vincent, particularly (and despite its limitations) with the Probation of First Offenders Act, cannot be overestimated. And the change in ministers in the Home Office as a result of the 1906 election was equally important.

In the next chapter we examine the 1907 Act and the early development of probation.

2 The first decade

The Probation of Offenders Act 1907

Compared with many Acts of Parliament today, the Probation of Offenders Act 1907 was fairly brief, comprising only a handful of pages. The Act has, of course, been seen as a hugely significant development, a major leap forward for criminal justice, but, while its significance is easy to acknowledge with hindsight, a close inspection of its contents suggests that it was more a hesitant step forward rather than a leap.

The Act applied to any person charged before a court of summary jurisdiction, and also to those 'convicted on indictment of any offence punishable with imprisonment' (section 1 (2)). Thus it widened the scope for probation beyond that of the 1887 Act which had only focused upon first offenders. In deciding whether to use the powers contained in the Act, the court was enjoined to take account of the 'character, antecedents, age, health, or mental condition of the person charged, or to the trivial nature of the offence, or to the extenuating circumstances under which the offence was committed' (section 1 (1)). This list of factors that should have been considered before making an order covered a variety of issues, any one of which might have inclined the court towards probation; the court did not need to consider all or several of these before deciding on sentence. Again, therefore, this would seem to indicate a widening of the scope for probation. Perhaps, too, it is important to note the presence of 'age' as one factor for the court to consider. As we will see, for a considerable period of time, probation was seen as a sentence that was particularly applicable to young offenders, an impression that had been implanted by the 1887 Act where the court had to consider the 'youth' rather than the 'age' of the offender.

Another issue that has dogged the probation order for all of its history has been the accusation that it represents a 'soft option' or a 'let off'. One of the roots of this charge can be found in the first section of the Act where a court of summary jurisdiction, having considered the factors discussed above, then decides whether 'it is inexpedient to inflict any punishment or any other than a nominal punishment, or that it is expedient to release the offender on probation … without proceeding to conviction' (section 1 (1)). In these few lines it is implied that probation can be equated with no punishment at all; and the lack of a conviction could also imply that probation is not a 'proper' sentence of the court. It is worth emphasising here that a conviction *was* recorded if the individual was convicted of an indictable offence punishable by imprisonment, an 'odd state of affairs [that] lasted for forty years' (Hinde 1951: 199) and one that could only have led to some confusion. Consent was crucial as the offender had to agree to enter into a recognisance and to be bound by its conditions, and consent remained a distinguishing factor of the probation order for more than 80 years. Home Office guidance on the Act made it clear that probation should be seen as different from punishment: 'Probation really rests upon a promise, not upon compulsion. This is the essential difference between probation and punishment' (Le Mesurier 1935: 237).

The probation order itself is somewhat difficult to distinguish as three different disposals were possible within the Act when the case had been proved and the court had considered the factors discussed:

- dismissal of the charge;
- releasing the offender on a recognisance without supervision (binding over);
- releasing the offender on a recognisance with supervision (probation order).

The existence of these three options within the Act served to complicate matters as the term probation could be applied to any of them. The crucial matter, however, was the use of supervision for the third option and it is this which has set probation apart from other sentences (and which we shall recognise as the probation order), although the legal ambiguities of the Act were not clarified for a further 40 years.

The probation order was, in fact, a condition that could be contained in a recognisance, along with three other conditions:

- prohibiting the offender from associating with thieves and other undesirable persons, or from frequenting undesirable places;
- causing the offender to abstain from intoxicating liquor, where the offence was drunkenness or an offence committed under the influence of drink;
- generally securing the offender to lead an honest and industrious life.

No minimum length for a probation order was specified, although the maximum period was three years. Interestingly, the offender could also be ordered to pay 'damages for injury or compensation for loss' (section 1 (3)), although this does not seem to have been used often by the courts.

The appointment of probation officers for petty sessional divisions (PSDs) was discretionary, not mandatory, thereby leaving it up to the local justices to decide whether or not to appoint. And a positive decision was not encouraged by the fact that payment for probation officers was to come from the PSD; government funds were not made available. Indeed, the method of payment itself was vague as it was left to the court to decide whether to pay by salary or by some other means (a fee-based system). Even with regard to the appointment of 'special probation officers' for those under 16 years of age the Act remained rather vague, as it allowed such appointments 'where circumstances permit' (section 3 (2)). There is, therefore, very little clear guidance about who probation officers might be, how they should be appointed or how they should be paid – all issues that were to be significant during the following decades. Indeed, section 3 (3) b of the Act allowed supervision to be carried out by 'a person who has not been appointed to be a probation officer for any petty sessional division'.

The duties of probation officers were set out in the Act, and these were:

- to visit or receive reports from the person under supervision at such reasonable intervals as may be specified in the probation order or, subject thereto, as the probation officer may think fit;
- to see that he observes the conditions of his recognisance;
- to report to the court as to his behaviour;
- to advise, assist and befriend him, and, when necessary, to endeavour to find him suitable employment

It should be noted that there is no mention here of carrying out preliminary enquiries into the situation and character of the defendant, tasks which police court missionaries were already undertaking on an ad hoc basis and which justices considered to be useful.

While the significance of the Act in introducing the probation order cannot be overestimated, the details are – on the whole – surprisingly vague and diffident. The vagueness may well have been deliberate, giving courts the widest possible opportunity to make use of the Act and to be innovative. Who was to run the incipient probation service? It was certainly not a national body, as government refused to take responsibility for it, except for two instances. First, the Home Office would be responsible for probation in London, although this task was left to the courts in all other parts of the country. Second, the Home Secretary was empowered to make Probation Rules that would guide the work and organisation of probation (the first were issued in 1908). Thus, despite obvious Home Office reluctance to control directly the new disposal, the door had not been closed firmly on this option. From the start, probation was very much a local service driven by local courts and must be understood as such. This, of course, does not mean that national and local tensions did not exist from the beginning; state intervention in criminal justice had begun to get underway seriously following the deliberations of the Gladstone Committee, and the Probation of Offenders Act can be seen as another step, albeit a small one, in this direction.

What was different about the probation order? Three different choices were available to the courts if they decided to release an offender 'on probation'. The key to probation as we know it is the supervision element, but in 1907 the possibility of confusion about the meaning of probation was evident (and would be all too clear in some of the accounts provided by witnesses to the Departmental Committee set up to investigate the workings of the Act). Probation was not clearly distinguished from the other two options in the Act and this fact alone did not encourage the use of the new disposal. There was also unnecessary confusion about whether a probation order required a conviction to be recorded.

The appointment of probation officers, their qualifications and training, and their remuneration were all missing from the Act, and the duties of officers were set out in very general terms. The failure to clarify these issues meant that tensions that had been bubbling under for some years (particularly concerning the abilities of police court missionaries) emerged more forcefully in the next few years. Probation was not, therefore, introduced to unanimous acclaim; indeed it would be more true to say that while there was little in the way of Parliamentary opposition there were certainly noises of discontent from various individuals and organisations (for a flavour of some of the discussions, debates, arguments and tensions that were carried on see, for example, Bochel 1976; Garland 1985; Page 1992; Vanstone 2004a). While direct Home Office control would not have been welcomed, the lack of Home Office funding was a limiting factor.

Viewing the Act in isolation may well have encouraged a tendency to overstate its importance. It is worth remembering that in 1908 two Acts were passed that have claims to be at least as significant as the Probation of Offenders Act: the Children Act which introduced juvenile courts, abolished imprisonment for children under the age of 14 and limited the use of imprisonment for those aged 14–16; and the Prevention of Crime Act which introduced the statutory power to sentence those aged 16–20 to detention in a borstal institution (an experimental scheme had been running since the beginning of the century). And if we take a slightly wider perspective and follow Garland (1985) by looking at the period 1894–1914 we are faced with 30 official reports on penal and social regulation and more than 15 Acts of Parliament covering penal matters. From this point of view, the Probation of Offenders Act 1907 is only one of a series of measures that, taken together, constitutes a penal–welfare complex that dominated the treatment of offenders for most of the following 100 years.

David Garland points to the significance of the Act, which he sees as constituting

> an important extension and transformation of the sanctions of the criminal law. In establishing a state-authorised system of social work, financed from the rates and ordered by the courts, the Act heralded a profound revision of the state's proper functions with regard to the offender. At the same time, section 4 of the Act established measures of investigation, surveillance and normalisation that extended and refined the field of vision and intervention available to the court. And precisely because these duties of 'visiting', 'reporting' and 'advising' were the stipulated duties of a paid and accountable official – unlike the vaguer status of investigation and reform in prisons – they were all the more likely to operate in actual practice.
>
> (Garland 1985: 218–19)

But this is to overestimate the contents of the Act. By using terms such as investigation, surveillance and normalisation Garland gives a late-twentieth-century sheen to the 1907 Act which it cannot really support. And, although the duties of a probation officer were set down in the Act, the appointment of officers was permissive so that, where courts decided not to appoint them, there was no question of financing from the rates being necessary, and it is difficult to envisage how the statutory duties could be carried out at all. The 1907 Act was an important step on the journey that had begun in 1887, but it was not the first step and it would not be the last by any means.

Planning for implementation

In the months following Royal Assent to the Bill (21 August 1907), the Home Office appointed a Committee to advise how the Act should be implemented in London, where the Home Office was responsible for the implementation of the Act.

In the months leading up to the Act, and for the remainder of the year, discussion continued regarding who might be the appropriate people to be appointed as probation officers. As noted in Chapter 1, the Chairman of the Prison Commissioners, Evelyn Ruggles-Brise, was keen on using police officers for the work, especially as he wanted to see probation being used as an alternative to imprisonment for adult offenders (Bochel 1976: Chapter 2). While an influential figure, however, Ruggles-Brise had few supporters – even the Metropolitan Police Commissioner was opposed to such an arrangement. Some argued that the new probation officers should not be drawn from the ranks of any existing body but should represent a completely new organisation:

> They would be known in their various localities as interested in philanthropic work, and frequently would be men of position and influence which would help them in obtaining work for their young protégés. Some, no doubt, would be supplied by charitable societies, but, on the whole, independent gentlemen with leisure at their disposal would prove the most satisfactory. An officer provided by a denominational body would be under a certain obligation to promote its aims, and would often in the mind of the probationer be open to the suspicion of trying to 'get at' him for religious purposes.
>
> (Russell and Rigby 1906: 145–6)

The CETS missionaries, of course, had a strong claim. In the first place, they were already available and familiar with the work of the courts; second, they represented no financial demands upon the government; and, third, they appeared to have the confidence of magistrates. In 1906, members of the Society had met with the Home Secretary to press their case:

> They expressed their Society's willingness to fall in with any arrangements that might be made about court probation officers and pointed out that the Society, being a ready-made organisation and having well over a hundred agents already familiar with police court work, could easily provide probation

officers, and indeed find voluntary workers to give assistance. They had a hundred and nine missionaries employed in the work, and in addition sixteen lady missionaries. Although its management was in the hands of the Temperance Society the police court work was, they claimed, 'absolutely unsectarian'.

(Bochel 1976: 37)

According to a contemporary study by Gamon (1907), this was not the case, and the quote from Russell and Rigby suggests they agreed with him. He seems to have fully appreciated the work done by the missionaries in court but considered them to be 'tainted with the sectarian brush' (Gamon 1907: 181), overly focused upon temperance issues, not especially well-educated (which might prove a drawback in dealing with magistrates), untrained and trying to serve two masters (the courts and the societies that employed them). Not surprisingly, Gamon argues for a trained body of probation officers and, implicitly, for a greater degree of professionalism.

There was little agreement, then, about who would best be suited to act as probation officers and the Home Office Committee did not clarify the matter by advocating a policy of diversity when it came to appointments. In practice, this meant that for London the CETS and other religious bodies (the Church Army, the Federation of Local Free Church Councils and the Roman Catholic Westminster Education Fund) in addition to the National British Women's Temperance Association and the Reformatory and Refuge Union agreed that their staff might be appointed as probation officers.[1] As for the rest of England and Wales, it can be assumed that for the most part those who were being used prior to the Act (generally missionaries) continued to perform the duties of a probation officer.

The Home Office Committee also prepared the first Probation Rules that the Act empowered the Home Secretary to issue, and these went a little way to filling out some of the gaps in the legislation:

- Probation appointments were to be made by justices on an annual basis.
- Probation officers were expected to ensure that the offender understood the conditions of the order.
- They were expected to visit offenders (weekly for the first month) rather than have them report.
- Uniforms were not to be worn.
- Annual returns about the details of cases (including the results of their work) had to be made by probation officers to their justices' clerk.

A Memorandum was also sent out by the Home Office to all justices reminding them of the Act, making suggestions about the appointment of suitable persons as probation officers, and outlining the fee-payment method adopted for London. The Memorandum emphasised the responsibility of the magistrates for making the Act a success. But a lot was being left up to individual petty sessional divisions.

As Bochel (1976: 43–5) points out such a Memorandum was 'purely advisory … Apathy and misunderstanding on [the part of magistrates] could be disastrous'.

The Act began operating on 1 January 1908.

The Departmental Committee on the Probation of Offenders Act

Given that a rudimentary system of probation had existed formally since 1887, and that the 1907 Act represented an extension of that system rather than a radical change, it is likely that probation supervision in 1908 was very much what it had been for the previous two decades. Newton (1956: 123), from a distance of 50 years, summed up police court missionary work as follows:

> These founder fathers were missionaries in the true sense of the word and they used the methods of missionaries – changing behaviour by changing feeling – through 'conversion'. Their methods were persuasion, exhortation and support. They strengthened weak resolution by administering solemn pledges to renounce drink; they gently admonished the sinner while at the same time they offered him the helping hand of friendship; they advised him for his own good; they assisted him in many ways to improve his social and economic condition; and finally they prayed for guidance for him and for themselves. These men believed in the supreme importance of the individual to God and the parables of the lost sheep and the prodigal son were their casework manuals.

Missionaries worked in the courts, visited offenders in their homes, found them jobs and places to stay if they were homeless. The accounts of practice quoted in Page (1992) and Vanstone (2004a) suggest energetic individuals struggling with people who desperately needed help but who were not always able or willing to accept it easily. It is not surprising that there is little evidence in the accounts of early practice of what we might call developed theories of crime as these were not widely available at the time; but the language used is profoundly religious and the dramatic structure of many of the accounts reads like traditional Christian narratives of the conversion of sinners and is redolent of writing that can be found in the work of John Bunyan more than 200 years earlier. The missionaries were practical men driven by their Christian faith.

In summing up one account of practical work by a missionary, Maurice Vanstone (2004a: 55) sets out what is probably as accurate a general description of early probation work as is possible. The methods used involved:

> first, the development, not of what would be classified later in the history of social work as a professional relationship but rather an intense personal relationship characterized by personal commitment, concreteness, concern and trust; second, the use of moral and religious persuasion and influence; and third, the use of authority and coercion.

As the work was, for the missionaries, literally a struggle for souls, and intensive efforts were sometimes necessary, we should bear in mind that the words 'advise, assist and befriend' might be best interpreted widely rather than in the more narrow, sentimental sense that has tended to be attributed to them. Coercion was a part of probation work from the start.

However the probation order was being used, it is clear that neither frequency nor consistency characterised its first year in operation. Early in 1909 the Home Secretary set up a Departmental Committee to inquire into the workings of the Act and it is worth examining the Committee's report in some detail. Their description of the work of the probation officer is somewhat idealised, but it does move away from the religious language noted above and it also introduces a medical model which would become highly influential. The Committee emphasised

> the direct personal influence of a man or woman chosen for excellence of character and for strength of personal influence ...
>
> ... 4. There are many persons on whom the effect of such influence, applied at the moment when the commission of an offence reveals the special need of it, may be as valuable as the skilled help of a doctor to a person suffering from disease. Often without friends of their own, more often with friends only of a degraded type, out of touch with any civilising influence, the probation officer comes to them from a different level of society, giving a helping hand to lift them out of the groove that leads to serious crime. He assists the man out of work to find employment. He puts the lad into touch with the managers of a boys' club, where he can be brought under healthy influences. He helps to improve the bad homes which are the breeding ground of child offenders. He persuades the careless to open accounts in the savings bank. Securing for him a respectful hearing, and furnishing a motive for acceptance of his counsels, there is always in the background the sanction of the penal law – the knowledge that the probation officer is the eye of the magistrate; that misbehaviour will be reported to the court, and will bring its penalty. So great, however, is the influence which a good probation officer is able to exercise over an offender during the specified period of probation, that his friendly interest is often sought after that period has expired, and his advice continues to carry weight, although the powers that supported it are ended.
>
> ... 5. To the magistrate also the probation officer may be of much assistance. The reports furnished by the probation officer inform him of the results, in practice, of his action; he can tell whether his clemency has been justified or not. He gathers material to guide him in future cases.
>
> (Home Office 1910a: 2)

As at least three of the five Committee members were strong supporters of the probation system, it is not surprising that the work of probation officers should be seen in so positive a light, and the Committee's report is driven to a large degree by the first of its 36 conclusions and recommendations: 'That the Act has already proved to be of great value in a large number of cases, and that actively used, when the conditions allow, it may become in the future a most useful factor in our penal law' (Home Office 1910a: 13).

During 1908 a total of 8,023 individuals were released on probation. The great majority of these (71 per cent) had been convicted of indictable offences that had been tried in courts of summary jurisdiction; a further 23 per cent had been convicted of non-indictable offences; and the remaining 6 per cent had been convicted on indictment. By far the most common offence was theft, comprising around 66 per cent of offences; offences of drunkenness were next most common making up 6 per cent of offences. Interestingly, one female offender aged between 16 and 21 was given a probation order for an offence of manslaughter.

Just over three-quarters (76 per cent) of those given probation orders were male, which meant that a remarkably high percentage of orders were made on female offenders. Just over one-third (35 per cent) were aged under 16; just under one-third (31 per cent) were aged between 16 and 21; and one-third were over 21. In other words, two-thirds of those who received probation orders in 1908 were aged 21 or younger. Women were much more likely to be given a probation order if they were older – 38 per cent of those aged over 21 were female, while only 12 per cent were under 16. Despite the provision in the Act for special children's probation officers, these seem to have been used in only a handful of cases, including London where two female officers had been specifically appointed for this purpose.

Three-quarters of those placed on probation received an order lasting between 3 and 12 months; one in ten orders were for 3 months or less and only 5 per cent were for between 2 and 3 years. The Committee, using police returns, claimed that 'the statistics available for the year 1908 show that ... less than 5 per cent [of those given probation orders] had to be recalled before the court and penalties imposed' (Home Office 1910a: 2), but this is choosing the better of two possible measures of outcome. Using data supplied by probation officers to the justices (Home Office 1910b: Appendix IV) a rather different picture of 'success' can be presented, one the Committee chose to ignore: by adding four of the columns under the 'Result of Probation in Completed Cases' (Conduct Satisfactory, Sentenced or Reconvicted, Probation Extended, and Absconded) there are 2,685 cases of which 807 (30 per cent) come under the last three categories and can be counted as 'unsatisfactory' – a much greater proportion than 5 per cent (we have ignored those classified as Other Cases, Died or Removed to Other Districts, or where the case was not complete).

In all, a total of 1,043 courts of summary jurisdiction supplied data to the Home Office and, of these, 27 per cent had appointed no probation officers. This left 763 courts where such appointments had been made, but of these 25 per cent had made no probation orders. Thus, almost half of the courts of summary jurisdiction (45 per cent) had not made any use of the 1907 Act. There was also considerable variation in the use of probation orders between areas where similarities might have been expected: 'at Liverpool 478 probation orders were made, at Manchester 77, at Birmingham 59, and at Newcastle 19' (Home Office 1910a: 3). And a reading of the evidence presented to the Committee suggests that where courts did use probation orders very different approaches were followed.

Twenty-nine witnesses appeared before the Committee, around half of whom were sentencers and justices' clerks, with the remainder split approximately evenly between probation officers and members of penal reform groups and organisations who supplied probation officers. One issue that appears regularly in the Minutes of Evidence is that there is considerable confusion amongst sentencers about what a probation order is; some see no difference between what was available prior to the 1907 Act, while others mix up binding over with probation. Such confusion cannot have encouraged use of the new order. The perception remained that probation was for the young and first offenders; one magistrate pointed out that 'it has never occurred to me to use the probation principle for a grown man' (Home Office 1910b: 96). Some magistrates felt that the conditions in the Act did not give them such scope for attaching conditions as was available in the Summary Jurisdiction Act of 1879, particularly with regard to residence in a specified institution. Some witnesses argued that the visits of a probation officer to an offender and his or her family were intrusive and unwelcome and would not contribute to leading the offender away from crime. Difficulties about finding appropriate individuals to serve as probation officers, the additional costs to local authorities, extra work for clerks to the justices, and the fact that the Act was only just over a year old were also cited as reasons for the lack of use of the Act. But the Committee was not convinced by many of these arguments:

> partly owing to misapprehension of its scope, partly to its novelty, and partly to objections that have no solid foundation, the courts in many places have not made use of the powers of the Act in a considerable proportion of the cases in which they might properly be applied.
>
> (Home Office 1910a: 13)

It consequently recommended that the Home Office should contact every magistrate (again) to remind them of the Act and to encourage them to make use of it appropriately. This meant considering probation for 'a great number of cases where the person charged is neither a first offender nor a child' (Home Office 1910b: 5) and might even include a serious offence where the nature of the offence and the character of the offender were suitable.

The probation officers who presented evidence to the Committee were clear about one aspect of the Act: it gave them much more power over the offender than had been possible under previous legislation. 'It [the Act] gives one more control over the people who have been placed on probation than before. One finds one is able to exercise greater influence over them because they realise that if they infringe their recognisance they may be brought up' (Home Office 1910b: 97). And some magistrates too considered that the probation order provided greater control. This view was endorsed by the Committee.

While the Committee did not comment directly upon the lack of probation officers in many courts, they were very clear about the significance of the individual who acted as probation officer:

> The value of probation must necessarily depend on the efficiency of the probation officer. It is a system in which rules are comparatively unimportant, and personality is everything. The probation officer must be a picked man or woman, endowed not only with intelligence and zeal, but, in a high degree, with sympathy and tact and firmness. On his or her individuality the success or failure of the system depends. Probation is what the officer makes it.
>
> (Home Office 1910a: 5)

What is perhaps most interesting about this description of the characteristics of the probation officer is that there is no mention of any kind of formal qualifications; personality is the crucial factor and that has little to do with education or training. Perhaps the main reason for this emphasis is the reliance on police court missionaries to perform the duties of probation officer – a reliance that the Committee was aware of and appreciated. Indeed, given the lack of Home Office funding, it is difficult to see how probation could have developed at all in the absence of the missionaries. At times, it is possible to discern in the evidence presented by witnesses to the Committee an emerging tension between missionaries and probation officers, for example in the way offenders were dealt with and in home visits. Similarly, there is also a sense of competition between the various societies that were involved in missionary work. These tensions are not noted by the Committee although they were to become rather more pronounced over time.

With regard to staffing, the Committee was in favour of using educated young men as voluntary probation officers to deal particularly with youths aged 16–20 who were considered to be difficult cases. Honorary probation officers might be used in rural areas where there was not enough work to justify a full-time, paid officer. And, while the Committee did not definitively rule against it, they did recommend that 'as a general rule' police officers should not be appointed as probation officers (Home Office 1910a: 14).

The topic of pay was just as significant 100 years ago as it remains today, and not surprisingly given the messy situation left by the Act. The Committee found that most of the missionaries carried out their probation duties without remuneration (they were paid by the societies that employed them); where payment was made this varied in the amount; and that payment by fee was much more common than by salary. Consequently, it was recommended that salaries should be paid, that actual on-the-job expenses should be refunded, and that the fees paid by the Home Office to probation officers in London were too low.

With regard to the duties of probation officers, the Committee made it clear that it accepted that the preliminary inquiries made by them on behalf of magistrates were useful, but urged that these should never have anything to do with the merits of the charge and that any such information should not be used until the charge had been proved. Although attendance in court was preferable when a probation order was made, the absence of the officer should not be an obstacle to the court making such an order. Probation officers had to guard against being seen as a soft touch (obviously considered to be as much of a problem then as it remains for probation today), but they were to be allowed some discretion in whether or not to bring probationers back to court:

> We do not wish to suggest that the probation officer should regard it as his duty to bring the probationer again before the court for any slight breach of decorum or even for infraction, if it is trivial, of one of the conditions of the order. But he should be careful to make him feel – and the magistrates may be expected to support their officer in so doing – that probation is a reality, that it is not equivalent to acquittal and discharge. Too much laxity can only result in an unwillingness on the part of the magistrates to use the probation officer's services at all.
>
> (Home Office 1910a: 8)

The Committee was adamant that probation should not be seen as the provision of charitable relief and they firmly condemned the practice of Mr Wheatley, head of the St Giles Christian Mission and an experienced London missionary, who claimed to have dealt with 414 cases during 1908. During his evidence the Committee felt that Wheatley had given the impression that 'he regarded the personal influence of the probation officer upon the probationer as quite secondary to the relief, in money or goods, which might be given to him, and which was in fact given to a very large proportion of the probationers in his charge' (Home Office 1910a: 8). Nor did the Committee think that probation officers should be used to collect fines.

The Committee also examined whether changes were necessary in the operation of the probation order, and it is evident that conditions were already a key aspect of the probation order. The key recommendations in this respect were:

- Probation orders of less than six months were rarely useful.
- 12-month orders were probably most useful, though longer terms might be necessary in some cases.
- The Act should be amended to ensure that courts were clear that the period of probation could be extended.
- A condition of residence should be introduced for those over the age of 16 (this was already possible for those aged up to 16).
- The condition of abstention from intoxicating liquor should be extended to cover cases where the offence was directly or indirectly attributable to excessive use of alcohol.

The final topic addressed by the Committee was the organisation of probation work, both at micro and macro level. The number of cases that a probation officer could supervise satisfactorily at the same time was examined in detail. To some extent, this depended upon the geographical area covered by individual courts (the Committee recommended that 'the district assigned to a probation officer should not be unmanageable through its extent') and the number of orders made, but the evidence from witnesses regarding personal caseloads ranged from around 30 to 300–400; the latter figure, the Committee noted with considerable understatement, 'we cannot regard as adequate supervision' (Home Office 1910a: 9). Their recommendation was that in urban areas 60 cases were the maximum that a probation officer should be expected to supervise at one time if the orders were on average for six months; where the average length of an order was longer, they suggested that a larger number might be supervised. Adequate record-keeping and reporting back to the court when required to do so were also suggested.

At the wider level, the Committee was firmly against the proposal put forward by some witnesses for chief probation officers to be appointed. Its reasoning is worth quoting in detail as it is not especially convincing and one is left with the impression that the real reason for recommending against the proposal is the financial one:

> We do not recommend the general adoption of this plan. In the first place, unless the number of probation cases increased to a remarkable extent, the districts would be few, if indeed there were any, in which there would be work enough to occupy a chief probation officer. To keep him fully employed it would be necessary for him to be attached to a large number of courts, so large a number that he could not properly keep in touch with the magistrates at all of them or be sufficiently cognisant of the hundreds of cases ostensibly placed in his charge. Nor would the expenditure on the salary of such an officer be justified, in our opinion, by the services he would perform. Second, there would be a danger that the sense of responsibility of the probation officer actually in daily contact with the probationers would be weakened by the position of subordination in which he would be placed, His individuality, on which everything depends, would have less play; he would feel himself a mere agent acting under instructions. Lastly, the magistrate himself would lose touch with his cases. At many of the stipendiary magistrates' courts the magistrate takes a close personal interest in the outcome of the probation orders he has made. In many of the justices' courts one or more of the magistrates, or sometimes the clerk, take a similar interest. If the communications of the court were with the chief probation officer alone, and the actual supervision of the probationer were entrusted to a subordinate, this personal interest, highly desirable to maintain as it is, would inevitably be diminished and even disappear. The reports to the magistrate would be at second hand. The probation work, instead of being, as it should be, essentially human and alive, would soon lapse into officialism and proceed by routine.

(Home Office 1910a: 9–10)

The feeling that probation was still a cottage industry in its early stages and based on personal relationships is confirmed by a couple of further recommendations. First, that there was no need for any kind of permanent central commission that would oversee probation work, advise about methods of working and publish periodical reports on the probation system. The Committee acknowledged that something of this nature was already being done by a Home Office official and suggested that this should continue. Second, that oversight of probation work in petty sessional divisions should be left on an informal basis to one or more of the justices.

There were, however, three recommendations regarding organisational issues that were to have important consequences. The first suggested that justices might form local committees to encourage interest in probation work. Second, a directory of probation officers should be prepared by the Home Office and revised annually (and one purpose of this would be to facilitate the transfer of cases from one area to another). Third, 'it would be useful if a Probation Officers' Society were formed to assist in the dissemination of information and in the development of probation work' (Home Office 1910a: 14) and the proposed directory would contribute to the establishment of such an organisation.[2]

Developments, 1910–18

Following the Committee's report, the Home Office sent information to all magistrates reminding them of the availability of the probation order, and they appointed the Secretary to the Committee as the official with special responsibility for probation work. He in turn began to compile the directory of officers that had been recommended and it was published in 1911. Pay was increased for London probation officers (those for whom the Home Secretary had responsibility) and a move from fees to salaries began.

In 1910 Sydney Edridge, Clerk to the Justices at Croydon, called a meeting of probation officers to discuss the formation of a staff association, and in 1912 the National Association of Probation Officers (Napo) was formed. While its objectives were concerned with the advancement of probation work by bringing probation officers together and sharing experience of work, Napo's longer-term significance lay in the potential it offered for developing professionalism and thereby the need for training and qualifications for probation officers. One recent commentator has summed up well the position in the missionary/probation officer debate at the start of the war:

By 1914, a well established system of Police Court Missionaries, now called Missionary Probation Officers, worked in the adult courts and continued with a method of work rooted in a combination of Mission and COS [Charity Organisations Society]. Their methods and organization had altered little since their foundation in the 1880s, though it had expanded.

Bolted onto this, and at this stage rather tenuously, were a handful of Children's Probation Officers working in the newly formed Children's Courts of London. Their origins and working methods were rooted in a different view of social work which owed more to a belief in the power of 'character' and 'influence' of an interested and educated middle-class adult working with the family to divert from a life of crime.

(Gard 2007: 952)

The Criminal Justice Administration Act 1914 took forward several more of the Committee's recommendations. The Act changed the law with regard to the use of conditions, widening them in respect of alcohol use and introducing a residence condition. The court was permitted to vary the conditions of an order or the length of the order (as long as it did not exceed three years). The Act also made provision for the payment by government of any society 'formed or already in existence having as its object or amongst its objects the care and control of persons under the age of twenty-one whilst on probation' (section 7 (1)). Bochel (1976) notes that the CETS originally regarded this with some concern as the words 'already in existence' were not in the original Bill, leading them to conclude that any such payments would not be made to them. The CETS arranged for one of their supporters in Parliament, William Joynson-Hicks (later to become Home Secretary in 1924), to put forward the amendment, which was accepted. This relatively minor issue suggests that, where finances were concerned, competition would lead to tensions between the organisations providing probation officers. But this clause of the Act was never implemented due to the outbreak of war and by 1918 the situation had changed (see below). The money payment supervision order is foreshadowed in the Act as section 1 (3) introduced the possibility of supervision for offenders aged between 16 and 21 who were fined, but the provision was rarely used.

One fairly predictable result of the war was an increase in juvenile crime. As Bailey (1987: 17) notes: 'A pre-war total of 37,500 young persons under sixteen charged before the juvenile courts each year went up to 51,000 cases by 1917' – a rise of 36 per cent. This increase, as might be expected, put pressure on the Home Office, and, given the use of probation for young offenders, it also meant that the probation system was under scrutiny. As Table 2.1 shows, the total number of persons tried in all courts was lower during the war years than in the previous six years, while the number of juveniles tried was higher than in the preceding years. The number of all persons given a probation order increased by 11 per cent between 1913 and 1916, while the figure for juveniles over the same period was 52 per cent; and between 1915 and 1918 more than half of probation orders were made on juveniles. For the period 1908–19 as a whole, slightly more than 1 in 10 juveniles tried received probation orders, compared with approximately 2 in 100 of all offenders tried. It is notable that with the end of hostilities the number of offenders placed on probation fell to pre-war levels.

Four books published between 1914 and 1917 all praised the probation system, especially when dealing with young offenders. But they also made pointed criticisms regarding the tensions we have already noted. Cecil Leeson's (1914) *The Probation System*, the first full-length study of probation, was heavily influenced by the example of probation in America and Leeson's experience working as a

Table 2.1 Number of persons tried in all courts and number placed on probation, with similar figures for juvenile courts, 1908–19

	Persons tried in all courts			Persons tried in juvenile courts		
Year	Total no.	No. on probation	%	Total no.	No. on probation	%
1908	757,080	8,023	1.06	Particulars not available		
1909	726,256	8,962	1.23	Particulars not available		
1910	698,305	10,223	1.46	33,598	3,568	10.62
1911	697,463	9,521	1.37	32,977	3,454	10.47
1912	730,669	11,219	1.54	38,351	4,537	11.83
1913	743,559	11,071	1.49	37,520	4,465	11.90
1914	685,324	10,747	1.57	36,929	4,496	12.17
1915	587,979	10,676	1.82	43,981	5,719	13.00
1916	668,835	12,329	1.84	47,342	6,781	14.32
1917	508,763	12,505	2.46	51,323	6,548	12.76
1918	433,476	11,719	2.70	49,915	5,868	11.76
1919	546,588	9,655	1.77	40,473	4,188	10.35

Source: Home Office 1922: Table II.

probation officer (he was to become secretary of the Howard Association in 1916 and secretary of the Magistrates' Association in 1920 when it was founded). He was in favour of much greater use of probation and was convinced of the need for preliminary inquiries before an order was made: 'so far from the preliminary inquiry being a desirable proceeding merely, it is a proceeding which the very nature of the probation system makes essential' (Leeson 1914: 67). He was anxious that probation was being used too often because it was cheap, argued for payment by salary rather than fees, and was a supporter of having chief probation officers and using voluntary probation officers. He also advocated training for probation officers, whereas the Departmental Committee on the Probation of Offenders Act had noted only the need for character and personality:

> The emphasis laid on the importance of personality in probation work has tended to obscure the necessity for special training. Given the right kind of man, it is possible for him to do good probation work, even though possessed of no special knowledge. But since the best probation work does necessitate special knowledge, and a peculiar skill in dealing with people, no man lacking such knowledge and skill can hope to do quite the best work; nor can he take his own share in improving the work by contributing to its technique. Besides character and personality, therefore, probation officers are required to satisfy specific demands as to age, education, training and experience … As the system expands in England, and the demand for probation officers increases, it may be found possible to modify the Social Study Courses already possessed by most of the newer universities, to meet their needs.
>
> (Leeson 1914: 87–9)

Leeson noted four specific problems of the probation system. First, to ensure that competent probation officers were appointed and that they were given enough time for their work and not overloaded with cases. Second, the use of probation in 'unsuitable cases. No offender should be released on probation, reclaimable or otherwise, unless his individual interests are reconcilable with the interests of the community' (Leeson 1914: 177). Third, making orders for only a few months was a waste of time. And, fourth, there was a serious lack of organisation, which could be remedied by the Home Office taking control of the system as a whole.

He produced another book, *The Child and the War* (Leeson 1917), as a direct response to the 'grave increase in the numbers of juvenile offenders' during the war. Again he argued powerfully for probation, although he was worried that often it was seen as a soft option. He called for an increase in the number of salaried probation officers while acknowledging that juvenile offending would almost certainly decrease after the war, and again advocated making more use of voluntary workers.

William Clarke Hall was a leading magistrate and, like Leeson, a highly influential supporter of probation. In 1917 he published *The State and the Child* where he too argued in favour of a more co-ordinated, professional system. He castigated the dual control that characterised probation officers, pointing out that in London three authorities were involved: the court, the voluntary societies such as CETS, and the Home Office. While careful to pay tribute to the work of the missionaries, he was certain that there was no doubt 'that professional probation officers are necessary, or that they should be selected and trained with the utmost care' (Clarke Hall 1917: 109). Like Leeson, he urged greater use of voluntary workers alongside trained probation officers and was in favour of having chief probation officers as could be found in America. Douglas Pepler (1915) too, in *Justice and the Child*, urged the claims of probation – particularly for juvenile offenders.

Besides these books, various penal reform organisations were making their criticisms about the abilities of missionaries and the dual control system known to the Home Office during the war. Napo, too, not surprisingly, made the case for a more professional and fully trained probation service (see Bailey 1987; Bochel 1976). By the end of the war, new ideas about delinquency were emerging that would not have helped a case for retention of the missionaries.

> A gradual shift in approach to the explanation of juvenile delinquency took place in the 1920s. The original emphasis on social and economic factors, on the effects of unemployment, and on the material conditions of the home, was slowly replaced by a modified environmental approach in which the psychological conditions obtaining in the home and family were given greater prominence.
>
> (Bailey 1987: 12)

Indeed, the very existence of the 1907 Act, which legislated for something that had been done voluntarily by police court missionaries, thereby implicitly routinising what had been a religious process at its core, can be seen as heralding the end of police court missionaries.

A decade of achievement?

What had actually been achieved in the ten years subsequent to the implementation of the 1907 Act? Although the Act itself was no great leap forward, it represented a small but significant development of the 1887 Act by widening the scope for the use of probation and by including the use of supervision by a specified individual. The Act remained rather vague on detail but this did leave the door open for creative use by justices. Key issues such as who were to be appointed as probation officers, how they were to be organised, and how they were to be paid were all, however, too important to be left to individual courts to decide. At best, a situation lacking any coherence might have been expected. At worst, the growth of probation might have been stifled as tensions emerged with various individuals and organisations arguing over these key issues. It is all too clear that the Home Office did not wish to get heavily involved in the new probation system – apart from its oversight of London, which meant that there was a governmental foot in the door – and, while this can be seen as having advantages as well as disadvantages, the lack of Home Office funding meant that the new system was hobbled from the start.

The Departmental Committee that reported in 1910 probably came too soon on the heels of the Act. It did not permit the new legislation any time to settle down and work through its teething problems and it could also be seen as only applying to London as it was only in London that the Home Office had any direct power. On the other hand, it did pick up the potentially problematic issues we have identified in the Act: organisation (especially the dual control question), pay (not only how much, but on what basis) and appointments (the probation officer/missionary debate is apparent). And these issues were to remain important for some time. The Committee recommended what quickly became Napo and the significance of the birth of this organisation for the development of probation cannot be overestimated. Napo not only encouraged the idea of professionalism, but also began the task of constructing a probation culture and tradition – which have proved to be vital sources of strength (as well as sometimes drawbacks) in the growth of probation. By insisting on the need for specialised knowledge and skills, Napo was a vital factor in transforming a disparate group of individuals into a highly professional organisation.

The probation system had influential supporters, but the First World War may have proved to be at least as influential as individuals. The increase in juvenile crime during the war led to a focus on probation, and what had been seen as tensions began to be redefined as problems – and problems required solutions of some kind. Cecil Leeson and William Clarke Hall urged the reorganisation of probation on a national basis and greater training for probation officers and, given the timing of their books, they may have been listened to more seriously than might have been the case.

At the very least, in 1919 after 10 years of existence, the probation system seems to have been reasonably firmly established. The disruption caused by the war worked, on the whole, in probation's favour. In 1919 there were almost 10,000 probation orders made by the courts, 43 per cent of which were for juveniles. There were between 700 and 800 probation officers, although the number of courts at which officers were appointed had only increased from 763 in 1908 to 819 in 1919, leaving 215 courts of summary jurisdiction with no officers. The vast majority of probation orders (94 per cent) were made in the summary courts.

Probation had begun with a solid, if unspectacular ten years. In the next chapter we explore how the system developed during its second decade of existence.

3   Consolidation

Probation certainly cannot be said to have taken off and grown significantly in its first decade of existence. The war seems to have contributed to an increase in the use of probation, but this was to a considerable degree the result of increased use for juvenile offenders. There was a sudden drop in the use of probation from 11,719 in 1918 to 9,655 in 1919, with the bulk of this decrease the result of almost 1,700 fewer juvenile offenders being given probation. This may have been a cause for some worry, but it must be emphasised that probation had demonstrated its worth during the war, and a strong case had been made for developing it along more organised, professional lines by supporters such as Leeson, Clarke Hall and Pepler (see Chapter 2). Any such development would have had resource implications, however, and – despite the initial euphoria that came with the end of the war – economic reality had reared its head by 1920.

In spite of the immediate post-war economic boom, Britain emerged from the war 'a debtor nation, where before the war it had been a creditor … The collapse began in 1920 with an increase in government borrowing rates, a fall in prices and the beginnings of a rise in unemployment' (Stevenson 1984: 106–7). In 1921, the Prime Minister, David Lloyd George, appointed a Committee on National Expenditure chaired by Sir Eric Geddes to investigate where savings could be found in government expenditure. Social spending fell from £205.8 million in 1920–21 to £182.1 million in 1922–3 and £175.5 million in 1923–4, before beginning to recover (Peden 2000). It is worth recalling that the government had been spending very little indeed on probation but with the need to make savings it is unlikely that increased spending on this rather marginal item would have been welcomed as the 1920s began.

While it is difficult to be certain due to the lack of information, it is probable that the number of probation officers had scarcely grown between 1913 and 1919. This claim is partly based on the number of courts where probation officers had been appointed increasing only by around 45, partly based on the impact of the war, and partly on the stability in the numbers placed on probation during those years. The questions regarding pay, appointment and control – all of which had been raised during the war – had not disappeared in 1919; indeed Napo was complaining to the Home Office about these matters in 1918. While Mike Nellis's view that 'The post-War probation service was in poor shape' (Nellis 2007: 32) may be overly pessimistic (although one might justifiably ask whether a probation service as such existed), there can be little doubt that probation was in need of a boost and that the time was not particularly propitious if increased spending was needed.

But the Home Office was aware that probation was facing problems, as Victor Bailey points out:

> In the course of the First World War, however, Home Office opinion on the issue of central control seemed to change. This was due most probably to a number of factors. Demands for the abolition of dual control became more insistent as bodies like the National Association of Probation Officers made themselves heard. The Church of England Temperance Society were forced on the defensive, as a number of courts began to appoint their own probation officers. Moreover, it became evident to the Home Office from the replies of justices' clerks to the circular of 11 January 1919, that the existing system was unsatisfactory. Rarely were probation officers able to give their undivided attention to juvenile cases; the remuneration of officers was decidedly inadequate.
>
> (Bailey 1987: 38)

In 1920, the Home Secretary Edward Shortt, appointed a Departmental Committee to inquire into the training, appointment and payment of probation officers. This may well have been seen as seriously raising expectations as its remit covered the very issues that were causing problems for probation.

The departmental committee on the training, appointment and payment of probation officers, 1922

The Committee heard evidence from 49 witnesses, with approximately one-third of these being probation officers and one-quarter sentencers, so that there was a good deal of practical experience available. Just as the 1910 Committee had done, this one began its report with praise for the 'great value of probation as a means of reformation and the prevention of crime' (Home Office 1922: 4), so it was clear from the start it was not going to be harshly critical of probation (if this had not been clear already by the membership of the Committee of five, the Chair being the Under-Secretary at the Home Office, and another member a senior Home Office official with responsibility for probation). The core of probation work was set out by the Committee, but essentially this remained somewhat vague and mystical whereby the personal influence of a good person (the probation officer) transformed a bad one (the offender):

> The underlying idea is the value of the influence which a man or woman of strong personality may exercise over one of weaker or immature character, who, owing to lack of discipline, bad associations or other circumstances, has been led to commit offences, and is liable to fall into or persist in criminal habits.
>
> (Home Office 1922: 4)

Just how this influence worked in practice was opaque, but it is interesting to note that the causes of crime are seen as not especially complex or threatening: 'lack of discipline, bad associations'. From the mid-1920s onwards, this view of the roots of crime began to change and became more complicated necessitating more specialised knowledge on the part of probation officers.

But, although probation was perceived to be generally effective, it was not to be used indiscriminately. The Committee noted that some offences were simply too serious to be dealt with by a probation order, and for some offenders who had been steeped in crime for too long probation was unlikely to be helpful. Targeting was, therefore, an essential part of good probation work and what we now term responsivity, and take as an essential component of effectiveness since the What Works initiative (see, for example, Andrews 1995; Raynor and Vanstone 2002), seems to have been implicitly recognised as early as 1922:

> Indeed, positive harm may be done by releasing on probation an offender to whom its application is entirely unsuitable. Whether a particular offender can with advantage be put under a probation order must depend on the circumstances of each case, and the decision must be left to the judicial authorities.
>
> (Home Office 1922: 4)

So probation should be used early in an offender's career and should not be used repeatedly. Probation was not only useful in preventing offending, but the Committee also considered that its use had contributed to a decrease in the prison population and in the use of reformatory and industrial schools, and the cost implications of this were not insignificant at the time.

The statistics available to the Committee (some of which have been discussed in Chapter 2) showed that in 1919:

- 43 per cent of probation orders were made on juveniles.
- 27 per cent of orders were made on females.
- 94 per cent of orders were made by courts of summary jurisdiction.
- Of the 580 orders made by the higher courts, 80 per cent were made by the London Sessions.
- 5 per cent of those released on probation appeared for sentence (a crude measure of reconviction).
- The use of probation varied from 0.74 per cent in one town to 5.75 per cent in another (for all cases).
- For juveniles, use varied from 1.45 per cent to 43.61 per cent.
- One-fifth of courts of summary jurisdiction had not appointed a probation officer.

Such differential use of probation suggests that there was considerable scope for greater use of the order and one of the first recommendations of the Committee was that 'Probation could with advantage be used much more freely in many Courts. Every Court should have a Probation Officer at its disposal' (Home Office 1922: 22).

Since 1907, probation officers had been subject to two different methods of appointment (and also, therefore, of payment): most were appointed by Justices of petty sessional divisions (PSDs) except in London where they were appointed by the Home Secretary. One method of moving forward on this early recommendation would be to have probation officers appointed and paid by the state, a proposal that was put to the Committee by the newly constituted Howard League for Penal Reform. But this suggestion was not accepted as the Committee felt that the local elements of probation were key to its success. Probation officers appointed by local Justices were more likely to work closely with their courts; and if they became 'a new class of Civil Servants' (Home Office 1922: 7) they would tend to be seen as an official rather than a friend by their probationers and this, in turn, would have a negative impact upon the influence they could bring to bear. The Committee did, however, recommend the scrapping of the annual renewal of probation officers' appointments, thereby giving greater job security.

The great majority of the 784 probation officers employed at the time were agents of religious and social organisations: the Church of England Temperance Society, the Discharged Prisoners' Aid Society, the Catholic Aid Society, the British Women's Temperance Society, the Church Army, the Salvation Army. The work carried out by these individuals covered more than just probation work and the Committee recognised the value of this:

> in addition to probation work, properly so-called, these agents frequently perform duties of an analogous character which are conveniently included under the description of 'missionary work'. The missionary work of the Police Courts is of the greatest value to magistrates when they need enquiries to be made as to the circumstances of the persons who come before them, and when a helping hand can be given, or a word in due season can be spoken. Frequently the missionaries are employed in arranging disputes or differences, especially between husbands and wives. All the witnesses, including magistrates whom we consulted, were unanimous in attaching great importance to the missionary work of the Courts and expressed the opinion that it is essential to the proper administration of justice. We agree with this view, and we are strongly of opinion that in appointing and fixing the remuneration of Probation Officers, Courts and local authorities should not discriminate too narrowly between probation work and missionary work.
>
> (Home Office 1922: 8)

It is interesting to note that such 'missionary work' became, over time, aspects of official probation work: social inquiry reports, matrimonial work; it is possible to see a hint of crime prevention work too.

Given the preponderance of religious organisations involved in delivering probation work, and the Committee's acknowledgement of their contribution to probation work, it comes as no surprise that there was no serious consideration given to moderating their influence:

> While we think there is room for improvement in their organisation, we should feel reluctant to make any recommendation which would have the effect of putting any check on the development of their work. It must be remembered that in this country much of the best social work has been accomplished by voluntary organisations, and probation offers a field in which private enterprise may be looked upon to yield good results.
>
> (Home Office 1922: 10)

Thus the system of appointing probation officers was to remain as it had been, with voluntary organisations responsible for supplying most of those employed. There was some criticism of the organisation of CETS: probation work and temperance were rather too closely related; and those employed by CETS had to be members of the Church of England, thus limiting recruitment of adequately qualified individuals. In response to such criticism, the Committee recommended the Police Court Mission part of CETS should be separated from any association with temperance work, that recruitment of probation officers should not be limited to members of the Church of England, and that probation officers attached to the Mission should not take any part in fund-raising for CETS.

Personality was still the most important characteristic for an effective probation officer and the Committee acknowledged that 'sympathy, tact, common sense, firmness' were all desirable and, in addition, 'there was general agreement that a keen missionary spirit, based on religious conviction, is essential' (Home Office 1922: 13). Thus, despite the fact that some witnesses argued that probation officers were not adequately trained and had a limited outlook as a result of their belonging to religious organisations, the Committee was reluctant to recommend any official training scheme, although the various societies who provided probation officers were encouraged to improve training for their recruits. University training was not considered to be necessary as character and personality were the key qualities, and the status of probation officers was made remarkably clear:

> It must be remembered, however, that men and women who go to the universities usually do so to fit themselves for a professional career, and it is doubtful whether a probation service organised on the lines we consider desirable would provide opportunities or prospects which would usually attract candidates of university training.
>
> (Home Office 1922: 14)

And because probation work was not considered to be a profession, large salaries could not be expected; indeed some probation officers who provided evidence to the Committee 'even deprecated the granting of large salaries on the ground that it might attract to the work persons who did not enter upon it from a love of the work, but for the prospect of a well-paid career' (Home Office 1922: 15).

There was little doubt, however, that in terms of the amount of payment as well as in the way probation officers were paid, the system was inadequate. Some probation officers were paid by salaries, while payment by fees remained in force in more than 400 courts. In London, children's officers (Home Office appointees) were paid considerably more than their Police Court Mission counterparts although two-thirds of the latter's salaries were paid by the Home Office. Individuals who were not regular probation officers but used occasionally by the courts were paid on a fee basis. The situation was messy to say the least, and the Committee recommended an increase in pay and that this should be by salary, with payment by fees scrapped except for those who carried out occasional probation work. Although the increased cost of this recommendation would not have been high, it was made at a time when the Geddes Committee restrictions on public expenditure were biting; they can be seen as a vote of confidence in the work of probation officers. But a general superannuation scheme was not recommended.

The final significant issue addressed by the Departmental Committee was how probation was organised, an issue that is intimately related to the other topics considered in the report. Training, pay, appointment, the development of probation work – the fragmentary and uncoordinated nature of all of these would have been very different if probation had been organised differently. The Committee was opposed to the idea of a government department taking control of the probation system, partly because this would diminish the local relationships that were felt to be so significant for probation, and partly because of the cost of such a proposal. Instead, the current arrangement whereby the Home Office Children's Department oversaw probation was to continue, with the assistance of a small Advisory Committee consisting of key stakeholders. In London, a single Police Court Mission was recommended while outside the capital collaboration was encouraged and the beginnings of probation committees can be seen.

> In provincial towns the magistrates should appoint a small committee of their own members to select Probation Officers and generally supervise their work. In counties endeavour should be made in suitable cases to organise the work on County lines.
>
> (Home Office 1922: 24)

The need for more funding for probation was made fairly robustly by the Committee, although they were fully aware of the financial restrictions the government was facing. The cheapness of probation was emphasised, especially in comparison to prison, borstal or reformatory or industrial schools. A government grant towards the costs of probation was recommended 'when the financial position is clearer' (Home Office 1922: 21), although the Committee acknowledged that such a grant would carry greater accountability to central government.

Overall, the message of the Departmental Committee might be summarised as 'Carry on as normal'. There is nothing radical in the report; it is a cautious and careful examination of probation that proposes no real change in the topics it had

been appointed to pursue. With regard to training and the appointment of probation officers no changes were considered necessary. Pay needed to be improved
and this should be on a salaried rather than a fee basis. But the power of the various societies that provided probation officers was scarcely touched. This is not so
surprising given that the great majority of probation officers were agents of these
societies and paid by them, so that without them there would have been – quite
literally – no probation system. The societies' position was further enhanced by
the government's efforts to cut expenditure.

Having said that, it should be emphasised that, with the benefit of hindsight,
and despite the relative blandness of the report, it does contain the seeds of
significant developments. Perhaps most importantly, there was some criticism –
albeit rather muted – of the societies, and in particular of the organisation of
the CETS. This did not go far enough for those who wanted more professional,
better qualified probation officers, but it was the beginning of the end for the
missionaries. Similarly, although no official training scheme was recommended,
better trained and qualified probation officers were agreed to be desirable. If more
university-based training were to be introduced, this would almost inevitably
lead to a diminution in the power of the societies. The tension between local
and central came through in the report, but although the idea of a national
service was turned down this was an issue that would not be finally settled
for many years. And the need to have a probation officer available at all
courts was a vital endorsement of the value of probation and a spur to further
development.

The Departmental Committee was only making recommendations, of course,
and it was up to government as to how far these might be taken on board. But,
bearing in mind the membership of the Committee, it was always likely that their
recommendations would chime with official Home Office thinking and implementation began almost immediately with the appointment of the Advisory
Committee recommended in the report. It is also notable that just over a year after
its publication, the first *Report on the Work of the Children's Branch* (Home
Office 1923) was published with a section on probation (following a suggestion
by the Departmental Committee) not only endorsing the Committee's work but
encouraging greater use of probation by the courts. This included the letter sent
by the Home Secretary (along with the Departmental Committee report) to all
magistrates' Benches in the country which urged magistrates to take on board
the key recommendations made by the Committee. This first report from the
Children's Branch noted the continuing differential use of probation across the
country, and suggested that there was still some misunderstanding by magistrates
about the kinds of offence that probation could be used for. Evidence from the
Prison Commissioners and individual prison governors was used to argue that
probation could be used more often as an alternative to short sentences of imprisonment especially for offenders aged between 16 and 21. The report was also
clear about the key problems of probation – and it is possible to discern here some
disagreement with the Departmental Committee's approach to organisation and
training:

The probation system still suffers to some extent from the defects of youth. There are no generally recognised standards or methods – as, for instance, in America, where in the large cities probation is highly organised. The development of probation in this country is on more individual lines which undoubtedly offers many advantages, but there are certain disadvantages. There is no 'carriere ouverte aux talents', and it does not necessarily secure the men and women with the best qualifications or highest training.

(Home Office 1923: 57)

Some figures were given to indicate the effectiveness of probation, with estimates varying from 90–95 per cent to around 50 per cent success (as measured by not reappearing in court for a number of years). These were acknowledged to be fairly crude indicators and the methods used to calculate them differed, but these early efforts should be recognised.

The next two reports on the work of the Children's Branch covered the same issues (Home Office 1924, 1925), although in addition both commented upon moves towards specialisms in specific areas, for example in after-care work with children, in helping offenders to employment, in supervising those who had been fined. Such developments were viewed positively, but they also led to the uneven development of probation in different areas – something that was not discouraged by the organisation of the system on a local basis.

In 1924 only 1,891 children were committed to Home Office Schools, a decrease of almost 90 per cent since 1919 which can be partly attributed to the increased use of probation, although as Bailey (1987: 53) argues, the costs of such schools, perceptions that they relied on old-fashioned penal methods, 'a general improvement in the social and economic health of the country since 1917, and a consequent decline in cases of neglect and delinquency' all played a part. Table 3.1 shows the growth of probation in the first half of the 1920s. In terms of numbers, those placed on probation increased by 43 per cent in the five-year-period 1919–24, but it is the increased proportionate use for juveniles

Table 3.1 Number of persons tried in all courts and in juvenile courts, with the number placed on probation, 1919–24

Year	Persons tried in all courts			Persons tried in juvenile courts		
	Total no.	No. on probation	%	Total no.	No. on probation	%
1919	546,588	9,655	1.77	40,473	4,188	10.35
1920	672,438	10,735	1.60	36,064	4,691	13.01
1921	585,073	10,293	1.76	30,253	4,147	13.71
1922	582,855	11,030	1.89	31,056	4,715	15.18
1923	603,370	12,666	2.10	28,769	5,448	18.94
1924	641,713	13,838	2.16	29,624	5,812	19.62

Source: Home Office 1925: Table VII.

that is most striking, from 10.35 per cent of those tried in juvenile courts to 19.62 per cent (although it should be acknowledged that this is, to some extent, a result of a large drop in the number of juveniles tried). In all, 42 per cent of probation orders were made on juveniles in 1924.

Probation's main customers were juvenile males, although it was also favoured for adult females: 18 per cent of all probation orders were made on females; for those aged over 21 the figure was 37 per cent, while for those under 16 it was 8 per cent (Home Office 1925: Table VIII). In 1921, offences of larceny were by far the most common offence (64 per cent) committed by those placed on probation; and 80 per cent of all orders were made as a result of indictable offences (Home Office 1923: Table XII).

The Criminal Justice Act 1925

Some recommendations of the 1922 Committee could be acted upon without legislation (e.g. the Advisory Committee was appointed by the Home Secretary within a few months of the publication of the report). The CETS reacted quickly to the report's criticisms by sending a deputation to the Home Office to discuss how they might respond.

> They were prepared ... to meet Home Office requirements by dropping the Society's name from the title of the Police Court Mission; by basing the latter on county or Quarter-Sessional, rather than diocesan areas, and by increasing lay membership of their Committees and including, where possible, local magistrates and philanthropists. Their police court missionaries would no longer be required to take an active part in raising funds; and the Missions would endeavour to improve their salaries, which the deputation admitted had been inadequate in the past.
>
> (Bochel 1976: 91)

However, the CETS had two sticking points. They wished to retain the right to appoint members of the Anglican Church as their agents, and the right for their probation officers to carry out temperance work if they wished to do so. If the Home Office was willing to go along with these points, the CETS undertook to consider the appointment of probation officers on an individual basis and not necessarily always to appoint Anglicans; and they agreed that their missionaries would not be forced to carry out temperance work. The two CETS branches in London were amalgamated to become the London Police Court Mission. So the CETS responded positively in the hope that their power would not be eroded.

The costs of probation on the public purse were not high – in 1919–20 they were estimated at around £27,000, and in 1924–5 at £47,000 (Home Office 1925) – and they were met almost exclusively by local authorities. Despite the restrictions on government spending, in 1924–5 the Home Office decided to follow the Departmental Committee's recommendation and make a grant towards the cost of probation and £22,500 was duly made available. This was a significant development in several ways: it was the first time that government funding for probation had been made available; it was voted through in advance of the Criminal Justice Bill, which was being held up as a result of the political situation, implying that the Home Office was keen to support probation; and, perhaps most importantly, with the benefit of hindsight, by providing funds the Home Office was taking another step towards control of probation – especially outside London.

The three general elections that took place in 1922, 1923 and 1924 delayed the Criminal Justice Bill that had first been introduced in 1923, but with the return of a Conservative administration in 1924 the Criminal Justice Act 1925 eventually received Royal Assent in December. The main provisions of the Act as far as probation was concerned were:

- A probation officer had to be appointed for each probation area.
- The task of probation officers was the supervision of those who were placed on probation by courts of summary jurisdiction, courts of assize or quarter sessions.
- Every petty sessional division (PSD) was designated as a probation area.
- A probation committee, consisting of at least three magistrates, would be responsible for the pay, appointment and supervision of the work of probation officers in each area.
- Smaller PSDs would be combined where necessary in order to form a probation area.
- The agents of voluntary societies could be employed as probation officers.
- The Home Secretary would make rules regarding the power of probation committees, for confirming the appointment of probation officers, and for fixing salaries and expenses.

These provisions made significant steps to consolidate probation. For the first time, every court would have the services of a probation officer. In 1924 there had still been almost 150 courts of summary jurisdiction which had not made such an appointment (Home Office 1925), and the use of probation was confined almost exclusively to courts where a probation officer had been appointed. In addition, the Act made it clear that probation supervision applied equally to the higher courts, presumably in an effort to encourage its use. The organisation of probation was formalised with the designation of probation areas, and by providing the power to combine areas excuses about a PSD being too small to support the work of a probation officer would no longer apply. The role of the voluntary societies was confirmed, thereby allaying some of their fears – originally the clause covering this had not been included in the Bill. Indeed, it was on the personal intervention of the Home Secretary, William Joynson-Hicks, that an amendment to include the clause was moved on the second reading of the Bill. Finally, the power of the Home Secretary was strengthened with regard to rules, and this was in addition to the increased power that came with the provision of a grant.

1926–30

The five years following the Act were hugely significant for probation. The 1922 Departmental Committee had decided against a general superannuation scheme for probation officers, mainly on the grounds of the number of different organisations that employed them. Despite this, the 1925 Act included the power for the Home Secretary to provide a superannuation scheme and a small committee was charged with designing and setting up such a scheme (Home Office 1926a), which duly came into operation in 1926. The details of the scheme need not detain us, but the implications are significant: at a time when government expenditure was under pressure the Home Office showed itself willing to improve the financial arrangements for probation officers, a clear gesture of the importance accorded to probation; as Bochel (1976: 103) notes, it supports the impression that probation work was a full-time occupation 'comparable in status with other public servants, such as local government officers'; by providing a pension scheme good candidates would be encouraged to become probation officers, and another small step in the direction of central control was made.

A new, and much fuller, set of Probation Rules was published in 1926 (Home Office 1926b), and the most important of these also demonstrated the slow but steady spread of Home Office control.

- The organisation, size and functions of probation committees were set out.
- Details of the appointment and qualifications of probation officers were specified (after a year appointments were subject to confirmation by the Home Secretary; police officers were not permitted to act as probation officers; age at appointment had to be between 25 and 40; and, in addition to the usual emphasis on personality when making appointments, training, experience and educational qualifications had to be taken into account).
- The duties of probation officers were defined (and, in an early example of what would become National Standards 60 years later, the frequency of meetings with offenders was set – at least once a week for the first month, and for those under 16 meetings every fortnight at least for the first six months).
- A formal system of record-keeping was prescribed.
- Pay scales were fixed and would be by salary; extra pay could be made to a principal probation officer, or to an officer with approved university qualifications (thereby sanctioning the appointment of principal officers, and encouraging the recruitment of more highly qualified staff).

Despite the fact that the number of juvenile offenders brought before the courts had been dropping since the end of the war (from almost 50,000 in 1918 to 27,800 in 1925), there was continuing anxiety about young offenders generally and, in particular, the number of 16–21-year-olds who were being sent to prison with no previous conviction, a matter the Home Secretary had commented upon during a debate on the 1925 Criminal Justice Bill (Mair 1991). As a result, another Departmental Committee was set up in 1925 to inquire into 'the treatment of young offenders and young people who owing to bad associations or surroundings require protection and training' (Home Office 1927). Not surprisingly, given that since the beginning of the decade around three-quarters of those placed on probation were aged 21 or under, the Committee had some important points to make about probation, not least their comment that the Home Office was 'now a partner in the development of the probation system' (Home Office 1927: 48).

Probation was to be encouraged in all suitable cases and the 1925 Act was seen as a positive development. However, it was noted that the term 'probation' still covered three different ways of dealing with offenders (as had been provided in the 1907 Act): dismissal, conditional discharge on a recognisance (binding over), and release under the supervision of a probation officer. This led to confusion and misconceptions about what probation involved and the Committee was clear that probation should only apply to the last of these. Clarity about what probation was would also help to minimise the idea that the disposal was a soft option leading to dismissal, an issue that is mentioned several times in the report:

> If the offender is merely placed on probation, the injured citizen may feel that justice has not been done, and that such a step will weaken the healthy fear of breaking the law which ought to exist in the minds of all. These are natural feelings, and it would be a mistake to take no account of them. Moreover, there may be substance in the criticism if release on probation is merely regarded by the offender as being 'let off'. The sufferer should be satisfied, and public interest should be safeguarded, by taking care that probation is made a reality, and by making the offender and the public understand that it is so. Both should know that probation is strictly a period of trial, and that if the offender fails he will be deprived of his liberty; and may be deprived of it, too, for a longer period than would have been the case had he been sentenced to imprisonment in the first instance.
>
> (Home Office 1927: 49)

As early as 1923, possible misuse of the condition of residence which could be inserted as part of a probation order had been noted by the Children's Branch (Home Office 1923). Essentially, this involved cases where the condition was used to remove an offender from his home for quite lengthy periods, for example in 1923, of the 518 probationers so dealt with (61 per cent of whom were female), 42 per cent were sent for periods of two or more years. While the Committee was keen to encourage the greater use of hostels where offenders could live and go out to work (a recommendation that was to have considerable significance), they were adamant that sending a probationer to a residential home for training was not acceptable:

> We do not think that when Parliament provided that a condition as to residence could be inserted in a probation order it contemplated that it would be used to remove an offender from his home and secure his detention, frequently for long periods, in an institution without any of the safeguards

as to control and inspection which are applied when an offender is sent to a certified school or to a borstal institution.

(Home Office 1927: 54)

Conditions that were more closely related to the specific circumstances of offenders were recommended, such as a requirement to attend evening classes, and courts were encouraged to use the power in the 1907 Act to order restitution where offences of theft or damage were concerned.

Close supervision of the work of probation officers was urged on probation committees, as was the need to secure the best available candidates, and the Committee endorsed the need for better education and the suggestion in the Probation Rules that university qualifications should lead to higher salaries.

One of the aims of the Committee was to try to reduce the number of young offenders sent to prison – 'Is it desirable that over 2,000 lads and girls between 17 and 21 should be sent to prison every year, and if not, how can it be avoided?' (Home Office 1927: 80). While only around 530 young offenders had been committed to prison for fine default in 1925–6, the Committee wanted this figure to be reduced even further and urged greater use of the power contained in the Criminal Justice Administration Act 1914 whereby those aged 16–21 who had been fined and allowed time to pay could be placed under supervision. The Committee recommended that 'there should be no committal to prison unless supervision has been tried and has failed' (Home Office 1927: 84), adding that probation officers were probably most suitable to undertake such work. But probation's role as an alternative to custody for young offenders could be developed even further:

> we are convinced that a considerable number of offenders under 21 who are now sent to prison could be dealt with more satisfactorily by the use of probation. This view has been frequently expressed by Governors and other prison officials from their personal knowledge of the character and behaviour of young prisoners. Confirmation of our opinion that probation is not tried often enough is also afforded by an examination of the extent to which it is used by different courts.... [T]here is a marked diversity of practice, partly no doubt due to the fact that some courts have not fully appreciated the value of the system, and have not in the past obtained the services of qualified probation officers.

(Home Office 1927: 85)

Finally, it is worth noting several other points in the report that with the benefit of hindsight can now be seen as indicators of future significant developments. First, there was a brief discussion about the desirability of appointing chief probation officers (CPOs) and, while the Committee could not be said to be keen, they did not recommend against this, only commenting that, as supervision of probation officers rested with the courts, if a CPO was to be appointed care would have to be taken not to jeopardise this relationship. Second, although the Committee did not go so far as recommending inspection of probation work, they did recommend that the Home Office should 'satisfy itself as to the manner in which the work is being carried on' (Home Office 1927: 124). Third, the importance of after-care was affirmed and the role of probation officers in such work was emphasised, but the Committee went on to recommend that the Advisory Committee on probation that had been appointed as a result of the 1922 Departmental Committee should also consider the issue of after-care (and the Advisory Committee was reconstituted to take account of this in March 1928). And finally, even as the work done by the voluntary societies was acknowledged, the Committee also noted the 'controversy as to the desirability of employing agents of voluntary societies as probation officers' (Home Office 1927: 60).

The Howard League convened a conference in October 1927, attended by more than 60 societies ranging from the Magistrates' Association and Napo to the National Council for Mental Hygiene and the Theosophical Order of Service, to try to push forward some of the recommendations contained in the *Report of the Departmental Committee on the Treatment of Young Offenders*. Again, the importance of probation was emphasised; indeed, Rose (1961: 189) has claimed that, as far as the League was concerned, 'The main interest in the 1920s was to get probation established, especially in the juvenile courts.' A motion that all vacancies for probation officers should be advertised and candidates interviewed by probation committees was carried unanimously. The recommendation for hostels was claimed to be 'the most valuable ... in the Report' (Howard League 1927: 11), although the fact that very few existed was also noted and another resolution was carried urging probation committees to ensure that hostels were made available for young offenders of both sexes.

Another report on the Children's Branch was published in November 1928 (Home Office 1928) and this sums up the position with regard to probation after all of the activity of the 1920s. In 1927, only 16 courts were without probation officers – a considerable improvement since the figure of 147 in 1925, and almost certainly a result of the Criminal Justice Act 1925 requirement that a probation officer should be appointed for all probation areas. It was estimated that in December 1927 there were 711 probation officers, 442 (62 per cent) of whom were male and 269 (38 per cent) female; only 255 of these were full-time, however, and the need for more full-time probation officers and for more female officers was emphasised.[1]

The Young Offenders' Committee recommendation with regard to the use of hostels was endorsed by the Home Office. Indeed, the foundations of what are now known as Approved Premises were laid in the report.

> It may be desirable in some cases that the hostel should be under the direct control of the probation officer ... To encourage the extension of this system the Secretary of State, with the approval of the Treasury, has decided to contribute towards the cost of maintaining probationers in hostels if the local authority is willing to give similar support.
>
> (Home Office 1928: 21)

It was estimated that the cost of probation for the financial year 1927–8 was around £106,400, half of which was paid by government and half by the local authorities. The various voluntary societies were thought to spend between £50,000 and £60,000, taking the total cost to about £160,000 – one-third of which, therefore, came from the voluntary societies, a not inconsiderable sum that points to the continuing heavy involvement of the societies in probation work.

In 1927 a total of around 15,950 offenders were placed on probation (2.54 per cent of those found guilty).[2] 42 per cent of these were under 16 years old, 31 per cent were aged between 16 and 21, and the remaining 27 per cent were over 21. The probation order was (if we ignore dismissal, which occurred in 29.98 per cent of cases in 1927) the most popular disposal in the juvenile courts even when compared with fines (26.6 per cent of cases compared with 28.07 per cent for probation). Almost one-fifth (17 per cent) of those who received probation orders were female, but the proportion varied directly with age, with only 7 per cent of those aged under 16 being female compared with 18 per cent of those between 16 and 21, and 34 per cent of those aged over 21.

The vast majority of probation orders (97 per cent) were made at courts of summary jurisdiction, and four out of five orders made at these courts were for indictable offences (76 per cent of orders in ordinary courts and 87 per cent in juvenile courts). But, while the use of probation had increased by more than 50 per cent since 1921, there were still 'marked differences of practice in different parts of the country, and whereas in some areas probation is probably being used to its greatest extent, in other areas there is room for a wider exercise of the beneficent powers vested in Courts by the Probation of Offenders Act' (Home Office 1928: 25). To take just a few examples of these differences (and not the most extreme): in the Berkshire Ordinary Court probation orders made up 7.56 per cent of the 119 charges proved compared with Northampton, where the figure was 20.19 per cent of 104 charges proved; in Hull and Bristol the figures were 54.36 of 344 cases and 10 per cent of 330 cases respectively (and similar differences could be found in the juvenile courts). Despite the growing influence of the Home Office, local discretion remained powerful.

Important changes took place in Napo. In 1928, Sidney Edridge, who had been Chair of the Association since its foundation in 1912, retired. His replacement was William Clarke Hall, the Metropolitan magistrate who, as we have seen, was a strong supporter of probation but not so keen on the religious test imposed by the Police Court Mission. Gertrude Tuckwell, a trade unionist and one of the first women to be appointed Justice of the Peace, became president and the Earl of Feversham, who had worked as a probation officer in South Africa, became vice-president. A new journal, *Probation*, began publication in 1929 and an examination of its first few issues sets out what were probably agreed by Napo to be the key issues facing probation at the end of the decade.

Training was one of these issues. Clarke Hall (1929: 8) was in favour of training – 'it is desirable and a very great advantage to a Probation Officer to have had a high standard of education' – but not at the expense of marginalising personality and religious spirit. He advocated a system of training that covered both the pre-appointment and post-appointment stage. Related to this, the idea of probation as a profession and probation officers as professionals appears repeatedly in these early issues. Napo was obviously in the business of professionalising probation as far as it could, and distancing itself from the rather more amateur efforts of the missionaries was one way of doing this, although care had to be taken not to alienate the religious organisations. Feversham himself refers to the tensions between Napo and the religious societies:

> In the past there has existed a fruitless divergence of opinion between members of certain religious societies and the members of the Napo. The new officials of the Napo ... have only one aim, which is for probation officers to cease internally bleeding probation, but rather to unite in what I should like to term the National Christian Association of Probation Officers.
>
> (Feversham 1929a: 4)

And at a Home Office conference of probation officers in May 1929 he mentioned 'strife and bitterness' between different organisations, arguing that 'They should try to put aside any question of denomination, or of the points of view of the different Societies of which they were members' (Feversham 1929b: 7). While Napo's wish to become the only organisation to represent probation is understandable (and explains the close relationship that was cultivated with the Home Office), some of Feversham's language is striking. An editorial in *Probation* commented upon 'rivalry or hostility' between Napo and the Police Court Mission (Anon. 1929a: 20) and was followed by a short contribution by the Secretary of the London Police Court Mission which wished the new journal success but pointedly insisted upon the separate nature of the Mission, noting that the majority of probation officers were still agents of religious or voluntary societies (Pearson 1929).

Particularly noticeable in these early issues of *Probation* (which run to around 13–14 pages) is the emphasis on psychology and psychiatry. In the first issue, there is an article on 'The Unconscious Motive of the Juvenile Delinquent' (Creighton-Miller 1929); in the second, a piece on 'Juvenile Courts in America' (Chinn 1929), which emphasises the importance of psychiatry; while the third contains an article on 'The Psychology of the Criminal' (Burns 1930). In addition, in a short list of relevant books in issue 2, the first four are all to do with psychology. Indeed, the first on the list is Cyril Burt's *The Young Delinquent* first published in 1925 and destined to become highly influential in its explanation of the origins of juvenile delinquency. Burt was a supporter of probation and recommended that children's probation officers should be trained in psychology. By the end of the 1920s, then, there is evidence of changes in views about delinquency (see Bailey's summation in Chapter 2, p. 41).

Maurice Vanstone (2004a) has traced the gradual changes in probation discourse as the language of psychology entered the lexicon of probation officers around this time and increasingly shaped their work. Bochel (1976) and Vanstone (2004a) both point to this period as a time when ideas about casework began to make their appearance. And Bill McWilliams (1985) has argued convincingly that it was during the late 1920s that diagnosis became a key foundational concept for probation:

> Diagnosis was, of course, but one facet of the broader, treatment-based philosophy which came to be embraced by very many members of the probation service during this period, but it was diagnosis which lay at the foundation of the whole elaborate edifice. In these years from the late 1920s social workers in general and probation officers in particular came to see their task as akin to that of the physician and adopted, in large part, the so-called medical model as the basis and justification for their work.
>
> (McWilliams 1985: 260)

Psychology, casework and diagnosis all suggested the need for greater training for probation officers if they were to go down this route. But there were other reasons, too, for taking up such ideas: because they were associated with education and training they were related to increased professionalism; they were also associated with the latest thinking about crime and how to treat it; and they would help to sweep away the vestiges of old-fashioned probation work as practised by (some) missionaries.[3] In other words, they would contribute significantly to improving the status and authority of probation officers.

So too would a career structure and this was another topic that appeared in the first issues of *Probation*. The idea of introducing a grade of assistant probation officer for those younger than 25 when a full-time appointment could then be made was suggested by Clarke Hall (1929) and by the author of an unsigned article eight months later (Anon. 1929b). The latter's piece was entitled 'Chief Probation Officers' and made a strong case (which is worth quoting at length) for such a post:[4]

> in every great city [there should be appointed] a chief probation officer at a substantially higher salary ... He should be responsible for the complete organisation of the system throughout his area. He should be in direct touch with all the charitable societies, religious bodies, voluntary workers, clubs, institutions, etc., who could help, and with employers who could give work. He should be able in every town and village throughout a scattered area to invoke the assistance of some particular person who would befriend and take an interest in any probationer living in that town or village, and finally should supervise the work of his ... subordinates.
>
> Every county in England and Wales should under this scheme appoint a chief probation officer. At present there are still counties where there is no full-time probation officer at all. In such districts the existence of a 'chief' would be invaluable. He could supervise all the half-time workers and help to organise their districts, thus rendering their work far more systematic and efficient than it is at present ... The supervision of a chief probation officer would do away with many of the drawbacks which exist at present.
>
> (Anon. 1929b: 25)

Practice was yet another topic that *Probation* focused on and the first three issues contained pieces on the use of hostels and homes, the pros and cons of seeing probationers in their homes or in the office, the importance of finding jobs for those probationers who were unemployed, and the difficulties in supervising those with mental health problems. One article suggested a list of ways of avoiding failure on probation (Anon. 1930) – a list that looks surprisingly modern:

- Probation orders should not be made without full knowledge of the 'mental and physical condition or surroundings of the delinquent'.
- Orders should be strictly enforced.
- Orders should not contain conditions that are difficult to enforce.
- Conditions of residence should be used cautiously.
- Caseloads should not be excessive or geographical areas too wide to cover effectively.
- Probation officers should have an office away from the court.
- Those made subject to a probation order should be carefully selected.

A conference presentation that was reproduced in the first issue of *Probation* on 'The Technique of Probation' remains relevant today with its discussion of the need for preliminary inquiries, careful diagnosis, making 'an individualised plan in each case worked out with the probationer himself', regular reviews of the plan, cooperation with outside agencies, home visiting, regular reporting and taking account of the 'disciplinary side to Probation' (Warner 1929: 11). Apart from the reference to home visiting, there is very little that is out of place for probation practice in the first decade of the twenty-first century.

While the CETS had introduced training for their missionaries in 1926, a major development occurred in 1930 with the start of a Home Office-initiated training scheme. It began with a handful of individuals who were trained at various institutions 'where adequate facilities exist both for practical probation training and for university education in social subjects' (Le Mesurier 1935: 67); at the same time, the candidates were appointed as assistants in probation areas and were mentored by an experienced officer. While the numbers involved were small, the significance of the training scheme should not be underestimated: it represented yet another small step towards Home Office control and therefore another small diminution in the power of the religious agencies. Social work was already being taught in universities and its methods and language were infiltrating probation work. It was only a matter of time before social work took over from religion as the core of probation.

A key decade?

It would be an exaggeration to claim that in 1920 the probation system was in an especially weak position, but it was certainly not flourishing after a dozen years of existence, and the economic climate was not conducive to increased government spending – indeed, government spending on probation was minimal, and whatever growth probation had enjoyed since 1908 cannot be laid at the door of direct governmental support. By the end of the decade, however, the situation had changed and probation was firmly entrenched in the criminal justice system.

In 1920, 10,700 individuals had received a probation order (see Table 3.1 above), while by 1930 this figure had risen to 18,000 (Home Office 1932), an increase of 68 per cent. Government had begun to contribute to the funding of probation officers, a training scheme had been initiated, and rules for probation work were specified. While the religious and other voluntary agencies still played an important part in probation, there is little doubt that their grip (particularly that of CETS) had been loosened and government was slowly taking control. This struggle for probation was carried out quietly and rather politely and continued for another decade, but the result was never in doubt. Probation had powerful supporters in the Home Office and these individuals – whether or not they looked favourably on the missionaries, as Joynson-Hicks certainly did – could not help but increase Home Office control by encouraging the development of probation.

The position of the agencies was weakened still further simply by the passing of time. As probation became more and more a common court disposal, supervision would have become more routinised and, as such, codification and regulation became more possible – with the Probation Rules a prime example of this. Napo, as would only be expected from such an organisation, was keen to encourage the professionalisation of probation and, as one way of developing this, wished for more education and training for probation officers (although specific details were sparse). Systematic record-keeping began, and demands for a career structure. Overall, this process can be characterised as a move from the more individual, charismatic approach of the old-style police court missionaries to the more modern, bureaucratic, scientific approach that evolved over time. Such an evolution seems to have been inevitable – it was only a question of when it would occur and what form it would take. The general direction of government had, for some time, been towards increasing intervention in public affairs and it would have been very surprising if the direction had been different for probation. Government intervention meant bureaucratisation in the widest sense. Similarly (and it is worth recalling it was government that encouraged the formation of Napo), it would have been more surprising if an organisation such as Napo had failed to emerge. Academic developments in social work, criminology and psychology provided the wider cultural context in which probation could grow. Faced with such developments, it is difficult to envisage anything other than a marginal role for the religious agencies.

By 1930, probation meant not only the supervision of offenders, but also preliminary inquiries, matrimonial work and after-care work with released prisoners, though none of these was carried out consistently by all probation officers. A probation order was recognised as providing an alternative to a custodial sentence; it was acknowledged as a more humane sentence than prison, probably more effective, and cheaper. More than 20 years after the 1907 Act, probation was well entrenched as a court disposal and, having consolidated its position, a period of growth could be expected.

4 'A major part of our penal system?'

The claim that forms the title of this chapter was made in the context of an over-view of general trends in crime in the first half of the twentieth century, where one of the arguments advanced was that from the beginning of the century there had been 'a change in penal philosophy from one which was predominantly puni-tive to one which is primarily reformative' (McClintock and Avison 1968: 20). Probation was seen to be a key indicator of this change and throughout the 1930s its significance was acknowledged repeatedly in official reports. In this chapter we will examine how probation developed from 1930 up to the 1948 Criminal Justice Act, a period dominated first by mass unemployment as a result of the depression following the Wall Street crash of 1929, and then by a second world war only 30 years after the so-called Great War had ended. It is not our intention to try to tease out just how far these two issues may have impacted upon proba-tion's development, but it is necessary to bear them in mind as the backcloth against which this development took place. And, although we certainly do not wish to claim any simplistic causal relationships between unemployment or war and recorded crime, there is no doubt that crime increased considerably during this period; for example, between 1931 and 1951 indictable crimes recorded by the police rose from 159,278 to 524,506, an increase of 230 per cent, while during the preceding 20 years the increase had been only 64 per cent (McClintock and Avison 1968: 23).

Before examining the development of probation during this period, we will briefly discuss probation's position in 1930.

Probation in 1930

In 1930, a total of 17,989 offenders were given a probation order by the courts. The great majority of these – 95 per cent – were made by magistrates in courts of summary jurisdiction; slightly fewer than 800 probation orders were passed by the higher courts. But most orders – 84 per cent – were made for indictable offences, leaving around one in six orders made for the less serious summary offences, which suggests that probation was regarded as a useful disposal by magistrates at least. Most of those who received a probation order were male (85 per cent), but with 15 per cent of orders being made on female offenders

Table 4.1 Sentences passed in courts of summary jurisdiction for indictable offences by type of offence, 1930 (%)

Sentence	Violence	Sexual	Theft	Fraud	Other	Total
Dismissal	6	3	10	6	15	10
Recognisance	15	8	15	12	17	15
Probation	5	21	29	16	51	29
Industrial School	–	–	1	–	5	1
Custody	42	43	18	38	2	20
Police Cells	–	–	–	–	–	–
Reformatory	–	2	1	–	5	1
Fine	30	18	23	27	4	23
Whipping	–	1	–	–	–	–
Other	1	4	1	1	1	1
Total No.	851	867	42,070	3,717	2,341	49,846

Note: Numbers have been rounded and may not necessarily add up to 100%.

probation already seems to have been perceived as an appropriate disposal for women (who made up 12 per cent of all those found guilty). As we have noted previously, women were increasingly more likely to be given a probation order as they got older: for offenders under 16, only 6 per cent of orders were made for females; for those aged 16–21, 15 per cent were for females; while for those aged 21 and over, almost one-third (31 per cent) of those who were subjected to a probation order were female.

The significance of probation as a sentence for juvenile offenders is evident by the fact that, of the 17,989 orders made by the courts, 40 per cent were made on offenders aged under 16. Indeed, probation was the most popular disposal in the juvenile courts where 24,662 persons were proceeded against in 1930; probation made up 29 per cent of all disposals, with dismissals the next most commonly used (27 per cent), followed by fines (21 per cent) and recognisances (7 per cent). But probation was not only a significant sentence for juveniles as Table 4.1 shows.

Taking courts of summary jurisdiction as a whole (including juvenile courts), where more than nine out of ten probation orders were made, probation was the most commonly used disposal, surpassing custody and the fine. The two disposals regularly confused with probation – dismissal and recognisances – were used in 25 per cent of cases. Even in the higher courts, where only 781 probation orders were made, they accounted for 11 per cent of disposals, making probation the third most commonly used sentence (imprisonment made up 57 per cent and recognisances without a probation order 15 per cent).

Probation orders were made for all kinds of offence, but by far the most common was theft; in 1930, almost three-quarters (73 per cent) of probation orders made in the summary courts were for offences of theft and a further 16 per cent were for summary offences, as Table 4.2 shows. Interestingly, the use of orders for summary offences increased with age which encourages the view that probation was perceived by the courts as a disposal for young offenders.

Table 4.2 Probation orders made in courts of summary jurisdiction by type of offence and age group, 1930 (%)

Offence	Under 14	14–15	16–20	21 and over	All ages
Violence	–	–	–	–	–
Sexual	–	2	1	1	1
Theft	70	74	79	67	73
Fraud	–	1	2	6	2
Other indictable	16	10	–	3	7
Summary	13	13	17	23	16
Total No.	4,346	3,195	5,533	4,105	17,179

Note: Numbers have been rounded and may not necessarily add up to 100%.

It would be difficult to deny probation's importance as a court disposal by 1930. It was especially significant in the Summary Courts for juveniles who had been found guilty of offences of theft, where a probation order was virtually the default disposal. It is not surprising that Clarke Hall (1933: 278) pointed to the 'paramount importance' of the Juvenile Courts for probation, as it was in these that the beginnings of habitual criminality could be dealt with effectively at an early age.

Clarke Hall's early death in 1932 robbed probation of one of its most influential supporters. As we have noted previously, he was also a moderniser and in one of the last pieces he wrote before his death he returned again to arguing for a better organised probation service (Clarke Hall 1933: 278). Around 1930, there were 792 probation officers working in the courts and 31 per cent of these were members of religious societies. Clarke Hall deprecated the continuing influence of these societies – they influenced the appointment of probation officers, they could lead to 'sectarian difficulties' (Clarke Hall 1933: 284) and they meant that the system of dual control over probation officers continued. He seems to have viewed them as an obstruction to the progressive development of probation. He advocated the appointment of full-time probation officers wherever possible, but also encouraged the use of voluntary workers whereby religious societies could continue to play a role in helping offenders. At the time he was writing (the early 1930s) there were only three chief probation officers in England and he was keen to see more such appointments at a higher salary, as this would provide a career path for probation officers and encourage applicants with more educational qualifications. The interest shown by the Home Office in probation was welcomed, but this was shared by the local authorities who were responsible for the appointment and supervision of probation officers. While he did not spell out his own views on the matter, he did note that 'the more advanced reformers ... are striving for a uniform state service under which all probation officers would be appointed by the Home Office and paid directly by the Treasury' (Clarke Hall 1933: 289). The days of relying entirely on personality or a sense of vocation were numbered: 'Probation can never, and should never, be a mere untrained vocation' (Clarke Hall 1933: 291). And, in one paragraph, Clarke Hall articulated the balancing act that has characterised probation for much of its life.

Although to strangers the English system, here briefly indicated, may appear somewhat haphazard and unscientific, it does possess the supreme advantage of being both vital and vocational. The English probation officer is no mere official bound by regulation and routine, but a man or woman who is devoting his, or her, life to the doing of a great work for humanity and who is almost wholly untrammelled in the doing of it. To combine technical efficiency and regularity of practice with individual effort and effective personality is by no means easy. Some other countries lay greater stress upon the former; this country has undoubtedly tended to concentrate upon the latter.

(Clarke Hall 1933: 286)

Another advocate for probation was Roy Calvert, who was associated with the Howard League and the National Council for the Abolition of the Death Penalty. In 1933 he and his wife published *The Lawbreaker*, a well-written and acute study of crime and its treatment. The Calverts noted that there was still confusion about what probation was, especially as it was all too easily seen in the same light as a dismissal or binding over (see Chapter 1); there were too few probation officers and they needed better training, and careful selection of cases based upon a thorough investigation of the offender and his or her background was the key to success. They were in favour of conditions of treatment and opposed to the continuing influence of religious organisations which was open to 'grave objections on many grounds' (Calvert and Calvert 1933: 183). Interestingly, in a discussion of the results of probation, they note the comparative costs of various sentences:

- £44 for a year in a local prison;
- £66 for a year in a convict prison;
- £58 for a year in borstal;
- £1,000 for preventive detention;
- £8 for a year under the supervision of a probation officer.

They concluded that 'There is every argument in favour of trying the more effective and less expensive method of treatment whenever the occasion warrants it' (Calvert and Calvert 1933: 180). Like other modernisers, they too were in favour of a national service paid fully out of public funds.

Two Departmental Committees

In April 1931 a Departmental Committee was set up by the Home Secretary to investigate methods of dealing with persistent offenders who were 'sentenced again and again to short terms of imprisonment' (Home Office 1932: 4). The Committee's main proposals centred upon the introduction of two new sentences of detention and prolonged detention and they had little to say about probation directly. Probation was acknowledged as being useful for a wide range of offenders, but repeated use of probation if it had previously failed was not encouraged. Perhaps more significant was their discussion of the need for more effective after-care arrangements for those released from custody. A single organisation with responsibility for after-care was proposed, perhaps by bringing together the two organisations then involved in such work (the Borstal Association and the Central Association for the Aid of Discharged Convicts). While the probation service was not mentioned as a possible body for this task, a few paragraphs later the Committee described the kind of personal help that could be vital for a released prisoner and it is difficult to see how they could have missed the obvious answer to their proposal:

> much good could be done by arranging for some suitable person to give individual attention and friendship to a man discharged from preventive detention. The difficulty of finding a large number of individuals who would take on such tasks is obvious; but in dealing with these men, many of whom feel themselves to be social outcasts and easily take the view that it is useless for them to try to renounce their past, the personal touch is of great value. If it were possible to find suitable people each of whom would befriend and help one or two ex-prisoners, we believe that such personal relations would often provide the incentive and moral support which many of these ex-prisoners need if they are to make and maintain efforts to follow honest courses.
>
> (Home Office 1932: 33)

Roy and Theodora Calvert too stressed the importance of after-care and argued that 'the simplest and most practical way of creating a national parole system would be to transfer the parole work after release to the probation officers' (Calvert and Calvert 1933: 158).

Another Departmental Committee was set up in 1933 (Home Office 1934) and it was aimed squarely at trying to avoid imprisonment in cases of fine default. Although there was no sign of rising prison numbers at this time (indeed, from 1920 until 1944 the average daily prison population remained at around 11,000–12,000 – see Rutherford 1984: Appendix), it is notable that more than 20 per cent of receptions to custody in 1932 were due to cases of fine default and almost as many again were a result of other failures to pay.

The Criminal Justice Administration Act 1914 had provided the power for offenders aged between 16 and 21 who had been fined and given time to pay to be placed under supervision until they had paid. This power was rarely used 'due to a view that the work of supervision is incompatible with the ordinary work of the Probation Officer and that this officer is the only person available to undertake it' (Home Office 1934: 31). The Committee dismissed such a view and argued that probation officers were eminently suitable for this task as a result of their training, experience and role of authority in the court. Whether or not they had the time to take on such work was another matter and the Committee noted that 'little progress could be made by merely throwing additional duties on to the existing officers' (Home Office 1934: 31). The valuable work done by probation officers in matrimonial cases was also noted by the Committee, although again whether they had adequate time to carry out such work was questioned.

The Committee made three recommendations that related to probation. The first two proposed extending work with offenders who had been fined:

> ... 11. Freer use should be made of the power to place offenders under supervision. The power should be enlarged to cover persons over 21, and to enable supervision to be ordered at any time between conviction and payment of the fine.
> ... 12. No offender under the age of 21 should be committed to prison in default of payment of a fine unless the Court certifies that the method of supervision has been tried and proved ineffectual or that there are special circumstances making the adoption of this method undesirable.
>
> (Home Office 1934: 88)

Both of these recommendations were accepted and provided for in the Money Payments (Justices Procedure) Act 1935. The third recommendation addressed an issue that had appeared throughout the report – the lack of court staff to work on fine default issues – and the Committee recommended the appointment of Investigating Officers who could inquire into an offender's means. As work of a similar nature was already done by probation officers (supervision of 16–21-year-olds who had been fined, and investigation of applications for maintenance orders) the Committee thought it best to make the investigating officer's work the responsibility of probation, either by appointing more full-time officers, making part-time officers full-time, or appointing assistants who could undertake such work.

Both Departmental Committees, therefore, had implications for the extension of probation work which would come to fruition in the future. Official confidence in probation would seem to have been high, although this was dented slightly by what probation officers saw as their being relegated to a secondary position in supplying information to juvenile courts by the Children and Young Persons Act 1932. Bochel (1976) details how, when the Bill was introduced in December 1931, a provision was included that required juvenile courts to be supplied with information about the young offenders before them and local authorities not probation officers were charged with making enquiries and reporting to the court. Despite strenuous efforts by Napo – 'Can the enquiry of a local authority, which is an end in itself, have the same value as the enquiry of a probation officer, which is a means to an end – that end being the re-education of the offender?' (Sander 1932: 196); 'the proper person to make full enquiries into the cases of children and young persons coming before the courts is the probation officer' (Tallerman 1933: 252) – speeches by the Earl of Feversham in the House of Lords, lobbying and the support of various penal reform groups, this part of the Bill was not amended. Although the Act made it clear that magistrates could direct enquiries to be made by probation officers, Napo was clearly not confident that this would happen often and that they would not be asked to assist with local authority enquiries. The Act did, however, extend the use of probation supervision to young people who were in need of care and protection and those who were considered by a parent or guardian to be beyond control.

The *Handbook of Probation*

By the early 1930s, the probation service had been operating for a quarter of a century but, despite the increasing power of Napo, it remained a somewhat ad hoc organisation. The missionary influence was still strong although this was diminishing slowly. The presence of two contrasting accounts of probation work published at this time show very clearly a somewhat old-fashioned, religious view of probation and a rather more scientific, rational approach (ironically, the latter account was written by a practising Roman Catholic probation officer).

Surprisingly, the first of these books to be published is by far the more modern in tone and content. Mary Ellison was a Roman Catholic who worked for six years before her marriage as a probation officer in London. She wrote *Sparks Beneath the Ashes* (Ellison 1934) about her experiences, but, although her religion was obviously important to her (e.g. the epigraph to the book is taken from the writing of Pope Pius XI), there is little of the missionary spirit discernible in her work. She comes across as a social worker dealing with the poor, the homeless and the feckless. Her view of probation work is objective and unsentimental, based on training rather than vocational:

> This curative form of supervision is best undertaken by those who are properly trained and experienced in such methods. They are able to investigate and examine, from a detached point of view, the environmental difficulties which often surround the offender and the motives which lead to the commission of the offence. This is necessary for the benefit of the individual and for the community, for the maintenance of as perfect an equipoise as possible between the interests of both is essential.
>
> (Ellison 1934: xii)

Ellison is a sharp social critic, quite willing to question the role of the community in making young delinquents. Her accounts of cases show her sympathy with those she supervised, but also clearly point to the hardships of offenders' lives and the appalling conditions in the slums where many lived. At times she alludes to the concept of diagnosis, she notes that psychologists can be helpful, and she carries out matrimonial work. Indeed, she is also alert to the significance of international crime:

> The speeding up of means of communication has many results, one of which is the increase of international crime. Telephone, wireless, aeroplane, all offer endless possibilities to the educated crook, and international gangs are generally composed of the educated riff-raff of many countries.
>
> (Ellison 1934: 85)

Jo Harris, whose book *Probation: A Sheaf of Memories* was published in 1937, had worked as a Police Court missionary prior to the 1907 Act and became a probation officer following the Act. Harris's book, in contrast to Ellison's, is saturated in religious language and imagery; the words 'redeem', 'redemption' or their derivatives occur so often that, at times, it is easy to feel that one is reading a religious tract. Harris sees probation as 'redemption in the open':

> When the Probation Act was in its early and experimental stage it was difficult for people to believe or accept the idea that redemption in the open was possible. Even in these days there are still those who speak of probation as being 'let-off'. Of course it is nothing of the kind. It certainly is *not* a conviction, but is really redemption in the open. The offender is given the opportunity to redeem himself in his own environment.
>
> (Harris 1937: 20–21, emphasis in original)

While he acknowledges that the probation officer is a key part of the Police Court, Harris carried out his work at home, chatting with offenders, making friends with them and trying to point out the error of their ways. There is considerable sentimentality in his account of his work, though here and there one can find some hints of more up-to-date approaches. The anonymous reviewer of his book in *Probation* is condescendingly dismissive, noting that Harris 'writes in a way that reflects the kind-hearted sympathy with human frailty that has always distinguished the old missionary officer. Upon the principles of modern social work he attempts no statement' (Anon. 1937/8: 170). Typical of his style is this account of one of his cases, where the religious symbolism is heavy (and suitable employment is clearly an effective mode of treatment):

> In our first conversation I discovered that he had a great desire to be a shepherd. He was soon able to get work on a farm where, after a few months, he was made under-shepherd. At this work his whole character seemed to change. His work was his joy, his sheep were his friends, and his letters were some of the most descriptive I have ever received. In the lambing season his hours were long and difficult, but the tenderness with which he related his experiences showed how truly his work was his redemption. At the end of his period of probation, when we said good-bye to each other, I gave him a framed picture of the Good Shepherd, just in remembrance. His rough curly head bent over it, and his dark eyes answered in their own way. I often see him, but I know that he can safely be left working out his own salvation amongst the creatures he loves.
>
> (Harris 1937: 68)

Examining successive numbers of *Probation* for the first half of the 1930s one finds relatively few contributions directly concerned with religion and the religious impulse in probation. Articles are concerned with the psychology of offenders (staff at the Tavistock Clinic are well represented), with how to make probation effective – investigations or inquiries are seen to be crucial – and with a wide range of practical issues: juvenile courts, home visits, after-care, caseloads, the role of the family, hostels, alcoholism, domestic courts. McWilliams (1985) has argued that it was during the 1930s that professionalism really began to take hold of probation, and this can be seen in the pieces published in Napo's own journal.

Perhaps the most significant publication during this period, however, was the publication of *A Handbook of Probation* in 1935. Although Page (1992: 145) finds it 'disappointing in a number of respects' – a judgement that follows McWilliams (1985), who points to several instances where he considers the *Handbook* should have gone further, although he does note its significance – Maurice Vanstone (2004a: 90) recognises fully its importance as

> the first attempt to draw together the diversity of practice and theories into a coherent set of guidelines for probation officers. In so doing, it attempts to create a professional identity for a vocation set within both [sic] an historical, legal and theoretical framework.

The *Handbook* aims to give a 'complete picture of the working of the probation system at the present time' (Le Mesurier 1935: 5). It not only describes the origins and development of probation, thereby giving authority to the foundation narrative of the police court missionaries, but also codifies the work of probation officers; it is partly a job description and partly an early example of national standards. It exemplifies what its contributors consider to be good practice in order that probation work might be improved, that magistrates will note what probation can offer, and that the public will begin to acknowledge the efforts of probation officers. Most of the 21 contributors mentioned in the Preface were (or had been) probation officers, but there were also four psychologists and two court clerks. The *Handbook* can be seen as yet another step by Napo to take full control of probation work, to be recognised as the authoritative voice on practice. The power of the religious organisations was, by this time, on the wane although at least half of all full-time probation officers were missionaries in 1934 and probably at least a similar proportion of part-timers (Le Mesurier 1935).

Interestingly, the *Handbook* opens by correcting several misconceptions about probation: it is *not* intended primarily for young offenders or first time offenders; it is *not* a suspended sentence; and it should only be understood as release on a recognisance and under supervision. Having established what probation is, the chapters then cover various aspects of probation work with investigation and supervision seen as the two major tasks of probation officers. Considerable time is spent on investigation as this is held to be the key to successful work; if courts encourage probation officers to investigate the circumstances of offenders then sentencers will be able to choose the most appropriate individuals for supervision and not waste probation on those cases where other sentences would be more suitable. Investigation is, therefore, one of the main ways of achieving success. McWilliams (1985: 266–67) recognises the *Handbook*'s discussion of investigation as containing a core of 'causal, diagnostic thought', which he argues shows the shift from saving souls to professional assessment, although he points out that

probation officers still lacked 'a body of theoretical and empirical knowledge …
which would guide the selection of "facts" and order their significance'.

While the pioneering work of the missionaries is acknowledged, it is made
clear that it is the missionary spirit which is important, not links with religious
organisations. Indeed, the importance of psychology to the probation officer is
explicitly noted:

> A study that is becoming increasingly necessary to all engaged in the work
> of education is that of psychology, and to few can it be more important than
> to probation officers. For their work is the re-formation of character, and that
> is based on re-education in its true meaning. They must try and influence
> the behaviour of their probationer and raise it to a higher standard, and to do
> this successfully they must be able to appreciate the motives which underlie
> behaviour. They must realise that there are unconscious motives as well as
> conscious ones, and that these affect their own conduct as well as those whom
> they are trying to help. It is not to be supposed, nor indeed wished, that they
> can make a deep and thorough study of this subject, which is one for trained
> experts. But they can and should learn enough to recognize certain symptoms
> and avoid many dangerous mistakes and – above all – to know when it is wise
> to consult the expert.
>
> (Le Mesurier 1935: 62)

The *Handbook* also comments on a variety of issues that Napo was keen to push,
many of which continued to resonate for probation throughout the ensuing
decades:

- the need for the use of conditions to be carefully considered and appropriate
  for the individual offender;
- whether probation should become a national, or remain a local, service;
- variations in the use of probation by different courts;
- the need for more rigorous evaluation of the effectiveness of probation
  supervision;
- the tension that existed between the probation officer as social worker and
  as court officer;
- the importance of employment for rehabilitation.

The *Handbook* concludes with a number of recommendations: the need for a
Consolidating Probation Act which would do away with the confusion about
what probation was and require courts to use their powers for preliminary inquiries; the need for more full-time probation officers and more female officers; better
standards of education and training for officers; the need for more medical
examination of delinquents. Whatever the merits or demerits of the *Handbook* in
the light of the development of probation since its publication, it represents a
claim to authoritative knowledge by a system that has come of age.

Official developments, 1936–8

The first half of the 1930s may have been a busy time for probation, but the second half (before the outbreak of war) was even more frenetic. The most significant development was the Departmental Committee on Social Services in courts of summary jurisdiction set up by the Home Secretary in 1934, and which reported in 1936. The report of the Committee (Home Office 1936) is probably the most important document in the first 50 years of probation's existence (and, ironically, the Committee was initially set up only to inquire into the matrimonial work of probation officers, not their work with offenders). The Committee was chaired by Sydney Harris, Head of the Children's Branch of the Home Office and a long-standing supporter of probation, and one of its members was the Earl of Feversham, president of Napo. Four of the remaining six members were 'directly connected in some way with the probation service' (Bochel 1976: 124). The Committee was, therefore, highly knowledgeable about the topic they were examining and also almost certainly keen to promote the further growth of probation.

It was recognised from the start that the probation officer was 'essential to the efficient administration of justice, but his status in the Court, his relations to the Bench, the Clerk, the police and other persons and authorities, have not yet been sufficiently defined' (Home Office 1936: viii). According to Sydney Harris, there were two main principles in the report:

> first of all, that the Courts need trained social workers to perform the various kinds of social work connected with the Courts, and secondly, that the probation service should be a wholly public service.
>
> (Harris 1936: 69)

Various problems are noted throughout the report: probation officers had too many tasks, and they were not clearly defined, the growth in the number of probation officers required supervision, greater accountability was needed, conditions of service needed clarification, dual control remained an anomaly, uniform training and education were required, there was still considerable variation in the use of probation, greater use could be made of it, and there remained several misconceptions (as the *Handbook of Probation* had noted) that urgently needed to be rectified. These misconceptions – such as that probation was primarily for young offenders or primarily for first offenders, that it was equivalent to being let off (partly due to its being confused with dismissal or binding) over and that it was therefore not taken as seriously as it should be – had dogged probation from the beginning. All of these problems meant that probation was practiced and organised inconsistently in different parts of the country. The problems addressed in the report were also precisely those that might have been expected after a quarter of a century of growth with little central coordination or control. Probation officers had been willing to take on extra duties partly as a result of a lack of clarification of what – statutorily – their duties were, and partly because by being willing to take on tasks they were making themselves increasingly indispensable to the courts.

The Committee's response to these problems was robust. Perhaps its most significant recommendation was that it would be 'essential for the efficient development of the probation service that in future it should be organised on a wholly public basis' (Home Office 1936: 143). This, on the face of it, rather innocuous statement hid the end of the role of the missionary societies and thus the end of dual control. The Committee paid tribute to the work of the societies and hoped that they would continue their involvement in court-related work, such as the development of probation hostels and as voluntary workers who might assist probation officers. But this was the end of an era, although as Nellis (2007) rightly points out it was by no means the end of Christian influence on probation work. The end of dual control, however, did not mean central control and the Committee made it quite clear that they did not wish to see the probation service under government control. To be successful in their work, probation officers had to work in close cooperation with the courts and to ensure that this situation continued it was imperative that probation officers should be selected and controlled by the local justices. Government control could lead to injustice:

> The probation officer is an officer of the Court and in the treatment of offenders and in other matters the Court must sometimes base its decisions on information provided by its probation officer. To place a Government official in such a position would inevitably raise questions of interference of the Executive with the Judiciary.
>
> (Home Office 1936: 96)

But in order to address the uncoordinated and inconsistent development of probation that the Committee acknowledged, a degree of central guidance was necessary 'to ensure efficiency, to act as a clearing house for new ideas, and to co-ordinate the work of the various authorities' (Home Office 1936: 116). The Committee recommended that a separate branch of the Home Office should be set up to carry out these functions, instead of them being left to the Children's Branch as had been the case since 1907. They also suggested that inspection should be carried out – again differentiating this from inspections that had previously been carried out by the Children's Branch – and this would ensure some accountability over how government money was being used.

Probation should be organised and overseen by a probation committees usually based on a county, assisted in most areas by local case committees. The Departmental Committee noted that, in some areas, probation committees, set up by the Criminal Justice Act 1925, had failed in their duties, and wished to emphasise the importance of such committees for the development of the service. Other recommendations covered the need for full-time probation officers both male and female, and encouraged a career structure by suggesting that in some areas probation assistants might be necessary, and that principal probation officers should be appointed in larger areas. Principal officers were already in post in some large areas such as Birmingham, Liverpool, Manchester and Sheffield. Deputy principal and senior probation officers might also be needed in some areas. Volunteers were acknowledged to be useful, but they should not take the place of paid probation officers. Indeed only probation officers should be permitted to supervise offenders.

The Committee also set out the various duties that probation officers might be expected to carry out in addition to the supervision of offenders and matrimonial conciliation:

- social investigation in cases where a probation order is unlikely to be made;
- investigation of means when a financial penalty is under consideration;
- supervision of those subject to a fine;
- receiving instalments of fines (but not collecting money);
- applications in bastardy;
- adoption enquiries;
- escorting to institutions;
- supervision of juveniles found to be in need of care or protection;
- administration of the poor box or court fund;
- after-care (but only for those released from approved schools and borstal, not in the case of those released from prison);
- miscellaneous advice.

The range of duties specified is wide and probation officers may have been at risk of becoming Jacks of all trades, but while noting that probation work was the main task of a probation officer the Committee also recognised that it would not be helpful to try to pin down precisely what probation officers might do.

> We have come to the conclusion that it would be unwise to attempt to define too closely the duties which a probation officer may be called upon to perform for the Court. It will be for each individual Court to decide which of the duties enumerated later, in addition to conciliation and probation work, should be entrusted to the probation staff having regard to local needs and circumstances. Care must be taken to see that the size of the staff is adequate to all the duties they are called upon to perform. We regard probation work as the probation officer's primary function and no additional work should be allowed to interfere, as is now too frequently the case, with the efficient performance of his duty towards his probationers ... While it is necessary in every Court to provide for all the essential social services, the probation officer should not be asked or expected to undertake forms of social work which are not directly the concern of the Court. The keen probation officer is tempted by his very keenness to enter new spheres of work and thus dissipate his energies for the services for which his salary is provided from public funds.
>
> (Home Office 1936: 78)

Widening the range of tasks that they were expected to carry out had implications for the kinds of individual who might be appointed as probation officers. There was a greater need than ever for educated individuals, preferably university graduates (and the introduction of promoted posts might help attract such candidates), and for specialised training in social work. The Committee suggested extending the Home Office training scheme that had begun in 1930, by appointing a Central Training Board which would oversee training that would be in two parts: first in social science – and psychology is mentioned specifically – and then a focused probation course.

Enquiring into the circumstances of those who were considered for probation was vital – not just to ensure that the most appropriate cases were chosen, but also to try to weed out those where there was little chance of success:

> In fairness then to society, the offender and the probation officer, no person should be placed on probation without full consideration of his previous history and present surroundings, as well as the immediate cause of his appearance before the Court. Without enquiry it is impossible adequately to take into account the conditions which the law prescribes as justifying the use of probation.
>
> (Home Office 1936: 46)

Finally, it is worth pointing out various issues discussed by the Committee that continue to resonate in the first decade of the twenty-first century. The need to enforce a probation order was emphasised; working with other agencies was encouraged as was a degree of specialisation; conditions had to be focused upon the individual offender; early ideas about restorative justice can be seen in a recommendation to increase the use of the power to order payment for compensation or damages when making a probation order; and sentence review is prefigured by the proposal that the higher courts and case committees might welcome progress reports on probationers.

Many of the issues discussed in the *Handbook of Probation* are explored in the Committee's report and it is no surprise that Napo was quite content with it; an editorial in *Probation* called it 'a very good report' (Anon. 1936: 49) and the Napo Chair, Gertrude Tuckwell, called it 'a great step forward' (Tuckwell 1936: 67). Despite encouraging greater government control of probation, there was still a considerable degree of local autonomy.

Sydney Harris returned to many of the Committee's concerns when he gave the third Clarke Hall lecture in 1937, but it is interesting to note that both he and the Chairman (Sir Herbert Samuel, who had been a Home Office minister when the 1907 Act was passed) specifically noted that probation had been to a certain degree responsible for the large drop in the prison population: 'The immense reduction in the prison population at the present day compared with thirty years ago is mainly due to two causes – the operation of the probation system and the giving of time for the payment of fines' (Harris 1937: 32). The following year the Committee's report was revisited again, this time by the Home Office in a booklet aimed at Justices of the Peace. *The Probation Service: Its Objects and Its Organisation* (Home Office 1938a) brought the key parts of the report to the attention of those who were seen as crucial to the success of probation:

It rests with the Justices not only to decide the cases in which the probation method can be properly used, but also largely to control and supervise the manner in which the method is carried out. The success or failure, therefore, of the probation system lies to a large extent in their hands.

(Home Office 1938a: 11)

It noted that some of the Committee's recommendations had already been acted upon, thus giving an impression of urgency to underline the importance of the proposals: the 1937 Summary Procedure (Domestic Proceedings) Act had provided courts with the authority to employ probation officers for conciliation; a Probation Branch had been set up in the Home Office; inspectors had been appointed (indeed the first inspector, appointed in 1936, was a female ex-probation officer); the Advisory Committee on Probation had been reconstituted; and a Probation Training Board had been established.

Yet another Departmental Committee reported in 1938. Corporal punishment was still available for boys under the age of 14 convicted of an indictable offence in the summary courts, for adults convicted of a range of mostly archaic offences (except robbery), and for boys under 16 convicted of certain specified indictable offences. It was also still used as a punishment for serious prison offences. Birching was mostly used for boys under 14, but, despite an increase of more than 100 per cent in the number of persons aged 16 and under proceeded against for indictable offences between 1930 and 1936, the use of corporal punishment had decreased; indeed birching was 'used by the summary courts in less than 2 per cent of the total number of cases in which there was power to apply it' (Home Office 1938b: 20). The Departmental Committee recommended the repeal of corporal punishment as a court sentence, only suggesting that it be retained for use in prison. The significance of probation was noted insofar as courts that made use of birching tended to be those where probation was rarely used – another argument for trying to encourage more consistent use of probation throughout England and Wales and increasing the number of probation officers. But probation was not always a sensible alternative to corporal punishment and the Committee argued that another form of punishment was needed:

[Where] the offence is due solely to a misdirection of the spirit of adventure which should be the natural characteristic of any normal adolescent boy ... probation is also unsuitable: for probation is a form of non-institutional training, and in many cases what the offender really needs is not prolonged supervision and training but some form of short and sharp punishment which will pull him up and give him the lesson he needs.

(Home Office 1938b: 46)

The arrival of Sir Samuel Hoare as Home Secretary in May 1937, with a Quaker background and a long-standing interest in penal reform (his great-grandfather was Samuel Hoare, who had played a significant role in the abolition of slavery, and his great-grandmother's sister was Elizabeth Fry: see Templewood 1954), and recommendations from the various Departmental Committees that had reported since the late 1920s still to be acted upon, led to the introduction of a Criminal Justice Bill in 1938.

As far as probation was concerned, the Bill was of considerable importance as it included many of the provisions of the Departmental Committee on Social Services in courts of summary jurisdiction. It tried to clarify the confusion regarding probation, binding over without supervision and dismissal by referring to probation separately. It also did not mention age as a condition of probation, thereby hoping to put a stop to the idea that probation was only for young offenders. It proposed to treat probation as a conviction which would be likely to weaken the perception of the order as a let-off. The possibility of a condition of mental health treatment being included in a probation order was introduced. The Departmental Committee's proposals concerning the appointment of probation officers, and the roles of probation committees and case committees, were provided for. The agents of voluntary societies could no longer be appointed as probation officers, and a sufficient number of officers had to be appointed for each area – including at least one female officer. Expenditure for training was to be made available. Other clauses had implications for probation: the 1938 Departmental Committee's recommendations regarding the abolition of corporal punishment were included; and imprisonment was to be abolished for all those under 16, for those under 21 in the lower courts, and restrictions were to be placed on those aged 16–21. In addition, Howard Houses (residential hostels for those aged 16–21) and compulsory attendance centres for those aged between 12 and 21 were to be introduced, the latter partly in response to the Departmental Committee on Corporal Punishment's recommendation for a tough alternative to probation.

Despite the number and scope of the proposed changes, Napo pointed to several omissions: there was no attempt to define the probation officer role, so the status and duties associated with the job remained unclear; the need for the courts to take account of inquiries made by the probation officer before making a probation order was missing; and the proposal to register a conviction when making a probation order was not welcomed (Norman 1939). It is interesting to speculate what the impact on probation would have been if this major set of changes had become law in 1938–9, but the Bill was dropped due to the imminence of war.

The war and the 1948 Criminal Justice Act

In 1938, a total of 29,301 offenders were placed on probation – an increase of 63 per cent since 1930. More than half (55 per cent) were under the age of 17, and 86 per cent were male. The vast majority of probation orders were made in the Summary Courts where probation was the most common disposal for indictable offences: 34 per cent of disposals were for probation orders compared with around 17 per cent each for custody and fines. The number of probation orders made in the higher courts had more than doubled since 1930. Almost nine out of ten probation orders (86 per cent) were made for indictable offences.

Despite a considerable increase in crime since the start of the decade – particularly amongst the young, where the number of young persons aged under 16 found guilty of indictable offences had doubled since the start of the decade – probation remained a significant penalty. The 1938 *Criminal Statistics* noted that the use of probation decreased for every age group after the age of 17 and that 'in every age group the proportion of female offenders placed under a Probation Order was higher than the proportion of male offenders' (Home Office 1940: xv). An analysis of reconviction rates found that the overall rate for males placed on probation was 29.7 per cent – the highest found in comparison to prison (19.7 per cent), a fine (17.8 per cent) or a dismissal/binding over (20.2 per cent) – although when age was taken into account the differences narrowed somewhat. For females, the reconviction rate was half that of males (15.2 per cent) and very close to the rates for imprisonment and dismissal/binding over. But, while the use of probation decreased as age increased, the reconviction rate too decreased, which strengthened the case for using probation more for adult offenders (a point that had also been noted by both the 1938 Departmental Committee and the Home Office 1938a booklet *The Probation Service: Its Objects and Its Organisation*).

The effectiveness of probation was also demonstrated by a study of probation-ers in Coventry published in 1945. The author claimed a success rate of 85 per cent when failure was measured by committal to approved school or prison, but went on to note that 'A more reliable figure was obtained from the five-year follow-up, which shows that 74 per cent of the cases were successful in that they did not appear before the court again, or that it was not considered necessary to remove them from their home environment' (Hughes 1945: 125). More intrigu-ingly, the study also showed the factors that were associated with success (none of which are surprising): shorter orders, first-time offenders, a good home, stable employment, positive leisure interests and favourable temperamental traits.

It might have been expected that the war would have brought a halt to the development of probation, but this was not the case. Despite probation being a reserved occupation, many male officers joined the armed forces, although the number of full-time officers continued to grow during the war years:

> a quarter of the full-time male officers soon departed the service … In spite of this loss, the number of full-time officers, which had increased from 299 in 1935 to 509 in 1939, continued to rise. By 1945, there were 750 employed in the service.
>
> (Bochel 1976: 161)

More small areas were combined, more female officers were employed, more senior and principal posts were established (indeed regular meetings of principal probation officers and the Probation Branch began in December 1942), and the training scheme that had been set up continued to run and produce trained proba-tion officers. Thus many of the recommendations made by the 1936 Departmental Committee were carried through.

All was not proceeding smoothly, however. The Home Office approach at times resulted in what Bochel (1976: 162) terms 'unwarranted interference' with the work of local probation committees, and Napo formally protested. B.J. Reynolds, Head of the Probation Branch in the Home Office, in an address to the 31st Napo national conference seemed to point to a threat for the service when he noted the growth of a number of social welfare services and the possibility of them all coming together: 'Will they remain separate and unrelated or will common or agency services hold the field or part of it?' (Reynolds 1943: 55). Would education, for example, take over probation work with those under the age of 18? And there were debates about the advantages and disadvantages of local and central control (reminiscent of similar debates in the 1990s):

> Those who wished to see the whole responsibility for the finance of the service transferred to the central government considered that the greater uniformity in service conditions, salaries for senior posts, size of case-loads and standard of work expected which would follow would benefit the officers and improve the quality of work performed by the service as a whole. Others, however, feared a change in the public's image of the probation officer if he became a kind of civil servant. They saw the probation officer cramped by official regulations and denied a sufficiently free hand in his work. Local control, they argued, meant that those responsible knew the needs and circumstances of the area in which their probation officers were working. The advocates of national control denied that membership of a nationally operated service was incompatible with a sense of vocation, and that a central authority could not appreciate the needs of various districts. Inspectors travelling about the country could see and compare the needs of different localities and view them in relation to the needs of the service as a whole.
>
> (Bochel 1976: 163)

The conditions that came with war complicated the task of supervision, especially with young offenders: the blackout, the closure of schools, time spent in shelters, evacuation, a diminution in parental controls as fathers joined the armed services and mothers worked, the general disruption of family life – all meant that keeping in touch with young offenders became much more difficult than it had been. Matrimonial work also increased due to the separation of husbands and wives.

Juvenile delinquency, however, was the most pressing problem, although an increase in youth crime had been evident during the 1930s leading to a major enquiry into the issue of juvenile crime being commissioned by the Home Office in 1938. The study confirmed that there had been a considerable increase in the number of boys under the age of 16 found guilty of indictable offences during the 1930s (Carr-Saunders et al. 1943). But during the war the problem worsened: between 1938 and 1945, the number of offenders found guilty of indictable offences increased by 44 per cent, but for those aged 21 and above the increase was 36 per cent, while for those under 17 it was 53 per cent and for the 17–20 age group it was 49 per cent. An examination of the Napo journal *Probation*

Table 4.3 Percentage of those found guilty of an indictable offence placed on a probation order, 1938 and 1946

	1938	1946
Males under 14	50	42
Males 14–16	51	41
Males 17–20	42	24
Males 21+	13	6
All males	32	22
Females under 14	56	47
Females 14–16	57	54
Females 17–20	63	45
Females 21+	25	17
All females	36	28

for the war years shows a large number of articles concerning juvenile crime and the juvenile courts particularly in the first three or four years of the war. And juveniles, of course, made up the bulk of probation's caseload.

In 1946, 27,027 offenders were placed on probation orders, a drop of 8 per cent from the 1938 total. Almost two-thirds (63 per cent) of these were under the age of 17, while 17 per cent were aged 17–20; and 83 per cent were male. While 91 per cent of orders were made at the magistrates' courts, the 2,420 made at the higher courts represented an increase of 43 per cent since 1938. At the magistrates' courts, the vast majority of orders were made for offences of theft (58 per cent) and burglary (22 per cent); 11 per cent of orders were made for summary offences. Table 4.3 shows the decline in the use of probation between 1938 and 1946, which affected all age groups and both male and female offenders.

The decrease in the use of probation took place against an increase in the numbers of those found guilty of indictable offences. So how did probation fare when compared to other court sentences? Table 4.4 shows changes in sentencing for indictable offences between 1938 and 1946 in the magistrates' courts. The drop in the use of probation is largely accounted for by an increase in the use of the fine, although for 17–20 year olds (young adult offenders) there was also an increase in the use of custody. In the higher courts, the use of probation for young adults and adults also dropped between 1938 and 1946 – from 35 per cent to 25 per cent for 17–20 year olds, and from 13 per cent to 9 per cent for adults. But, here, the drop seems to be accounted for by an increase in the use of custody, which increased by 12 per cent for young adults and 4 per cent for adults.

The increase in crime during the war seems to have led to more punitive sentencing, with the fine becoming a significant sentence for indictable offences in the magistrates' courts. The increased use of custody for young adults was to become a major issue for penal policy in the ensuing years. Probation was perhaps being used more discriminately – as had been suggested by the Departmental Committees – but it certainly seemed to be losing ground to the fine and, to a lesser extent, to custody.

Table 4.4 Disposals used by the magistrates' courts for those found guilty of indictable offences by age group, 1938 and 1946 (%)

Disposal	Under 14		14–16		17–20		21 and over	
	1938	*1946*	*1938*	*1946*	*1938*	*1946*	*1938*	*1946*
Probation	51	42	51	42	45	26	15	8
Dismissed/bound over	35	38	26	25	24	20	25	17
Fine	5	10	8	17	17	36	32	51
Custody*	8	7	13	13	10	15	26	23

Note: For those aged under 17, an approved school sentence has been included;
and for those aged 17–20 committal to a higher court with a view to a Borstal sentence has been included.
Note: Numbers have been rounded and may not necessarily add up to 100%.

With this as background, a Criminal Justice Bill was introduced in 1947 – largely replicating the Bill that had been lost in 1939 – becoming law in 1948. As far as probation is concerned, the Act can be seen as final confirmation of the significance of the supervision of offenders as a court disposal; the end point of a process that had begun 40 years previously with the Probation of Offenders Act. Probation was at last clearly distinguished from dismissal and binding over with these two disposals being replaced by the absolute and conditional discharge. There was no mention of age, previous convictions, or the trivial nature of the offence as reasons for making a probation order – indeed it was noted that a probation order could be made for any offence where the sentence was not fixed. The minimum period for which a probation order could be made was fixed at 12 months (the maximum remained at three years). A new condition requiring that a probationer undergo mental treatment for a period of up to 12 months was introduced. The Act made it quite clear that inquiries for the courts and the supervision of certain categories of offenders released from custody were part of the probation officer's duties:

> It shall be the duty of probation officers to supervise the probationers and other persons placed under their supervision and to advise, assist and befriend them, to inquire, in accordance with any directions of the court, into the circumstances or home surroundings of any person with a view to assisting the court in determining the most suitable method of dealing with his case, to advise, assist and befriend, in such cases and in such manner as may be prescribed, persons who have been released from custody and to perform such other duties as may be prescribed or may be imposed by enactment.
>
> (11 & 12 Geo.6. Ch.58: Fifth Schedule)

When probation had been introduced in 1907, orders could be made in the summary courts without recording a conviction; in the higher courts, on the contrary, a conviction was recorded. The 1948 Act rectified this anomalous situation by requiring a conviction to be recorded before any probation order was made. The Act also clarified the respective duties of probation and case committees, one of which – as far as probation committees were concerned – was to ensure that each petty sessional division should have at least one male and one female probation officer.

The other main provisions of the Act had implications for probation:

- the abolition of corporal punishment as a sentence;
- the abolition of imprisonment as a sentence for those under the age of 17 in summary courts;
- the abolition of imprisonment as a sentence for those under 15 in the higher courts;
- restrictions on the use of imprisonment for those under 21;
- the introduction of detention centres for those aged 14–20;
- the introduction of attendance centres for those aged 12–20 found guilty in summary courts.

It was certainly possible that by placing restrictions on the use of imprisonment for those aged under 21 and abolishing corporal punishment (although the latter was rarely used), then probation might be used more often. Detention centres, on the other hand, where offenders aged between 14 and 20 could be detained for between one and six months, could bite into probation's market – especially as they were introduced partly to replace corporal punishment and partly as an alternative to imprisonment for young offenders. Finally, although they have never been nationally available and their development has been fragmented and uncoordinated, attendance centres represented the first (but by no means the last) non-custodial sentence to be introduced since probation itself 40 years earlier.

With the passing of the 1948 Criminal Justice Act, the first phase of probation's development came to an end. The number of probation orders made in the courts during 1948 was 32,633 – an increase of 21 per cent on the number made in 1946. By 1949 there were more than 1,000 probation officers, the great majority of whom (86 per cent) were full-time; included in that number were 38 principal and assistant principal probation officers and 92 senior probation officers (Chuter Ede 1949). Probation officers now had a range of tasks to carry out in the courts, with the after-care of released prisoners a potentially significant development. A new set of probation rules was issued in 1949 to reflect the changes that had taken place as a result of the Act. Dual control had ended and training was firmly embedded, although the missionary spirit had by no means disappeared. Most of what Napo had identified in the *Handbook of Probation* had been introduced. So probation seemed to be on a solid footing to face the challenges of the post-war era, although the close working relationship of the service with the Home Office was beginning to show some cracks. There can be little doubt that by the end of the 1940s probation was indeed a major part of the penal system.

5   1950–62: A golden age?

Probation appeared to be well-placed to face the Brave New World of post-war reconstruction; it would be difficult to disagree with Maurice Vanstone's comment that the early 1950s was 'an era of confidence', although it is notable that he adds a warning that this was 'Despite the fact that there was no research evidence that probation or the psychodynamic model on which probation practice was purportedly based reduced offending' (Vanstone 2004a: 106). It is also important to remember that, while there can be little doubt about the general optimism that came with the end of the war and the election of a Labour government in 1945 with its commitment to a welfare state, any such optimism may not have been long-lasting and may have been misplaced. David Kynaston calls his history of 1945–51 *Austerity Britain* and argues that the six years after the war were 'in some ways even harder than the war itself' (Kynaston 2007: 633). Rationing only ended in the summer of 1954; there was a serious fuel crisis in the winter of 1946–7; the country faced the prospect of economic collapse in 1949. On the other hand, Britain in the 1950s was a dull and complacent society as two different historians agree: 'Britain in the fifties was one of the most conservative, stable and contented societies in the world' (Sandbrook 2006: 31); 'A case could easily be made for mid-century Britain as the most settled, deferential, smug, un-dynamic society in the advanced world' (Hennessy 2006: 435).

Yet, during the same period, there were profound changes that – with hindsight – only really began to bite during the 1960s: the nationalisation of major industries and utilities; the end of empire as former colonies were granted independence; immigration (symbolically starting with the arrival at Tilbury of the *Empire Windrush* from Jamaica in 1948); the Suez crisis of 1956; the development of nuclear weapons; the growth of television; the emergence of the teenager and the rise of rock 'n' roll. There was also a considerable change in crime. Despite a fall in recorded crime between 1945 and 1950 that continued for the first half of the 1950s, members of the public saw a crime wave (Hennessy 2006; Kynaston 2007). And a hugely popular film – *The Blue Lamp* (1950) – only served to confirm this belief that crime was rampant.

In 1950 there were 461,435 indictable offences known to the police; by 1960 the figure was 743,713 – an increase of 61 per cent. But the rise in crime seemed to be concentrated on teenagers, particularly those aged between 14 and 20: while there was an overall increase of 42 per cent in those found guilty of indictable offences between 1950 and 1960, the increase for 17–20 year olds was 129 per cent, and for 14–16 year olds it was 69 per cent. The rise began after 1955 – perhaps not coincidentally 1956 was the year when the film *Rock Around the Clock* was shown in Britain and Elvis Presley had his first hit records; teenagers, loud music and loutish behaviour became linked inextricably in the popular mind (Sandbrook 2006). Crime was bound to follow.

There is some agreement that the 1950s were a golden age of policing, when public confidence and trust in the police was at its highest (Reiner 2000), and one might speculate that – if the public had been aware of the existence of the probation service – then at this time they might have had just as much confidence in probation as a means of dealing with offenders. But would such confidence have been well-founded? Sewell Stokes's memoir of working in the London probation service during the war (but not published until 1950) is well-observed and amusing, written in a wry and self-deprecating tone and describes hard-working and caring probation officers, but essentially it foregrounds a well-meaning amateurism at work with offenders; the portrait of probation work could easily have come from the 1930s (Stokes 1950). The film *I Believe in You* (1950) was based on Stokes's book and it too shows a decent, caring group of probation officers working hard with delinquents in the kind of warm romantic manner we now associate with Ealing comedies (not surprisingly as the film was an Ealing production).[1] In contrast to Stokes's anecdotal account, Elizabeth Glover's textbook *Probation and Re-education* is full of discussions of treatment, of the importance of psychology and psychiatry, of careful planning, although it argues that it is 'friendship in probation ... that produces results, not "case work"' (Glover 1949: 262, and note the quotation marks round case work). It also, surprisingly often, recalls the days of the missionaries with its persistent references to the importance of Christian faith for the probation officer. Indeed, Glover insisted on the need to pull psychology and religion together:

> Good probation demands that its officers should be trained in psychology, that is to say in an understanding of the way the mind works, and that they should be persons of truly Christian magnanimity and discernment. (Some people who do not profess the Christian faith have these qualities.) A loving spirit of goodwill is not enough, neither is the enquiring, impersonal approach of the scientist. It is a combination of these two which is needed for probation to reach its highest efficacy. It is the merit of the probation system that it is consonant at once with modern psychiatric science, and with Christian faith and teaching.
>
> (Glover 1949: 270–71)

Similarly, a probation officer in London (A. G. Rose) listed a lengthy series of qualities necessary for the job which recall – as paraphrased by Vanstone – the emphasis on personality that was seen as so important for early probation officers:

> a professional outlook; high efficiency; the human motive of friendship; inner warmth and sincerity; sympathy; optimism about human nature; a capacity

to see the probationer's point of view; a preparedness to establish the right to be critical; knowledge of poverty and deprivation; knowledge of the probationer's neighbourhood; the skills of guidance not compulsion; being moralistic; good physical and mental health; a thought out philosophy; fluency in both verbal and written expression; streetwise attitudes; maturity; leadership qualities; flexibility and prescience; industriousness and decision-making skills; reliability; and a commitment to increasing self-confidence and self-reliance in the probationer.

(Vanstone 2004a: 96)

This list suggests that only superhuman beings might qualify as probation officers, but there is no room in it for the need of academic training in social science. And Rose concludes his article by self-consciously harking back to the religious basis of probation: 'Ultimately, however, it is on the interplay of personality and on the ability of the probation officer to give from his own spiritual resources that the value of the work will depend' (Rose 1947: 167).

Such accounts of probation make it look rather old-fashioned. Further, we have already noted (at the end of Chapter 4) that the proportionate use of probation by the courts had decreased considerably during the war – and matters had not improved by 1950. Finally, there was the Children's Act of 1948, which had introduced local authority children's departments to tackle child neglect and, as Nellis (2007: 37) perceptively points out, 'inevitably, the delinquency associated with it', thereby threatening probation's role in dealing with children who offend.

So, given that there were issues implying that probation was not in a position to be complacent, how were probation staff trained and how did they supervise offenders?

Training and casework

The Probation Training Board had been set up before the Second World War, separate from – but sharing most of its members with – the Probation Advisory Committee. After the war, these two bodies were amalgamated to form the Probation Advisory and Training Board as it was considered 'desirable for a single body to consider questions relating both to the training of probation officers and to the work of serving officers and the general administration of the probation system' (Chuter Ede 1949: 269). While it had been the aim of the Home Office that all new appointments as probation officers should be products of the formal training scheme, this did not prove to be possible as recruitment through the scheme did not keep pace with the demands arising as a result of the increased workload (between 1950 and 1960 the number of probation orders made by the courts increased by 10,500). Indeed, during the period from 1946 to 1961 about one in four probation officers were untrained 'direct entrants' to the service (Bochel 1976). This situation was compounded by a perceived lack of suitable candidates which the Home Office attempted to redress through the sponsorship of the film *Probation Officer* (1949) and the issue of an information booklet about the service, *Probation as a Career* (Home Office 1952). The former, sought to portray the 'typical' work of a probation officer and a review in *Probation* described it as showing

> the probation service helping an ordinary working class family. Mother applies for a summons against father and is referred to the probation officer; daughter runs away from home with a boyfriend and they are ultimately jointly charged with larceny. We see one probation officer dealing with the matrimonial problem, one dealing with the girl and a third with the boy. This situation enables the film to show the relation between an unhappy home and a delinquent child, and the difficulties of a child without a normal home background are underlined in the case of the boy who is an ex-inmate of an orphanage. Thus several problems are presented and the appropriate treatment hinted at on a very small canvas.
>
> (Anon. 1949: 274)

In fact, although the number of applications for training decreased for most of the period covered in this chapter (they more than halved between 1950 and 1956), the number accepted grew so that the percentage of successful applications more than doubled as Table 5.1 shows. In 1946, the Home Office had taken advice from the National Institute of Industrial Psychology in an effort to improve the selection of suitable individuals for training as probation officers. Applicants were formally rated by probation inspectors, with those who were successful invited to a selection committee of the Training Board where they had to undergo an intelligence test, observation in a group discussion, and interview by the selection committee. Those who were recommended for training then faced 'a general medical examination; if there is doubt about the temperamental stability or capacity to withstand emotional strain the medical examination is made by a psychiatrist' (Macrae 1958: 211).

Table 5.1 Number of applications for training and those accepted, 1949–60

Year	No. of applications	No. accepted	% accepted
1949	1,277	73	6
1950	1,401	78	6
1951	1,187	93	8
1952	1,185	68	6
1953	893	92	10
1954	605	61	10
1955	689	41	6
1956	568	76	13
1957	607	102	17
1958	693	131	19
1959	958	116	12
1960	1,012	132	13

Source: Home Office 1962a: 113.

Generally, the training received by a successful applicant depended upon age. If the individual was under 30, he or she was expected to undertake a full-time two-year university course for a qualification in social science, usually a diploma. If the student already had a degree, the course could be completed in one year. Following this, either a period of specialised training in probation practice and theory, or a one-year university course in applied social studies, was taken; the latter were generic courses in social casework and by the end of the 1950s were provided by half a dozen universities. The former involved

> lectures and seminars on the law related to probation officers' work, criminology, casework, human growth and development, medical aspects of delinquency, and matrimonial conciliation. Probation inspectors also undertake tutorial sessions. The practical training ... may be given anywhere in England and Wales under the supervision of experienced probation officers.
>
> (Home Office 1962a: 118)

For those aged over 30, training lasted about a year, with a mixture of theoretical and practical elements. But, despite the efforts given to training, in 1961 almost one-third of all full-time probation officers had been appointed with no relevant university qualifications or Home Office training (Home Office 1962a.). The moves towards a more 'scientific' approach to training can be seen in the following quotation from an article about training published in 1948:

> The main basis of the work, however, is the reaction of one character on another. The essential secret of this was possessed by the early pioneers. It becomes increasingly apparent that no amount of academic and scientific knowledge is of real and lasting avail in helping delinquents, unless it is backed by a strong element of human interest. Given this, the greater the knowledge of the complexities of human behavior the more effective will be the work. The study of the elements of psychology, followed by study of the character problems arising in the courts, is therefore essential. A probation officer is not expected to have specialized knowledge in this field, but he should be able to recognize types and pick out those people who need the help of specialists. This knowledge will help him to avoid a great deal of wasted effort, as it is now known that certain types of personality do not appear to respond to case work in the open, while other types do not respond to punitive methods. The application of the wrong form of treatment may be as dangerous to the community as to the individual concerned.
>
> (Minn 1948: 170)

On the one hand, there are obvious traces here of the early reliance on 'personality' and a clear reference to the work of the untrained missionaries. On the other hand, the importance of psychology is emphasised and an awareness of specialised knowledge. And 'case work' is mentioned, almost in passing. By the mid-1950s, casework had taken on a much greater significance and it is no coincidence that

Bochel (1976) in her discussion of the 1945–59 period entitles the chapter 'Social Casework for the Courts'. Indeed, it is notable that the winner of a Napo Literary Competition in 1945 was an essay entitled 'Relationships in Case Work' (Craig 1945).

Peter Raynor has recently defined casework succinctly as 'a process of therapeutic work in which the offender's needs and motivations, characteristically hidden behind a "presenting problem", could be revealed through a process of insight facilitated by a relationship with a probation officer' (Raynor 2007: 1067). In rather more detail, it is defined in a key probation text of the time:

> Casework is based on the belief in the intrinsic value of each human being and on his capacity for growth and change. Belief in the worth of the individual originally stemmed from religion and is part of the concept of democracy. How to use the individual's capacity for growth and change depends on some understanding of the nature of both man and society. This understanding, still incomplete, is derived from many disciplines: anthropology, sociology, medicine and psychiatry, and from the study of social work practice over the years. Informed by this body of knowledge, caseworkers have been able to formulate principles on which to base their methods of work; to gain clearer understanding of people, their social situations and the part that can be played in helping them. This knowledge also allows caseworkers to enter into and use conscious and controlled relationships with individuals as the means by which growth and change may be encouraged.
>
> (King 1958: 45)

With casework, probation officers became more self-conscious and reflexive about how they worked with offenders. They became more interested in examining offenders' feelings as well as needs that were emotional and material. The importance of psychology was further reinforced as casework was rooted in this. Casework used the language of diagnosis and treatment, and spoke of clients (although it is often lazily assumed that casework and a medical model of crime are virtually synonymous, it should be emphasised that this is not the case). Casework was grounded in the relationship between probation officer and offender and here difficulties emerged. In a 'normal' relationship both parties are free to continue or not, but in a probation casework relationship one party has been coerced by the courts into participating, and the offender has little choice but to take part as failure to do so could have undesirable consequences. David Smith (2006) has recently noted that, at this time, articles on probation in the journal *Case Conference* tended to focus on whether or not meaningful casework was possible given the legal power of the probation officer. And he goes on to show that some influential commentators on social work argued that – far from being a drawback – the authority of a probation officer could be a significant advantage as offenders were searching (subconsciously) for an authority figure.

But the open confidence that might be expected in a doctor/patient relationship may be much more problematic in a probation officer/offender relationship which is not based on the voluntary attendance of the offender. It may, therefore, be more difficult to get the offender to talk openly about his or her problems as a result of the serious power imbalance in the relationship. It may also not be a simple matter of agreeing on the offender's needs as the latter may be clear that accommodation or poverty might be the basis of the problem, while the probation officer might consider that there are more deeply rooted issues in the dynamics of the offender's family. Offenders may see no need, and have no desire, for change. The need for probation officers to be highly sensitive to how they build up relationships with their offenders, to be conscious of their own feelings and emotions, to learn how to react appropriately to and interpret carefully what offenders tell them, meant that training in casework required highly skilled probation trainers: 'It is through the medium of a supervisor that the young officer is helped towards self-awareness and so learns the meaning of, as well as the need for, controlled use of himself and his knowledge' (Newton 1956: 134).

As Dorothy Bochel (1976) points out, the significance of casework can be gauged by the fact that in the *Handbook of Probation* (Le Mesurier 1935) there is no mention of the term 'social casework', whereas, a quarter of a century later, the successor to the *Handbook* (King 1958) devotes approximately 25 per cent of its pages to a discussion of the principles and methods of casework and how they might be applied to probation work. Ultimately, however, it is difficult to know just how far the principles of casework that probation officers were trained in actually influenced their practice. George Newton, an assistant chief probation officer in London and a contributor to training, argued that most probation officers worked with offenders in two ways:

> The first is an attempt to relieve economic need where this is necessary, either directly by financial assistance or indirectly with the help of some other community service including the Employment Exchange, and so to equip a probationer to relieve his own economic needs. The second, by persuasive argument, encouragement, straight talking, exhortation and suggestion, attempts to change the direction of the probationer's behaviour towards an honest and industrious life, and, finally, to enforce a measure of control and a checking-up authority in order to prevent unlawful behaviour.
>
> (Newton 1956: 126)

There is little evidence of scientific casework here – indeed, little seems to have changed since the days of the missionaries. But Newton goes on to argue that now (in the mid-1950s) there is a much greater awareness of the 'effect of unmet emotional needs ... which, if unmet at the right stage in development, affect adversely the process of maturation and limit the sphere of rational conduct, leaving crippled personalities' (Newton 1956: 127). This – with its language of emotional needs, stages in development, rational conduct and crippled personalities – suggests a rather different kind of probation work. But, as Vanstone points out, a lot of the glamour of casework had to do with its rhetorical power – it helped to validate the work of probation officers by providing a language and a technique that further encouraged the claims of probation as a profession. And, no matter how attractive casework might have been in terms of being up to date, there was no evidence that it had any effect at all on offending behaviour – 'the assumption of a knowledge base' (Vanstone 2004a: 108) might well have been casework's real attraction.

Whatever the flaws and limitations of casework, and no matter how far practice failed to live up to the rarefied claims that were made for it in training, it became the foundation for probation work and remained so for many years despite attacks and modifications. Indeed, as Smith (2006) argues, it may currently be undergoing a renaissance as a result of developments in criminology that take account of offender biographies and emotions.

Matrimonial work and after-care

As we noted in the previous chapter, the matrimonial work of probation officers had increased during the war, and the immediate post-war conditions – especially the housing shortage – meant that marital difficulties continued to pose problems. Applications for divorce and the number of divorces obtained grew in the years after the war, just as the importance of the family was increasingly being recognised. Magistrates, under the Summary Procedure (Domestic Proceedings) Act 1937, had been given the statutory authority to request a probation officer to attempt reconciliation between husband and wife – a procedure that had been used informally since the early days of probation. In 1946, a Committee on Procedure in Matrimonial Causes was set up under the Chairmanship of Mr Justice (later Lord) Denning, to investigate the workings of the law on divorce, how this might be improved, and 'in particular, whether any (and if so, what) machinery should be made available for the purpose of attempting a reconciliation between the parties, either before or after proceedings have been commenced' (Lord Chancellor's Department 1947: 5). The Committee paid tribute to the efforts of probation officers in reconciliation work where marriages were in difficulty, noting that 'The probation officers have done their work so well that they have gained the confidence of the public' (Lord Chancellor's Department 1947: 7). But, despite their acknowledgement of the work done by probation officers, the Committee did not recommend extending probation's remit to take over marriage guidance work. Instead, they proposed a completely new marriage welfare service that would not only help individuals prepare for marriage, but also provide guidance when marriages were in difficulty. Their proposals for court welfare officers, however, suggested that probation was expected to play an important role – at least in the short term.

> ... (iv) Welfare Officers should be appointed to give guidance to parties who resort to the Divorce Court or are contemplating doing so. These Court Welfare Officers should be carefully selected. The aim should be to appoint men and women of such education, sympathy and understanding as to be able to obtain the confidence of persons in all sections of the community. They should preferably be persons holding a degree or diploma in social science

but this should not be regarded as essential. They should be trained in social service, particularly in marriage guidance and the welfare of children; and they should be given courses of instruction including refresher courses in these subjects.

(v) In order to make an immediate start, the first Court Welfare Officers could be appointed by selection from among the probation officers. Indeed there is no reason why the new Service should not be developed from the existing probation service. That service, despite its name, is already supplying Court Welfare Officers for the Magistrates' Courts, both in regard to reconciliation and the custody of children; and there is a number of suitable and experienced officers already available who could undertake work at once in connection with the Divorce Court. The probation service is moreover sufficiently flexible to allow for expansion and strengthening to deal with new work. Under the guidance of the Probation Training Board, those entering the service are so selected and trained that they are well suited for the work we have in mind, and there is no reason why the present system of pay and supervision in the service should not apply to those undertaking the new work.

(Lord Chancellor's Department 1947: 14)

The confidence that the Denning Committee seemed to have in the probation service in terms of supplying the first wave of court welfare officers is quite remarkable – particularly at a time when the service was having difficulties in recruiting staff. Despite the decision not to recommend that court welfare work should become a part of the probation task, probation seems to hold the key to the new position of court welfare officer, and, crucially, the new children's officers were not seen as being appropriate to act as court welfare officers and so posed no new threat to probation.

Following the Denning Committee, the Home Office set up a Departmental Committee to explore how marriage guidance could be developed via governmental grants. This Committee considered the obvious question of whether

the easiest and best way of providing marriage guidance ... would be to extend the probation service, especially as persons entering the service are selected for qualities of character and personality and are given a suitable training for matrimonial work as well as other branches of their duties as the social workers of the courts.

(Home Office 1948: 7)

The response was firmly in the negative, for several reasons: first, probation officers were too closely connected with the courts and offenders; second, those who tended to discuss their problems with probation officers were usually married and only rarely did unmarried individuals seek help from probation, and this latter group would be likely to make up a significant part of marriage guidance work; and, third, probation did not have the resources to cope with the level of demand that was envisaged.

The first court welfare officer was appointed to the Divorce Division of the High Court in London in June 1950 for an experimental period of six months. The individual was an ex-probation officer who had recently been working in the Probation Branch of the Home Office and his task seems to have been to assist the court in cases concerning children in divorce cases – a rather more limited task than had been envisaged by the Denning Committee. He seems to have been largely ignored until a chance meeting with a barrister he knew led to the latter mentioning his availability to a judge who made use of his services in a case, and this encouraged others to use him so the experiment continued (Page 1992). Indeed, the Royal Commission on Marriage and Divorce (set up in 1951 and reporting in 1956) commended the value of such work and recommended that the arrangements should continue and be expanded:

> the only existing statutory services which can suitably provide a [national] network are the probation service and the children's service. We have already said that there is an advantage in confining the work to a single service, and we recommend that the probation service should be selected.
> (Royal Commission on Marriage and Divorce 1956: 109)

Soon after the publication of the Royal Commission report, the government announced that the work of the probation service in the divorce courts was to be extended, and in 1959 the Probation Rules were amended to make such work a statutory duty for probation officers.

Another part of probation work that also expanded during the 1950s was the supervision of those released from custodial sentences. Like matrimonial work, work with those released from prison had been undertaken since the early days of the missionaries. Such work had become a statutory duty in the 1949 Probation Rules, following the changes in aftercare made as a result of the 1948 Criminal Justice Act, and the significance of this move is noted by Bochel (1976: 185): 'The decision was highly significant for the future of the service in setting it on a course of development destined in the long run to alter the balance of its work and to carry it closer to the custodial elements of the penal system.'

In general, the after-care of released prisoners was in the hands of local Discharged Prisoners' Aid Societies, where often probation officers acted as agents. As a result of the 1948 Act, probation officers were required to act as agents of the Central After-Care Council in respect of prisoners released on licence and borstal inmates released under supervision. Social work inside prison, however, was a different matter and while the National Association of Discharged Prisoners' Aid Societies (NADPAS) had taken responsibility for this following the recommendation of the 1936 Departmental Committee that probation should limit its work with prisoners, development had been slow. Indeed, by 1953 there were still only seven prisons with a full-time prison welfare officer.[2] Following the 1948 Act, after-care was taken increasingly seriously and in 1951 a committee was set up to examine the arrangements for dealing with the welfare of released prisoners (Home Office 1953). The Maxwell Committee quickly discovered that these arrangements were fragmented and haphazard: 'the present arrangements ... could not be advocated on grounds of administrative simplicity or practical convenience' (Home Office 1953: 11). Given that the framework of the welfare state could now meet the material requirements of those released from custody, the Committee suggested that the aid societies should focus their attention on something more like casework. They recommended that

> to assist the Aid Societies in the development of 'after-care', Prison Welfare Officers should be appointed at local prisons who should submit to the appropriate Aid Society recommendations for the after-care of such prisoners as are willing and able to benefit from their services and appear suitable for special attention and assistance.
>
> (Home Office 1953: 32)

The work envisaged for these welfare officers looked very similar to what probation officers were already doing; they were expected to be trained social workers, just like probation officers, their salaries would be similar to probation officers, and 'suitable candidates for these posts might often be found from within the ranks of the probation service' (Home Office 1953: 23). The work currently carried out by probation officers for the aid societies was commended by the Committee, which expressed the hope that it might be expanded. And it was suggested that statutory after-care could be further extended to other classes of prisoners when the new arrangements had bedded down. But, perhaps as a result of the competing demands being made on the probation service (e.g. matrimonial work) and the difficulties in recruiting trained staff, development continued to be slow for the remainder of the 1950s.

In 1957, a new Home Secretary, R.A. Butler, arrived in the Home Office and shortly after asked the Advisory Council on the Treatment of Offenders (ACTO) to examine the issue of compulsory after-care. The Council's report was generally in favour of the extension of after-care, but perhaps its most significant comment was to make it quite clear that only one organisation existed that could conceivably take on the after-care task:

> the probation service combines, like no other organised body, the two essentials for effective after-care. It is composed of trained social workers ... Secondly, it is so spread over the whole country that a discharged prisoner will seldom live more than a few miles from his supervisor, with the result that if a crisis occurs in his rehabilitation, help and advice are readily available.
>
> (ACTO 1958: 12)

The 1961 Criminal Justice Act made provision for the system of after-care recommended by ACTO, but a shortage of probation officers meant that such an expansion of probation work could not immediately be undertaken. As a result, only the provision of after-care for those released from detention centres (which catered for those aged 14–20) was implemented and the remaining after-care provisions were repealed by the Criminal Justice Act 1967, which introduced new provisions for the release of prisoners on licence.

Enter research

By 1957, the golden jubilee of the probation service, there were almost 1,300 full-time probation officers (excluding supervisory grades of whom there were probably around 150). Nellis (2007: 39) notes that by 'the year of its jubilee, the probation service demonstrably enjoyed an unprecedented level of official prestige, if not widespread public appreciation'. The celebrations included events with the Queen Mother and the ageing Viscount Herbert Samuel, who, as a government minister in the Home Office, had seen the 1907 Act through Parliament. A letter from the Home Secretary, R.A. Butler, congratulated Napo and in a speech to the Association he made it clear that he wanted more research to be carried out into probation. The 1948 Act had given the Home Secretary the authority to 'conduct research into the causes of delinquency and the treatment of offenders, and matters connected therewith' (11 & 12 Geo. 6. Ch.58: s.77), and by the mid-1950s a number of studies had been carried out discussing probation (not all of which had resulted from the Home Secretary's new power).

As early as 1948, Max Grunhut had judged probation to be a success. Reconviction rates – of 35 per cent – might look worse when compared with those associated with fines, dismissals and prison, but offenders with different sentences were not comparable. And, in any event,

> Even if probation did not diminish the number of relapses, something would be gained for the community if its security could be maintained on a tolerable level with less resort to degrading penalties. And such penalties probation does help to avoid: for it is a superior method of treatment which does not disrupt a man's life, but pursues its object by preserving, if not rebuilding, his social relations within his personal environment.
>
> (Grunhut 1948: 311)

Probation could, therefore, be used more widely. Hermann Mannheim (1955: 249) too, in 1950, was willing to explain away probation's failure to eliminate short custodial sentences: sentences were more punitive as an understandable result of public anxiety about crime, and sentencers might be more discriminating in selecting cases for probation.

The first Home Office research study to be published was a study exploring how to predict success or failure in those sentenced to borstal training (Mannheim and Wilkins 1955). One of the approaches followed was to compare those who had, prior to their borstal sentence, been subjected to a probation order and those who had not experienced probation. The results did not look promising: those who had been on probation in the past were more likely to be failures than those who had not; indeed, the former group were twice as likely to be reconvicted within three months than the latter and were far more likely to be reconvicted of four or more offences. But there was a good reason for this, as the authors pointed out: those who had been on probation before borstal were more likely to have started their criminal careers at a younger age than those with no probation experience (Mannheim and Wilkins 1955: 73–6). In another publication, one of the authors felt obliged to explain (or excuse?) this finding again: the higher failure rate for those who had been on probation before borstal

> might easily have been interpreted as indicating that a period on probation had had an unfavourable effect on these lads. The correct interpretation, however, may be this: first, boys who embark on their criminal careers at an early age are more likely to be placed on probation for their first offences than boys who commit their first offences somewhat later in adolescence. Secondly, it is now the prevailing view among criminologists that those who are early starters in delinquency are more likely to develop criminal habits than those who start later. The true (negative) correlation is therefore probably one between age at first crime and failure, not probation and failure; and if the age factor is eliminated by being held constant for both groups, the one with and the one without previous probation, the differential failure may disappear.
>
> (Mannheim 1955: 124)

An article by Grunhut (1952) describing a small-scale pilot study of offenders who had received probation orders tried to tease out the key factors that might be associated with success: his conclusions were that 'psychological conditions are more important than external circumstances', so that as far as probation work was concerned it should be focused

> in some cases [on] … the psychological effect of a new relation of trust and affection on persons who have yielded to the pressure of emotional stress and other inner conflicts. In other cases it is a change of residence, work or companionship wisely used or encouraged on the basis of a considerate understanding of the probationer's difficulties.
>
> (Grunhut 1952: 300)

Grunhut (1956) also discussed probation in a study of juvenile offenders and how they were dealt with by the courts. He noted that probation was by far the most popular sentence in the juvenile courts, but also that its proportionate use had fallen between 1938 and 1950, while the use of the fine had increased during the same period. Indeed, he argues that 'The outstanding feature in the changing trends of treatment practice between pre-war years and the post-war period is a shifting of the emphasis from probation to fines' (Grunhut 1956: 84).

Gibbens (1959) tried to tease out the factors that were related to success for adolescent girls under probation or supervision orders, but in breaking down his sample the numbers involved in the various categories became very small, and essentially his article served to underscore just how difficult it could be to measure success. He emphasised the role of the probation officer as supervisor and how flexible he or she had to be – indeed, the probation officer had to take on the role of a parent,

> at one moment a practical helper with finding a job or lodgings, at another an advisor about spending money or making friends, at another a skilful diplomat in smoothing over family crises, and all the time a therapist who watches for the receptive moments when the deeper perplexities and resentments, which are always present, can be ventilated and dealt with.
>
> (Gibbens 1959: 99)

A much less academic article, written by a probation officer, discussed the problems for probation work caused by seasonal employment in a seaside town (Hodges 1953).

Perhaps the two most important pieces of probation research, however, were a short article by Leslie Wilkins (1958), a member of the nascent Home Office Research Unit, and a report by the Cambridge Department of Criminal Science (1958), which had been supported by the Home Office. Wilkins started from the well-known fact that probation was used far more often by some courts than others and that differential use could not be explained simply by the different kinds of offender dealt with. His basic assumption was that those courts that used probation orders more often did so because they considered that probation was an effective sentence. He selected a court where probation was heavily used and another where use of the probation order was close to the national average for comparison purposes (both were courts of Quarter Sessions). His two objectives were to examine whether reconviction rates were related to the disposal policy of the courts – and more particularly the use of probation. No significant differences were found in reconviction rates: 'similar cases show similar success rates irrespective of variations in the treatment' (Wilkins 1958: 207). Heavy use of probation did not, therefore, result in greater success – not, perhaps, a ringing endorsement. Wilkins's conclusion, however, is to encourage greater use of probation orders, particularly for those who are given custodial sentences:

> It seems that a larger proportion of offenders who are now sent to prison or Borstal could be put on probation without any change in the reconviction rate as a whole, although with the selection of worse risks for probation the gross success rate for probation as a form of treatment might drop.
>
> (Wilkins 1958: 207)

Using probation as an alternative to custody was, therefore, judged to be an acceptable option even if this led to a higher rate of reconvictions for probation orders.

The Cambridge study carried a preface by the director of the department, Leon Radzinowicz, where he made a well-known statement about the importance of probation. Radzinowicz's claim was almost certainly made in the context of probation's golden jubilee, but it is notable that he claims probation to be British – choosing to downplay the American influence (which he acknowledges later) – a myth that Nellis (2007) argues had been successfully built up by the mid-1950s.

> If I were asked what was the most significant contribution made by this country to the new penological theory and practice which struck root in the twentieth century – the measure which would endure, while so many other methods of treatment might well fall into limbo, or be altered beyond recognition – my answer would be probation.
>
> (Cambridge Department of Criminal Science 1958: x)

The study used various measures of success, all of which showed probation to be more successful for adults than for juveniles:

- 79 per cent of adults and 73 per cent of juveniles completed their probation orders successfully (not returned to court for a breach or a further offence during the period of supervision).
- 70 per cent of adults and 58 per cent of juveniles were not breached or found guilty of a further offence while under supervision or for three years following the end of the order.
- 74 per cent of adults and 62 per cent of juveniles were not reconvicted for three years following the end of the order, despite an appearance in court while under supervision.

Probation was more successful with women than men and success was strongly related to age, but the conclusion was unequivocal: 'while the results are better for women than for men and for the older than for the younger offenders, yet probation emerges unquestionably as a generally effective measure of treatment whatever the sex and age of an offender happens to be' (Cambridge Department of Criminal Science 1958: 4).

Most of those who received a probation order were first offenders (two-thirds of adults and three-quarters of juveniles) and probation was especially successful with first offenders aged 21 and over with rates of success of almost 80 per cent for men and 90 per cent for women. Even for those with one previous conviction, probation was judged to be effective and capable of greater use, but the success rate for those with two or more previous convictions was not encouraging (Table 5.2). Previous experience of probation did not seem to have a particularly negative effect: 'the rates of success of probation, when ordered for a second time, differ little from the general results obtained for all recidivists' (Cambridge Department of Criminal Science 1958: 8). But a residence requirement was associated with higher rates of reconviction than probation orders with no such requirements – which to some extent could be explained by the fact that the more difficult cases had residence requirements (e.g. those with previous convictions).

Table 5.2 Success rate of probation for adults and juveniles by number of previous convictions (%)

	First offenders	*Offenders with 1 previous conviction*	*Offenders with 2+ previous convictions*
Adults	81.2	67.3	51.5
Juveniles	65.7	55.3	42.1
All offenders	72.4	60.3	49.0

Source: Cambridge Department of Criminal Science 1958: 7.

The Cambridge study was very positive about probation, but there was a serious limitation insofar as probation's success was not compared with any other court sentence, which made it difficult to judge just how effective probation was.

Probation never had it so good?

During the second half of the 1950s there was a great deal of government activity that was related, in one way or another, to probation. From 1955 onwards crime began to rise – 'The overall crime figures certainly show the 1955–60 quinquennium as a period of serious deterioration after a decade of *falling* crime' (Hennessy 2007: 515, emphasis in original) – and much of this rise was associated with teenagers. As Sandbrook (2006: 445) notes: 'Between 1955 and 1961, the number of boys between fourteen and seventeen convicted of serious offences more than doubled, with a similar increase among young men from seventeen to twenty-one. Teenage convictions overall doubled between 1955 and 1959.' At the same time, the austerity of the post-war years began to be replaced by a period of prosperity; it is no coincidence that the titles of both Hennessy's and Sandbrook's histories of the period refer to Harold Macmillan's famous phrase used in a speech in 1957 (which was actually warning about the perils of inflation):

> Let's be frank about it; most of our people have never had it so good. Go around the country, go to the industrial towns, go to the farms, and you will see a state of prosperity such as we have never had in our lifetime – nor indeed ever in the history of this country.
>
> (Macmillan quoted in Sandbrook 2006: 80)

Around the same time, prison overcrowding began to emerge as a problem, and in 1957 an ACTO report, *Alternatives to Short Terms of Imprisonment*, was published by the Home Office (ACTO 1957). The main recommendation was to set up an experimental attendance centre for 17–21-year-olds (it opened in Manchester in December 1958), but probation was seen as a possible option for alcoholic offenders, especially those with a mental health treatment condition. ACTO also reminded courts that they could make greater use of the provision of placing an offender who had been fined under the supervision of a probation officer. The Council reiterated the conclusions of an earlier report from 1952 which had made it clear that the suspended sentence was 'especially undesirable in conjunction with a probation order' (ACTO 1957: 32). A further ACTO report two years later urged the development of a system of detention centres for those aged between 16 and 21, and also recommended that statutory after-care was needed for those so sentenced. This would mean more work for probation and ACTO acknowledged that around 24 more probation officers might be necessary (ACTO 1959), although the service was short of staff at this time.

Perhaps predictably, given the rise in crime, there were demands for the reintroduction of corporal punishment and ACTO was asked to consider whether there was a case for this. Their conclusion was emphatic – 'corporal punishment should not be reintroduced as a judicial penalty in respect of any categories of offences or offenders' (ACTO 1960: 26). Interestingly, the Council mentioned that Napo had taken a vote of its members about whether they were in favour of bringing back corporal punishment and 10 per cent had supported it. Yet another ACTO report appeared in 1962, this one considering whether there were any possible new methods of non-residential treatment for offenders under the age of 21 (this age group was clearly causing a lot of problems), and in particular the feasibility of replicating a Citizenship Training Centre in Boston, Massachusetts, that appeared to be successful. ACTO did not recommend setting up such centres, but they were interested in developments in group work in probation:

> It was also suggested to us that there is insufficient scope in the present system of probation for stimulating positive qualities such as responsibility and resourcefulness, and that the probationer needs to be involved in a more active experience. We were interested to hear from the London Police Court Mission of their experiment in providing an adventure course for probation- ers and in encouraging an experiment in group counselling at a probation hostel for girls; and from the National Association of Probation Officers of a few experiments in group work or outdoor activities that have been carried out by individual officers on a limited scale.
>
> (ACTO 1962: 7)

As a result they recommended adding a new requirement to the probation order whereby the probation officer would guide the offender to make more construc- tive use of his or her leisure, using the facilities provided by the Youth Service or further education colleges. A voluntary agreement to attend was the preferred option, but ACTO was willing to countenance a legal requirement. This may be the first official acknowledgement of group work in probation and is one of the seeds that led to day training centres ten years later. Vanstone (2003) and Page (1992) both suggest that, while group work is discernible from the beginnings of probation work, its real emergence is apparent in the 1950s.

The government's anxiety about rising crime was made transparent in the White Paper *Penal Practice in a Changing Society* (Home Office 1959). The growth of crime was acknowledged (and set in historical context) as were its consequences in terms of prison overcrowding and strained resources in the probation service, borstals and approved schools. The White Paper focused on policing, prison and the criminal law as the ways to fight crime, so probation is notable by its almost complete absence except for an endorsement of the ACTO report on after-care (ACTO 1958; see also p. 94) where probation is welcomed as the only agency that could possibly take on the extra work: 'At the same time provision was made for the field-work of statutory after-care to be undertaken by the only nation-wide network of qualified social workers available to do it – the probation service' (Home Office 1959: 20).

From all of these reports, the probation service comes through as available, competent, keen, ambitious, professional, willing to take on more work, and experts in a defined area of working with offenders. Two official Home Office committees further support such an assessment. The Ingleby Committee was set up in 1956 to inquire into the juvenile court system, methods of dealing with juvenile offenders and the prevention of cruelty and neglect of juveniles. Its main recommendations with regard to probation were:

- Probation officers or the local authority children's department should be responsible for court reports on children.
- Probation orders should be replaced by supervision orders for children under 14 found guilty of an offence.
- Detention centre orders should be followed by a period of statutory after-care (following the ACTO report discussed above).
- Probation should be responsible, along with local children's authorities, for the after-care supervision of those released from approved schools.
- The existing 11 approved probation homes for young people aged between 15 and 20 suffered from staffing problems and were too small to offer adequate programmes for those sent there, so they should be discontinued as suitable approved schools and probation hostels became available (Home Office 1960).

The Streatfeild Committee was appointed in 1958 with the task of reviewing the arrangements for bringing to trial those charged with offences and for the provision of information to the courts that might assist them in deciding upon the most appropriate sentence. Its remit was restricted to the higher courts but its recommendations were seen to be relevant to magistrates' courts too. Streatfeild, like Ingleby, implicitly acknowledged the expertise of the probation service and its recommendations for probation looked to widen its role with regard to the provision of information for the courts. It was noted that probation reports were far more detailed than those prepared by the police and thus more relevant to the court in deciding what sentence to pass. They should include

> among other things, essential details of the offender's home surroundings, and family background; his attitude to his family and their response to him; his school and work record and spare time activities; his attitude to his employment; his attitude to the present offence; his attitude and response

to previous forms of treatment following any previous convictions; detailed histories about relevant physical and mental conditions; an assessment of personality and character.

(Home Office 1961: 95)

But reports were not valuable simply for such background and contextual information. The Committee also recommended that reports could contain an informed opinion (*not* a recommendation) about the impact of a particular sentence on an offender – and this could be a sentence other than probation. Only probation officers had the knowledge and expertise to provide such material to the court. Pre-trial inquiries were recommended, as long as the accused agreed, although these could not be carried out in every case due to a lack of resources. Such reports should be available to the courts when the accused was aged 30 or less, had not been convicted previously of an offence punishable with imprisonment, or had recently been in contact with the probation service. Once again, more work for a service that was already suffering from shortages of staff.

Moving into the 1960s

By 1960 the total number of persons found guilty of indictable offences was 163,482, an increase of 52 per cent since 1955 – and most of this increase could be laid at the door of offenders under the age of 21. Despite the rise in crime and the government's acknowledgement that this was a problem, on the surface probation seemed to be more than holding its own. In 1960, a total of 41,790 probation orders were made by the courts compared with 31,064 in 1950; most of these orders were made on male offenders with 15 per cent for females. The higher courts had increased their use of probation and were responsible in 1960 for 16 per cent of all orders. The great majority of probation orders were made for indictable offences, with only 12 per cent being made for summary offences. But the proportionate use of probation showed no signs of moving back to the position it had attained before the war, and this was due to changes in the distribution of sentences in the magistrates' courts (in the higher courts, the proportionate use of probation remained very similar to what it had been in 1938 although the absolute number of orders had increased considerably). Table 5.3 shows that absolute discharges decreased while conditional discharges increased, and fines increased markedly while at the same time the use of probation decreased.

As we have shown, the service was also taking on wider responsibilities for after-care, and matrimonial work; King (1958) suggests that probation officers saw around 70,000 marital cases annually. Staff shortages, however, remained a problem and research had by no means proved conclusively that probation was any more effective than other sentences of the court.

The service was certainly held in high regard officially; the number of government reports in the second half of the 1950s that simply took it for granted that the probation service could be relied upon to expand its work and take on new

Table 5.3 Sentences passed in magistrates' courts for indictable offences by age group, 1950 and 1960 (%)

Sentence	1950				1960			
	Under 14	14–16	17–20	21 and over	Under 14	14–16	17–20	21 and over
Abs. discharge	16	9	6	4	6	4	2	2
Cond. discharge	18	14	15	12	31	22	13	12
Fine	15	19	40	50	15	25	53	57
Probation	40	42	27	9	35	32	20	10
Approved school	7	12	–	–	5	2	–	–
Detention centre	–	–	–	–	–	9	1	–
Prison	–	–	5	21	–	–	5	16
Other	4	4	7	4	8	7	6	4
Total No.	26,222	15,688	8,902	48,200	29,916	26,198	19,660	59,938

Note: Numbers have been rounded and may not necessarily add up to 100%.

tasks is remarkable. But there was still a great deal of public ignorance about probation. Martin Page suggests that

> This public ignorance was no doubt associated with the veil of secrecy that seemed to be drawn across much probation work, with its confidentiality and delicate nature. Indeed, probation officers seemed a kind of secular priesthood, custodians of the 'sacred trust' vested in them by the courts, with probation officers sustained by a sense of vocation if not by religious beliefs as well, and with many of them leading lives as though they were observing vows of poverty, celibacy and obedience.
>
> (Page 1992: 228)

In 1959, however, a television series called *Probation Officer* began on Associated Television dramatising the work of probation officers. Napo dissociated itself from the series and questions were asked in Parliament about it, but there can be little doubt that the series brought probation to the notice of the general public (Page 1992). Given Napo's and MPs' responses to the series it seems that it was not an entirely uncritical portrait of probation. And two books published during the period also show a rather different view of probation – more realistic, less light-hearted and sentimental – from that found in Ellison (1934), Harris (1937) or Stokes (1950). John St John's (1961) *Probation: The Second Chance* provides a rounded picture of probation work in the criminal justice process, showing the difficulties and problems that could be encountered. St John discusses how probation officers use casework, how they work with the courts, with offenders and with other agencies. He examines popular conceptions about probation – for example, that it is only for first offenders, or confined to those who have committed minor offences – and shows them to be false. He presents probation officers who are tired and pessimistic, and emphasises the significance of psychiatry to their work. St John notices the decline in the proportionate use of probation and suggests various possible explanations:

> Perhaps this was caused by a desire not to add to the work of a service that is already overburdened? Perhaps fines are considered more suitable for an 'affluent' society? Perhaps the proportion of hardened professional criminals who are unsuitable for probation has increased? Perhaps courts nowadays select probationers with more care? The drop in the percentages is surely too great for these explanations. Despite the relative cheapness of probation, its – at worst – equal efficiency to prison or Borstal, it is difficult not to conclude that over the country as a whole the courts rely less than they once did on the kind of positive reform that probation is able to offer.
>
> (St John 1961: 263)

Despite the difficulty in conclusively showing that probation is effective – and he is fully aware of the problems in measuring success – St John is in favour of probation as it is 'ideally fitted to resolve the confusion and public fear that has arisen over this question of criminal responsibility … it does … protect society, as well as offer practical help to the offender' (St John 1961: 261). St John's is a more nuanced, more fully contextualised picture of probation than previous popular accounts – it would be too much to claim that it is warts and all, but it is moving in that direction.

Marjory Todd, too, in *Ever Such a Nice Lady* (1964), stresses the difficulties in being a probation officer (indeed, it is notable that incest is mentioned on the first page).[3] She discusses how tired she felt as a probation officer, how it all seemed to be a constant struggle against often insuperable problems, and the poverty of her clients is ever-present. At times she is almost overwhelmed by the futility of the work:

> How far is it possible for the probation officer to 'make over' the personality and developing sense of values of someone he can see for a quarter of an hour, perhaps, on one day of the week? … one is bound to wonder just how much can ever be crammed into a time so limited. Any belief that one will be able to effect dramatic changes is just not realistic and must bring far too many disappointments to those who start off as enthusiasts.
>
> (Todd 1964: 58–9)

So was this period a true golden age for probation? Perhaps, but only by default and if we look only at the surface. A series of official inquiries and reports validated the work of the probation service by recommending that its role be expanded, and casework had become the accepted weapon for treating offenders. Probation's professionalism was acknowledged by government and it was recognised as the agency responsible for social work in the courts. Napo was now self-supporting, 'the democratic organization of a professional body' and no longer reliant upon 'the patronage of the privileged' (King 1958: 212).

Probation had successfully carved out a clear role for itself. But in addition to the issues we have just discussed (the use of probation by the courts, staff shortages, and the rather darker vision of St John and Todd), it is worth noting that the development of the service had been fragmented and ad hoc – there was no sense of a carefully planned and coordinated process. And, while Napo's power had grown, its close relationship with the Home Office had begun to show signs of strain; there were tensions not just with the Home Office (over pay, amongst other things, although it is worth noting that equal pay for male and female officers was achieved in 1955), but also with children's officers and with the National Association of Discharged Prisoners' Aid Societies over areas of work. Prison overcrowding had become a policy issue and crime was rising – two significant factors that would, in one way or another, have serious implications for probation in the future.

In 1958, Frank Dawtry, the General Secretary of Napo, called for a full-scale review of the service and the following quotation from his article does not suggest that he was thinking in terms of a golden age:

> the time has come for a new departmental committee or royal commission to examine all aspects of the probation service. Its current problems, its local difficulties, the problems of recruitment, the training of a modern service, the best use of the inspectorate, the organization of the Probation Division, are matters of concern to every probation officer. There are also many matters in the daily work of the service to which no one has the time to sit back and give disinterested thought. Should the organization of aftercare or of matrimonial conciliation work involve specialization by certain officers? Can the newly developing prison welfare service be integrated and interchangeable with the probation service? Is the organization of approved probation homes and hostels on the best lines? Can the demand for more internal training be met? Is it satisfactory for the organization of the London probation service to be under direct Home Office control? Can a Government Department effectively administer a local and personal service? Is a principal probation officer to be a departmental head with somewhat remote control of a local service or to retain his present unique position in local services of knowing and partaking in the daily work of his staff? In a growing service seeking to keep pace with modern demands and modern skills, the list of matters now pressing for answer could be extended indefinitely.
>
> (Dawtry 1958: 187)

It would seem that there was no shortage of issues that required attention. In February 1959, the government announced that a full review of the probation service was to take place.

6 From Morison to Martinson, 1962–74

The 1960s, as Arthur Marwick (1998: 3) has noted, rouse 'strong emotions' in everyone – whether those individuals lived through them or not. They are perceived very differently: some would see them as a time of exciting changes that have improved the world for the better, while others view them as the moment when everything began to go wrong and blame them for every problem we have faced since then. Still others see the 1960s as a wasted time when fun and frivolity ruled and nothing changed. They were certainly a period when ordinary people saw considerable changes in their everyday lives: refrigerators, washing machines, television, vacuum cleaners were no longer only for the rich. Supermarkets began to appear in increasing numbers, car ownership more than doubled between 1960 and 1970, motorways began to be built, the expansion of higher education meant that increasing numbers of young people went on to universities and polytechnics after school – and school was increasingly likely to mean a comprehensive one (Marwick 1982; Sandbrook 2007).

The 1960s are also associated with youth culture: mods, rockers, hippies, rock music, drug taking and sexual permissiveness (the Profumo scandal that rocked Macmillan's government in 1963 can be seen as an early example of the last of these, although it had little to do with youth culture). It is no coincidence that in 1964 Mary Whitehouse began her campaign to clean-up television, which mutated into the National Viewers' and Listeners' Association (NVALA), campaigning against sex and violence in the media for many years and also succeeding in keeping these topics high in the public consciousness. Crime is, of course, closely related in the public mind with youth, drugs and sex and in 1964 the number of indictable offences known to the police topped the million mark for the first time; by 1970 the figure was more than 1.5 million. But despite any moral panics about youth and crime (and adults too were involved in crime – the Great Train Robbery, for example, took place in 1963), a great deal of liberalising reform went on under the Labour governments of 1964–70:

- 1965 Abolition of Capital Punishment Act – suspended for five years, confirmed in 1969.
- 1966 Race Relations Act – set up the Race Relations Board to conciliate in cases of discrimination.

- 1967 Abortion Act – made abortion much more widely available.
- 1967 Sexual Offences Act – decriminalised homosexual acts between consenting adults in private.
- 1967 National Health Service (Family Planning) Act – gave local authorities the power to provide contraceptives and contraceptive advice.
- 1968 Theatres Act – abolition of theatrical censorship.
- 1969 Divorce Reform Act – made divorce considerably easier.
- 1970 Matrimonial Property Act – the contribution of a wife within the home to be considered in cases of divorce.
- 1970 Equal Pay Act – the principle of equal pay for men and women was set out.

The Departmental Committee on the probation service that was set up in 1959 reported in 1962, two years before the Conservatives lost the general election after 13 years in government. As discussed at the end of the previous chapter, it would seem that a full-scale review of probation was over-due. How far did its recommendations prepare the probation service for the 1960s?

The Morison Report

The Morison Report was the most substantial inquiry into the probation service since that carried out by the 1936 Departmental Committee on the Social Services in courts of summary jurisdiction (see Chapter 4). It examined the various functions of the service, its organisation and administration, recruitment and training, and salaries and conditions of service. A second report was published – also in 1962 – looking into the approved hostel scheme. Both reports covered probation in Scotland as well as in England and Wales – and this is an important point (although, as we have noted in the Introduction, we have not included Scottish probation in this book), as within a decade probation north of the border would take a different organisational path. But despite the scope of the main report (or perhaps because of it), there was little in the way of radical change recommended; the overall impression given by the report is one of 'no change, steady as she goes'.

The Committee began by defining probation, and commenting on its value and effectiveness. Probation was defined as 'the submission of an offender while at liberty to a specified period of supervision by a social caseworker who is an officer of the court; during this period the offender remains liable, if not of good conduct, to be otherwise dealt with by the court' (Home Office 1962a: 2); the significance of casework is, therefore, officially acknowledged. But the Committee was quick to add that this did not mean that punishment had no part in probation; probation had a 'punitive element', a 'disciplinary aspect' that was important to emphasise as the old misconception of being 'let off' by the courts had not yet disappeared (Home Office 1962a: 3). Probation's value in acknowledging the human dignity of individuals, in helping to make offenders responsible members of the community, in avoiding the harms that result from imprisonment were all emphasised. The Committee's view was that four conditions needed to exist for the use of probation, and it is worth quoting these. It would be difficult to disagree with them even today, but no matter how well-meaning they might be it is hard to ignore their vagueness and the fact that sentencers, offenders, probation officers and other specialists might all be involved in making such decisions; and there is also the question of how differing assessments might be reconciled or prioritised:

> Firstly, the circumstances of the offence and the offender's record must not be such as to demand, in the interests of society, that some more severe method must be adopted in dealing with the offender; secondly, the risk, if any, to society through setting the offender at liberty must be outweighed by the moral, social and economic arguments for not depriving him of it; thirdly, the offender must need continuing attention, since otherwise, if the second condition is satisfied, a fine or discharge will suffice; and, fourthly, the offender must be capable of responding to this attention while he is at liberty.
>
> (Home Office 1962a: 4)

No definitive research was yet available to demonstrate that probation was a more effective disposal than fines, discharges or custody – indeed the Committee pointed out the limitations of such research. The problem remained of just how to measure 'the influence for good of one man or woman upon another' (Home Office 1962a: 9), which was, of course, the fundamental approach to probation supervision.

The report moved on to comment on the various aspects of probation work, none of which were seen as unnecessary. With regard to social enquiry reports (SERs; it was this Committee that recommended the term 'social enquiry report' should be used, partly to make it clear that such reports might be used whether or not a probation order was being considered), wherever possible a report should be prepared before a probation order was made, although courts were not obliged to request one. While most of the Committee's thinking on SERs followed the recommendations of the Streatfeild Committee (see previous chapter), they disagreed with Streatfeild's proposal that probation officers should be encouraged to offer an opinion about an offender's suitability for a sentence other than probation.

Probation was acknowledged to be a fully fledged profession which used a highly skilled approach – social casework. But, like any profession, probation officers had to be permitted 'reasonable discretion to use the supervisory techniques' thought to be most appropriate (Home Office 1962a: 26). The use of the term 'client' was deprecated, a suggestion that was ignored by probation officers until the Home Office made similar noises about it in the mid-1980s. While the number of probation orders had risen by more than 10,000 between 1950 and 1960, the proportion of offenders convicted of indictable offences placed on probation had declined, but the Committee brushed aside any suggestion that this might 'reflect any loss of confidence in probation by the courts' (Home Office 1962a: 28).

Instead, the possible reasons were judged to be more careful selection by the courts of those who were put on probation (which had always been seen as a key factor for effectiveness), the availability of alternative sentences, and awareness by sentencers that probation officers were struggling as a result of lack of resources. It was noted that the proportion of one-year orders had halved between 1951 and 1960, while three-year orders had doubled, a development that had clear implications for workload, and the Committee encouraged the early discharge of long orders wherever appropriate.

As for the other duties of probation officers, there was little sign of any perceived need for change. Supervision orders (for those under 17 who were in need of care and protection or beyond parental control) should continue to be a task for probation officers or a member of the local authority children's department. Money payment supervision orders, introduced by the Magistrates' Courts Act 1952, should not be seen as a substitute for a probation order and should be used only where there was a clear risk of default; collecting instalments of fines was not part of the work of money payment supervision. The supervision of children in matrimonial proceedings by probation officers (or a local authority) should continue. After-care of those released from custodial sentences had been a part of probation work for many years and – especially since the Criminal Justice Act 1961 – was becoming a task of considerable significance. This too was thought to be an appropriate duty for probation officers, although the Committee noted that considerable expansion of the probation service would be necessary to be able to deal with this area of work. It was emphasised that after-care should not be seen as a marginal aspect of probation work. Matrimonial conciliation was a statutory duty of the probation service and should continue, even in those cases where individuals contacted probation officers directly without reference to the courts. And the various relatively minor but important duties that had been taken on and grown over time were all necessary and should continue (e.g. enquiries in adoption cases, enquiries into applications for consent to marry, escorting young offenders to approved schools). Even the miscellaneous and voluntary activities carried out by probation officers should continue; they should be recognised by probation committees and taken into consideration when planning staffing. And, as Table 6.1 shows, such work was an odd mishmash of social work tasks that was growing in volume. It also suggests a touching faith in probation officers as social welfare workers; where they were known (and presumably many of those involved in such cases would be likely to have been in professional contact with, or know someone who had been in professional contact with, probation officers) probation officers would seem to be trusted as helpful in sorting out the problems of everyday working-class life.

As all of these tasks were judged to be appropriate for the probation service, and demand was likely to increase, the rest of the Morison Report focused on how the organisation, training, recruitment and pay of probation officers might be best arranged to cope with their initial conclusions about the work of the service.

There was some discussion about the administration of the service, with the Committee recommending the status quo. A local authority-run service was not

Table 6.1 Number of miscellaneous and voluntary work cases dealt with by the probation service, 1956, 1959 and 1960

Type of work	1956	1959	1960
Advice concerning difficult children	9,319	10,483	11,830
Voluntary supervision	5,457	5,884	6,924
Unmarried mothers – general welfare	1,215	1,124	1,425
Neighbours' quarrels	3,026	2,215	2,190
Financial assistance	6,729	7,618	8,140
Prostitutes referred by the police	–	–	64
Other cases	26,922	32,264	39,586

Source: Home Office 1962a: 62.

seen as being particularly efficient, nor were the arguments in favour of a national service accepted:

> A national service would permit economies in administration, would enable probation officers to be allocated nationally according to need, and would allow conditions of employment and local administration to be fully standardised. It could be accompanied by a system of local advisory committees to assist the administering authority to take account of local problems and opinion. These are arguments that deserve respect but we think that they are wholly outweighed by the desirability of preserving the employer–employee relationship between magistrates and probation officers; for we have no doubt that this relationship has been of prime importance in the growth of the probation system. It has fostered the courts' interest in probation and it has encouraged probation officers in their work by the assurance that their employers are people who are in daily touch with their practical problems. A merely advisory committee of magistrates could be no substitute for an administering committee in these respects. Nor, in our view, would the degree of uniformity possible in a national service necessarily be an advantage. We see greater merit in the present system whereby a local administrative committee can ensure that weight is given to local traditions, circumstances and personalities with which it alone can be fully familiar. A substantial degree of uniformity is, of course, desirable to give the service a sense of unity, to encourage movement within it and, since its efficiency is a matter of national concern, to preserve standards. But we are satisfied that this can be achieved through the discharge by the Home Office of its present function as central authority.
>
> (Home Office 1962a: 67–8)

Clearly, probation officers were to remain servants of the court; their relationship with magistrates was not one of equals. And local idiosyncrasies were to be preferred to national consistency.

Home Office control was removed from some minor areas (e.g. over the provision of cars or car loans, over the leasing of offices) and devolved to probation committees, and it was recommended that the Home Secretary should cease to be the probation authority for London with a London probation committee becoming responsible. But the overall significance of the Home Office (and the Probation Inspectorate) remained considerable. Indeed, the Committee noted that there was evidence of strain beginning to appear in what had always been considered to be a close relationship between the Home Office and the probation service. It is likely that the strain was, to some extent, due to the increasing confidence of Napo, but the Committee saw four causes: the increase in probation work without concomitant resources; opposition to probation salary claims; petty financial controls; and a failure by the Home Office to show 'its warm and genuine interest in the welfare of the service' (Home Office 1962a: 72). Home Office reports on the work of the service were recommended to meet this last point and four of these were published over the next 15 years (Home Office 1966a, 1969a, 1972, 1976).

At the time of the Morison Report, there were 103 probation areas, and further combinations were recommended; any areas which could not sustain at least six probation officers or where there were fewer than two female officers should be merged. The Committee wished all probation areas to have a principal probation officer who would be 'responsible to the probation committee for the efficiency of the service, to provide local leadership, to undertake or organise supervision of case-work and to give guidance with difficult cases' (Home Office 1962a: 69). The role of case committees in exercising supervision of probation officers was to be taken on by principal and senior officers.

In 1961 there were a total of 1,749 probation officers, of whom 30 per cent were female; included in the total were 62 principal probation officers and 158 senior officer posts. This represented a 40 per cent increase since 1956, and the training scheme had not been able to keep pace with such demand; 30 per cent of all probation officers employed in 1961 had neither a university qualification nor had undergone Home Office training (the 1936 Departmental Committee had recommended that no probation officer should be appointed without training). The Committee recommended the recruitment of graduates wherever possible, but did not stipulate that only graduates should be recruited nor did it fix a date when specified qualifications would be required prior to appointment as a probation officer. A workforce of more than 2,000 was considered to be required immediately, while 'a further increase to a strength of 2,750 may be necessary in the next few years' (Home Office 1962a: 110), but while greater flexibility was thought to be necessary in training and closer cooperation with the universities was advocated, there were no radical changes proposed for training (the suggestion that there might be a probation college with a full-time director and staff was turned down).

Finally, in order to improve recruitment generally, to improve the educational level of recruits, and to improve the prospects of those who were well qualified, 'bold increases in salaries' were proposed (Home Office 1962a: 141), with the prescription of pay to be determined by a national negotiating body rather than the Home Secretary.

The second report of the Morison Committee was in favour of approved probation hostels and recommended that a few more might be provided. For the most part the remaining recommendations walked a fine line between accepting that, while standardisation was not necessary, wide variations were not acceptable (Home Office 1962b).

The Morison Committee was certainly not pushing the boundaries of proba-tion, and it is perhaps an indicator of just how uncontentious the 177 conclusions and recommendations in the two Morison Reports were that in 1966 the Home Office could state that 'With a very few exceptions, the Government accepted these recommendations and ... most of them have since been implemented' (Home Office 1966a: 1). On the other hand, from Napo's point of view the main report 'seemed full of indecision and ambiguity and many questions which were considered important had been left unanswered' (Sanders 1962: 22).

One of these unanswered questions related to after-care, where the Committee had only made some general recommendations in the knowledge that the Advisory Council on the Treatment of Offenders had been asked to review the arrangements with regard to after-care. ACTO made it clear from the beginning that 'after-care is essentially a form of social casework' (ACTO 1963: i) and so it was no surprise that the Council's main recommendation had significant implications for probation: that 'after-care in the community, both compulsory and voluntary, should be under-taken by an expanded and reorganised probation and after-care service' (ACTO 1963: 30–31). There was some discussion about the possibility of setting up a new organisation to take on after-care, but the probation service was already available on a national basis, was trained in the techniques considered to be necessary for such work, and a new organisation would be costly and would not encourage a coherent approach to offenders. The government accepted this recommendation, acknowledging that considerably more staff would be required for probation to be able to cope with this expansion to their work, and by 1965 there were 2,319 estab-lished probation officers – an increase of 30 per cent since 1961, and numbers more than doubled between 1961 and 1971 (Home Office 1972).

But the other key ACTO recommendation was that prison welfare officers should be members of the prison service and not the probation service. In 1953, the Maxwell Committee had been opposed to welfare officers being part of the prison staff, so ACTO had reversed this recommendation, but they still consid-ered that prison welfare officers should have close links with probation (in fact, they would look very like probation officers):

> He would possess essentially the same qualities and skills as a probation officer and he would continue to be remunerated like a probation officer (or senior probation officer when appropriate) ... the Home Office inspectors of the reconstructed probation and after-care service ... should inspect the work of social workers in prison who, in turn, should have direct access to inspec-tors for advice on any matter of social case-work affecting a prisoner.
>
> (ACTO 1963: 24)

Much to the disappointment of the Prison Officers' Association (POA), two years after the ACTO report the Home Secretary decided that prison welfare posts should be filled by the secondment of probation officers and the scheme was implemented at the beginning of 1966 (see below).

Within the first half of the decade, then, probation's role had been expanded to take on after-care of released prisoners and prison welfare work. This was such a significant move that the service was renamed as the Probation and After-Care Service. Bochel (1976: 225) notes that these developments

> had the effect of drawing the service closer to the penal institutions and of extending a much greater proportion of its work beyond the courts. It also increased the possibility that the service would become associated in the public mind with custodial institutions and discharged adult offenders.

While prison-related work seemed to be a perfectly logical step for probation, it does seem clear that not all probation officers were happy with such a step. For them, prison was something that should be avoided and working in prisons was colluding with the enemy.

Losing juveniles … and more?

Despite the impression given by the Morison Report that essentially all was well with probation, major changes were imminent in approaches to dealing with juvenile offenders and these would lead to probation losing a key part of its work. In 1960 more than half (54 per cent) of all those placed on probation were under the age of 17, and 27 per cent were under 14; in other words, a substantial part of probation work was carried out with juvenile offenders. The 1963 Children and Young Persons Act raised the age of criminal responsibility from 8 to 10, thereby excluding the use of probation for this age group, and by 1972, the probation order was not available for offenders under the age of 17.

In 1964, before the general election of that year, a Labour Party Study Group (1964) under the chairmanship of Lord Longford published a report entitled *Crime: A Challenge To Us All*. One of the issues discussed in the report was juvenile delinquency: juvenile offenders were seen as the products of their environment; there was no real difference between children in need of care and control and juvenile offenders; and the family was the place to begin to deal with such young people. The report therefore argued that it was necessary 'to take juveniles out of the criminal courts and the penal system and to treat their problems in a family setting through the establishment of family advice centres, a family service, and, for a minority a family court' (Gelsthorpe and Morris 1994: 956). Soon after Labour's return to power in 1964, a White Paper was published taking up some of the ideas contained in the Longford Report. *The Child, the Family and the Young Offender* (Home Office 1965a) proposed scrapping the juvenile court for those under 16 and replacing it with family councils that would deal with juvenile offenders in a non-judicial way (family courts would only be used where agreement could not be reached by the family council). Thus, probation would lose its responsibility for offenders under 16. Predictably, magistrates were not particularly happy; Rutherford (1986: 54) talks of 'virulent opposition by the Magistrates' Association'. Nor were probation officers; Napo argued strongly in favour of retaining the juvenile court and for the continuing involvement of probation officers in dealing with juvenile offenders (Napo 1965). Indeed, the strength of the opposition was such that the White Paper was not taken forward.[1]

A new White Paper was published three years later (Home Office 1968) which took some account of the protests made over *The Child, the Family and the Young Offender. Children in Trouble* proposed retaining the juvenile courts, placing the supervision of children under 14 in the hands of local authority social services, and introducing intermediate treatment (IT) as a new approach to dealing with offenders under 17. Probation would, therefore, lose any immediate responsibility for juvenile offenders under the age of 14, but it would be left to the courts to decide whether the local authority or probation would be responsible for those aged 14–16. The supervision of IT could be by the local authority or the probation service, although as the responsibility for setting up IT schemes was to lie in the hands of the local authorities it would not be surprising if they favoured their social services departments to supervise those subject to IT.

The 1969 Children and Young Persons Act followed the White Paper proposals, introducing supervision orders for those under 17 and paving the way for a reduced role for probation for this age group. While efforts were made to amend the Bill as it was going through Parliament, these were unsuccessful and, as Bochel (1976: 236) points out, the Act 'foreshadowed the end of direct concern of the probation and after-care service with children under 14, the group perhaps uppermost in the minds of many who had sought the introduction of the probation system'.

With the loss of children as well as its increasing work with prisoners – both in custody and after release – the criminal justice focus of the probation service became noticeably stronger, thus raising questions about probation's identity. Was it a social service like local authority children's departments? Or was it a specialist service that worked largely with offenders (putting to one side its civil work)? Other developments during this period also began to throw such questions into greater relief.

Despite joining the Standing Conference of Organisations of Social Workers on its formation in 1963, Napo decided not to join the British Association of Social Workers (the 1969 successor to the Standing Conference, which aimed to unify trained social workers as far as possible) in an effort to ensure that it retained a separate professional identity (Haxby 1978). Following the Courts Act 1971, which established a national Crown Court (in place of the old Assizes and Quarter Sessions), there was some discussion about central control of the magistrates' courts which had implications for the organisation and identity of probation:

> If the magistrates' courts were to lose their local form of organisation under
> committees of magistrates (similar to that of the probation service) and if the
> magistracy itself were to become a national service, would it be practicable
> for the probation service to continue as a separate local service? And, if not,

should it be merged with the local authority social service or should it also become a national service administered by the Home Office?

(Home Office 1972: 2)

Perhaps the biggest threat to the continued separate identity of probation was the report of the Seebohm Committee which was tasked in 1965 'to review the organisation and responsibilities of the local authority social services in England and Wales, and to consider what changes are desirable to secure an effective family service' (Home Office et al. 1968). While Seebohm's terms of reference excluded any direct concern with probation, its main recommendation was for the unification of local authority personal social services, and thus the implications for probation were considerable, as the Committee acknowledged. Indeed, on one issue Seebohm went further than *Children in Trouble*:

> As far as children and young people under 17 are concerned, we are clear that the social service department, rather than the probation and aftercare service, should carry the responsibility for providing a social work service for the courts, for supervising and assisting young people in the community, and for aftercare work with young people who have left the new kinds of residential provision which are proposed.
>
> (Home Office et al. 1968: 78)

As we have seen, the 1969 Children and Young Persons Act did not go down this road, but the probation service was worried about the possibility of being merged with the proposed comprehensive local authority social service departments. While Napo was in favour of proposals for integrated social work departments and wanted probation officers to be regarded as social workers, it did not wish to become part of a unified social work department within local authorities (Napo 1966). The establishment of the Central Council for Education and Training in Social Work (CCETSW) at the end of 1970, which was to have oversight of the training of all social workers, again raised fears about probation losing its separate identity.

Even the Butterworth Committee (Department of Employment 1972), which was set up to look into the pay of probation officers and social workers, and which recommended relating the pay of local authority social workers to that of probation officers, could be seen as continuing a residual threat to the independence of probation.

Thus throughout the second half of the 1960s, probation was facing a dilemma; on the one hand, it was a social work service with a long and proud tradition, but it also wished to retain a clear identity of its own at a time when various developments were pushing for greater unification of all social workers.

Other official developments, 1965–74

Indictable offences known to the police had increased by 61 per cent in the decade 1950–60, but the 1960–65 increase was 52 per cent, so the crime problem was certainly not decreasing. Prison numbers continued to rise; in 1960 the average prison population was 27,099, while by 1965 it had risen to 30,421, an increase of 12 per cent. A 1969 White Paper on prisons admitted that 'Overcrowding is the worst feature of our prison system' (Home Office 1969b: 104). An indication of the seriousness of the problem can be seen from the title of a 1964 White Paper: *The War Against Crime in England and Wales 1959–1964* (Home Office 1964). The White Paper, of course, argued that the war would be won but it contained an implicit admission of failure; it announced a 'fundamental review of the whole penal system' (Home Office 1964: 13) to be carried out by a Royal Commission. In the event, the Royal Commission on the Penal System that was set up in 1964 was dissolved in 1966 without completing a report (the only Royal Commission ever to do so; for some discussion of the reasons see Radzinowicz 1999 and Windlesham 1993). The Central Council of Probation Committees, the Conference of Principal Probation Officers and Napo all gave evidence to the Royal Commission, but there was little sign of innovative or radical thinking (Royal Commission on the Penal System 1967a). Napo and the Conference of Principal Probation Officers were both opposed to current ideas about most juvenile offenders being dealt with by social services (see below), and the Central Council of Probation Committees was strongly in favour of more training for magistrates about probation's role. Perhaps the most radical proposal came from the Howard League, which suggested that courts should not be forced to choose

the right sentence at the moment of trial; except for the alternatives of absolute and conditional discharge, binding over or a fine. When it comes to choosing between supervision in freedom (probation) or in custody (imprisonment), we might envisage a new sentence to be called a supervision-or-custody order ... Under this procedure, the court (which would have the power to fix the maximum length of such an order) would impose a supervision-or-custody order of, say, up to three years. But whether the offender begins his sentence under supervision in freedom, and, should this fail for one reason or another, be moved into an institution for a spell, or vice versa, would depend on circumstances ... The procedure ... would entail even greater liaison between, and intermeshing of, the concepts of supervision in freedom and supervision in custody ... A supervision-or-custody order would tend to transform the two modes of treatment into a continuous process; and this is entirely desirable.

(Royal Commission on the Penal System 1967b: 146–47)

In their oral evidence to the Royal Commission, members of the Howard League admitted that this idea was probably far ahead of its time, but one can see in it ideas about the seamless sentence that came to fruition almost 40 years later.

The issue of drug misuse was – as we noted at the beginning of the chapter – a topic that began to assume some significance during the 1960s, and concern about the number of individuals dependent on drugs led to the reconvention of the Brain Committee which claimed there had been a disturbing increase in those addicted to heroin and cocaine during the 1960s, especially amongst the young (Ministry of Health/Scottish Home and Health Department 1965). The Committee also warned of increased use of amphetamines and cannabis, again among the young. Three years later, the Advisory Committee on Drug Dependence (1968) produced *The Rehabilitation of Drug Addicts*, and two of the Committee's recommendations touched on the probation service: first, that any community workers (including probation officers) who were working with addicts prior to hospital treatment should remain in contact with the addict during treatment; and, second, that courts, prison staff and probation officers should have a positive role in the rehabilitation of those offenders with drug problems. The Home Office endorsed these recommendations, noting that

> Through its contacts with young probationers whose difficulties are complicated by drug addiction, the probation and after-care service has been made very much alive to the many aspects of the problems, and the need for co-operative action is being met at local probation and after-care area level by organised study groups and work in liaison with other social services.
>
> (Home Office 1969a: 33)

That probation recognised the significance and potential demands of work with drug misusers can be seen by the introduction in the third edition of Joan King's *The Probation and After-Care Service* (King 1969) of a section discussing probation work with drug addicts.

In 1965, a few months after the publication of *The Child, the Family and the Young Offender* another White Paper was published, this one on *The Adult Offender* (Home Office 1965b). The key proposal was to introduce a system of parole whereby prisoners who had served at least one-third of their sentence (or 12 months, whichever was longer) would be released on licence to be supervised by a probation officer, with the licence running for a further one-third of the original sentence. Not only would this reduce prison overcrowding, but it would also improve the chances of rehabilitation:

> A considerable number of long-term prisoners reach a recognisable peak in their training at which they may respond to generous treatment, but after which, if kept in prison, they may go downhill. To give such prisoners the opportunity of supervised freedom at the right moment may be decisive in securing their return to decent citizenship.
>
> (Home Office 1965b: 4)

And it was the probation service which would be responsible for supervising prisoners while on licence. The White Paper also proposed the integration of the prison welfare service and the probation service, so that 'in future all Prison Welfare Officers will be Probation Officers on secondment' (Home Office 1965b: 10).

The use of volunteers had been associated with probation work since its beginnings, but there was renewed interest in the mid-1960s, to a large extent as a result of the increasing demands being made of probation in relation to after-care. The ACTO report on after-care (ACTO 1963) had encouraged the involvement of volunteers in an effort to make the increased probation workload manageable. And a Home Office working party produced two reports examining the use of volunteers and voluntary organisations and the kind of work in which they might be best involved (Home Office 1966b; 1967).[2] By the end of 1970 there were more than 2,100 volunteers 'actively engaged in a variety of tasks ranging from simple practical help in overcoming domestic difficulties to long-term friendships with prisoners and their families' (Home Office 1972: 45). Ancillary workers were introduced in 1968 on a trial basis in six probation areas with the aim of discovering 'whether there is a range of duties, intermediate between those of the clerical assistant and the fully trained professional probation officer, which can be delegated' (Home Office 1969a: 13–14). By 1974, there were 373 ancillaries employed on court and escort duties, maintaining registers of employers and accommodation, and helping run community service (which could involve direct work with offenders).

The 1967 Criminal Justice Act was focused on trying to keep offenders out of prison and various provisions were introduced in an effort to achieve this. The parole scheme proposed in *The Adult Offender* was included in the Act; the suspended sentence of imprisonment in theory would impact upon those sentenced to up to two years in custody; the use of fines was encouraged by increasing the maximum that could be imposed in the magistrates' courts from £100 to £400; and restrictions were placed on magistrates' power to imprison those who defaulted in paying fines. There were implications for probation in these developments. Parole would, of course, lead to increased work for a proba-tion service that was already hard-pressed in terms of resources, and Napo tried to have the implementation of parole delayed until more probation staff could be recruited. If the suspended sentence worked as planned, it would divert offenders from custody, but if it was used inappropriately it might be used for those who would have received a probation order and both Haxby (1978) and Sparks (1971) argued that this was indeed occurring. And increasing the level of fines could also bite into probation's share of the offender market.

The Act included several provisions for probation, with the two most significant being scrapping the need to have a female probation officer for a female offender, and encouraging greater use of social inquiry reports (the number of such reports prepared for the courts almost doubled between 1961 and 1972).

So despite the threat posed by losing juveniles and the possibility of being merged with social work departments, probation's work expanded during this period. Was this because probation had proved itself to be effective? There was certainly a considerable amount of research on the topic at this time, but just how positive it was about the effectiveness of probation is open to question.

Beginning in 1966, the Home Office Research Unit had devoted a major part of its work to probation research; indeed, around one-quarter of its publications during the ensuing ten years were on aspects of probation. There were studies of group work (Barr 1966), of the social environment of male probationers aged

17–20 and how this related to reconviction and casework (Davies 1969, 1973, 1974), of risk classification and prediction (Simon 1971), of after-care (Silberman et al. 1971), of probation hostels (Sinclair 1971), of social enquiry reports (Davies and Knopf 1973), of social work in prison (Shaw 1974), and of intensive probation (Folkard et al. 1974). While these studies all provided considerable amounts of potentially useful material, two things stand out: first, they demonstrate a very wide variety of approaches to probation work, confirming that there was little consistency; and, second, there was no accumulation of findings pointing unequivocally to effectiveness. With regard to the latter point, it should be noted that many of the studies were carried out more to discover what was going on rather than to explain outcomes; full outcome evaluations should have followed on from these studies. Even where there was some sign of success – as in Margaret Shaw's (1974) study of social work in prison – it is notable that in his Foreword to the report, John Croft (Head of the Research Unit) played down the significance of effectiveness. A discussion of reconviction rates was included in the second edition of *The Sentence of the Court* (Home Office 1969c), a handbook for sentencers describing the various disposals available to them. Probation was found to be more successful with those who had previous convictions than with first offenders, but Hood and Sparks were blunt about the significance of the study:

> The most important finding … is that fines and discharges are much more effective than either probation or imprisonment for first offenders and recidivists of all age groups.
>
> (Hood and Sparks 1970: 188–9)

It is difficult to see how this kind of information would encourage magistrates to make greater use of probation.

Nothing more encouraging emerged from other probation research. Max Grunhut suggested that mental treatment as a condition of a probation order (introduced by the Criminal Justice Act 1948) could have a positive prognosis (70 per cent of his sample were so classified), and the reconviction rate of such offenders was very similar to that found in the Cambridge study (see Chapter 5). But mental health conditions only accounted for 2 per cent of probation orders in 1958 (Grunhut 1963). Despite the growth in the number of social enquiry reports being prepared for the courts during the 1960s, they were not found to lead to reductions in reconviction rates or to greater use of probation (Hood 1966; Hood and Taylor 1968).

Overall, the conclusion might be that while there was little hard evidence to suggest that probation was an effective disposal of the courts, there did seem to be a firm belief that it was a good thing and it was only a matter of time (and more sophisticated research) before this could be proved conclusively. But the key piece of research to be published in this period washed away any such complacency.

Robert Martinson's notorious article 'What Works? Questions and answers about prison reform' was published in 1974, with its conclusion that 'With few and isolated exceptions, the rehabilitative efforts that have been reported so far have had no appreciable effect on recidivism' (Martinson 1974: 24). This conclusion cannot be reduced to 'Nothing Works' and it is important to remember that Martinson never used the phrase in the article, but the seductive clarity of 'Nothing Works' has had a lot to do with the development of probation since it appeared. Martinson's article has several serious limitations: first, it is littered with cautionary phrases such as 'impossible to interpret', 'no clear evidence', 'ambiguous results', 'equivocal' and 'important caveat', which could not lead to such a clear-cut conclusion as 'Nothing Works'; second, it relies on recidivism as the sole measure of success of a sentence, and reconviction rates (the usual measure of recidivism) have a number of methodological flaws that limit their usefulness (Lloyd et al. 1994); and, third, there is no consideration given to how the various programmes and projects included in the article were working in practice. Were they adequately resourced? Were they fully staffed by committed individuals? Were they targeting appropriate offenders? (Mair 1995a).

The common assumption has been that 'Nothing Works' hit probation hard, that it led to low morale and anxiety about the purpose of probation for more than a decade. But it is difficult to find any evidence for this; probation officers seem to have been unaware of the message that what they were doing was ineffective – 'its immediate significance for probation practitioners was minimal' (Mair 2004a: 15) and they carried on trying to rehabilitate offenders: 'In the post-diagnostic era the probation service has not actually lost its sense of mission' (McWilliams 1987: 114); 'the "nothing works" era actually became a period of creativity and enthusiasm in the development of new methods and approaches.' (Raynor 2002: 1182).

Among policy makers and researchers, however, 'Nothing Works' had a much greater impact, and it linked in well with other developments.

ACPS and the Criminal Justice Act 1972

The Advisory Council on the Penal System (ACPS) replaced the Advisory Council on the Treatment of Offenders (ACTO) following the collapse of the Royal Commission on the Penal System, and in 1966 it was asked by the Home Secretary to examine non-custodial penalties. The subsequent report – usually referred to as the Wootton Report, after its chair Baroness Wootton – is famous as the birthplace of community service, but its other key recommendations had implications for probation too (ACPS 1970):

- deferral of sentence;
- intermittent custody;
- probation combined with a fine or a suspended sentence.

There was a brief discussion of where the new sentence would be most suitably located – with the probation service or the prison service – but it was only too obvious that probation was its natural home. Community service was 'the most ambitious proposal' in the report (ACPS 1970: 12), and in an effort to make sure that it was taken up by government, the Committee sold it hard:

> in general the proposition that some offenders should be required to under-take community service should appeal to adherents of different variet-ies of penal philosophy. To some, it would be simply a more constructive and cheaper alternative to short sentences of imprisonment; by others it would be seen as introducing into the penal system a new dimension with an emphasis on reparation to the community; others again would regard it as a means of giving effect to the old adage that the punishment should fit the crime; while still others would stress the value of bringing offenders into close touch with those members of the community who are most in need of help and support.[3]
>
> (ACPS 1970: 13)

This vagueness about purpose has followed community service throughout its exist-ence and can be seen as negative (giving rise to inconsistency of practice, a key theme of Young's (1979) study, and a criticism that has followed community service since its inception) or positive, as one reviewer of Warren Young's study argued:

> Young is very critical of the ambiguity and muddle which continue, but sur-prisingly does not discuss the possibility that the community service will only be of use as long as the potential for ambiguity remains. In the absence of any coherent sentencing philosophy on which the actors can agree, ambiguity may be essential in a sentence which has to be recommended by probation officers, implemented by magistrates, consented to by offenders, financed by the Home Office, and tolerated by local communities.
>
> (Corden 1980: 262)

If a court decided to defer sentence, probation might well be involved in provid-ing evidence about the offender's behaviour during the deferral period. Intermittent custody would require a report regarding the offender's employment and residential status, and could divert some offenders away from probation. And combining probation with a fine or suspended sentence could lead to various complications with the supervision process (the probation organisations were in favour of combining probation with the suspended sentence, but opposed to combining it with a fine).

If the 1967 Criminal Justice Act had been based around trying to keep offend-ers out of custody, then the 1972 Act was even more focused on this; the Home Secretary, Reginald Maudling, made this quite clear when introducing the Second Reading of the Bill on 22 November 1971. In 1970, the average prison population was 39,028 – an increase of more than 25 per cent since 1965. Little wonder then that, as we noted above, the 1969 White Paper *People in Prison* (Home Office 1969b) acknowledged that overcrowding was the most serious problem facing the prison service. The Act introduced community service orders as the Wootton

Report had proposed but, as Warren Young points out, there were 'three significant departures from the Wootton Committee proposals ... All served to emphasize the penal content of the sentence and were designed to make it more attractive to sentencers' (Young 1979: 19).

First, while the ACPS had considered that community service should not be confined to those found guilty of imprisonable offences, the legislation restricted the new sentence to offences punishable with imprisonment. Second, the ACPS had proposed a maximum of 120 hours of community service and no minimum, while the Act doubled the proposed maximum to 240 hours and included a minimum of 40 hours. And, third, the ACPS had fudged the question of whether the proposed order should be a separate sentence or a condition of a probation order, suggesting that the decision should be left to the courts; the Act was clear that the order was a new and separate sentence (as with probation orders, the offender's consent was necessary).

Community service was a major development for the probation service. It was aimed squarely as an alternative to custody; it was a mixture of the punitive and the reparative with no necessary social work component; and it meant that probation had to work at making more community contacts, whether with voluntary organisations, trade unions or the general public. While officially the probation organisations welcomed the new order, it is by no means certain that all probation officers were happy about it: 'there was considerable ambivalence amongst probation officers about the introduction of the scheme' (Haxby 1978: 173); 'Many older, established probation officers still saw community service as alien to the social work ethos' (Nellis 2007: 48); 'The introduction of the community service order generated for the probation service a good deal of uncertainty and anxiety, disharmony and even outright opposition' (Roberts 1980: 116).

The 1972 Act also introduced the power to add supervision to suspended sentences of more than six months and to defer sentence (both proposed by the Wootton Report). More significant for the future of probation, day training centres (DTCs) were also included in the Act – although they had not been encouraged by Wootton. Attendance at a centre would be as a condition of a probation order for 5 days a week and up to 60 days; the centres would 'provide intensive supervision and social education for offenders with a history of short custodial sentences and a likely prospect of more to follow because of general social incompetence' (Home Office 1976: 25). Four DTCs were opened on an experimental basis in London, Liverpool, Sheffield and Glamorgan. Probation and after-care committees were also permitted to provide day activity centres similar to the day training centres 'but with the significant difference that clients generally attend them voluntarily rather than as a requirement of a court order' (Home Office 1976: 25). These two types of day centre came to symbolise two different kinds of probation work, highlighting the care vs. control debates that were emerging:

• Those in favour of voluntary attendance claimed that there was a much better chance of rehabilitating offenders if they chose to attend;

- Those who preferred statutory attendance argued that it was necessary to have an element of compulsion as this would be more likely to result in attendance and you could only work with offenders if they were actually present.

DTCs and day activity centres meant more intensive work with offenders and also more group work – significant developments for the probation service.

If some probation officers had been worried about the introduction of community service and the demands of day training centres, then another ACPS report on *Young Adult Offenders* (ACPS 1974) could only have exacerbated anxiety levels. The report proposed two new court sentences for offenders aged 17–21: the custody and control order, and the supervision and control order. The former would replace the three separate custodial sentences available for young adult offenders (imprisonment, borstal and detention centre) and would 'provide for a period spent in custody followed by supervision in the community by a probation officer: these periods would be regarded as a single continuum' (ACPS 1974: 8). The supervision and control order would be a more intensive probation order; as its name suggested, it would be more controlling. It would last for a maximum of two years and would include a number of requirements, none of which – as Haxby (1978: 163) noted – involved 'any new principle'. The ACPS argued that the proposed order was only going down the road that recent probation developments such as community service, day training centres and the suspended sentence supervision order had taken. As it was aimed at providing an alternative to custody, 'its operation would in our view be entirely consistent with the basic traditions of the probation service' (ACPS 1974: 12). But there were two major stumbling blocks for probation: first, the consent of the offender would not be necessary; and, second, if the probation officer thought that the order was about to break down (either by a breach of requirements or a belief that a breach or a new offence was about to take place) he or she could apply to a magistrate for a period of up to 72 hours detention. The Council acknowledged that increased resources would be necessary for probation if their proposals were implemented and they advocated an expansion of probation hostels and greater use of volunteers. It also recommended (as had the Wootton Report) the introduction of weekend detention, but added the idea of linking it with community service:

> as community service develops consideration should be given to the possible value of residential centres from which community service projects could be operated and at which offenders could be ordered by the courts to spend their weekends.
>
> (ACPS 1974: 62)

While probation officers welcomed the idea of keeping young adult offenders out of custody, they were unhappy about consent not being necessary for the supervision and control order, and about the 72 hour detention idea. They were also sceptical about the likelihood of more resources appearing (this was, after all, a time of increasingly stringent financial constraints) and about how far the proposed new order would simply displace the probation order (see Jarman 1974; Page 1974). Napo had 'serious reservations' about the report's proposals (Bruggen 1974: 117). Even Sir Kenneth Younger, the ACPS chair, acknowledged that the proposals were 'highly controversial within the Service' (Younger 1974: 99). As it happened, due to the economic problems in the early 1970s (inflation and the oil crisis) and the arrival of a Labour government in 1974 just before the report was published, its proposals were never taken up. But, with the benefit of hindsight, one might well wonder what the subsequent history of probation would have been like if the Younger Committee's proposed new sentences had been implemented.

A period of transition?

In 1963, when the Morison Committee reported, there were a total of 2,034 established probation officers; by 1975 this figure had increased to 4,735, an increase of 132 per cent. One-third of these were females. In 1975 there were 55 chief probation officers and 56 probation areas (a decrease since 1963 following local government reorganisation in 1972), with only the City of London area not having a CPO due to its size; in addition, there were 158 deputy and assistant chiefs and 869 senior probation officers, substantial increases since 1963. Table 6.2 shows the changes that took place in probation work during the period covered by this chapter.

Overall, the number of persons being supervised increased by 40 per cent, but this was a result of increases in the number of children and young persons subject to supervision orders, the number of cases of matrimonial supervision, and a considerable increase in after-care. The number of probation cases had dropped as a result of the Children and Young Persons Act 1969. The number of social enquiry reports carried out for the courts increased from 144,166 to 217,923. Community service had only just begun so numbers were still low.

In 1975, 30,051 probation orders were made by the courts (and 19,245 supervision orders), with three-quarters of these being for indictable offences. Just over

Table 6.2 Persons being supervised by the probation service at 31 December 1963 and 1974, by type of supervision

Type of supervision	1963	1974
Probation	76,531	52,110
Supervision	6,713	21,752
Matrimonial	1,687	12,224
Suspended sentence supervision	–	3,939
Money payment supervision	4,429	6,657
After-care	13,196	45,436
Total	102,556	142,118

Source: Home Office 1966a; 1976.

a quarter (28 per cent) were for female offenders; almost half (46 per cent) were for offences of theft; and almost one in five (19 per cent) were made by the Crown Court. Probation and supervision orders accounted for around 11 per cent of sentences passed by the magistrates' courts for indictable offences, and for 9 per cent of sentences passed by the Crown Court, but these figures represented a drop of around 6–7 per cent for both courts since 1966. The use of fines, on the other hand, had increased.

At least the organisational basis of probation seemed to have been finalised. The Expenditure Committee of the House of Commons report into probation had recommended that

> On the basis of the evidence given to us, we can see no reason for a change in the independent status of the probation service in England and Wales, while recognising that changing circumstances could require the point to be re-examined in the future.
>
> (House of Commons 1971: xxi)

And a government announcement was made in June 1972 that probation would continue as a separate service; at the same time, the government grant towards probation expenditure was increased from 50 per cent to 80 per cent. Some of the other recommendations of the Expenditure Committee are worth noting as they point towards the future:

- Matrimonial work should be removed to another agency if an offence was not involved (with the aim of relieving pressure of work).
- More use should be made of volunteers.
- Napo's suggestion of Regional Committees should be examined.
- A hostel enforcement order should be considered.
- More intensive probation schemes should be introduced.
- A national campaign to increase public awareness of the effectiveness of probation was needed.

Probation had certainly grown, not just in terms of the numbers of staff, but also in its tasks (prison welfare work, after-care, parole, community service). The demands on the service had led to the arrival of volunteers and ancillary workers. Group work was becoming an officially acknowledged approach to working with offenders (Vanstone 2003, 2004b). And, as Maurice Vanstone (2004a) suggests, the accepted probation approach of casework began to fragment during the 1960s as probation officers began to try out different approaches to working with offenders. Growth and diversification of practice led, almost inevitably, to a more bureaucratic structure, with an increasing emphasis upon management of staff.

At the same time, probation was moving away from a focus on the rehabilitation of offenders towards the aim of diverting offenders from custody. This was as a result of three different factors that, added together, forced probation down the path of alternatives to custody. First, prison overcrowding, as we have noted, was a constant problem during the 1960s and probation was the only available organisation that could be utilised to tackle the problem. The introduction of community service as an alternative to custody to be run by the probation service was one specific response to prison overcrowding. Second, research studies in the UK generally showed little evidence that probation was particularly effective in terms of reconviction rates, and so another rationale – diversion from custody – might demonstrate success. And, third, the Martinson review provided further, international 'evidence' that probation had little to offer in terms of reducing offending. Probation staff do not seem to have been unhappy with their new aim, but alongside it came demands for more intensive probation that would be more rigorous and more punitive – and this is a development that has had a consider-able effect on probation ever since.

The Morison Committee might be blamed for missing an opportunity to begin to build a probation service for the 1960s and beyond, but this is with hindsight. Perhaps more legitimately, the Morison Report can be accused of complacency as it never looked at probation with a critical eye. Following Morison, probation faced a period of continuous tension. As a firmly established organisation that had a long track record of working with offenders, as well as a certain vagueness about its aims, probation could be used to take on various new penal tasks – and it always appeared relatively willing to do so (perhaps too much so), although there were regular, well-founded complaints about resources. But growth and organisational stability may also have led to internal fissures as casework began to be questioned. The local base of probation was clearly one of its strengths, but it also represented a potential weakness as probation had no national voice (apart from Napo, which was more often in tension with the Home Office during this period, and increasingly likely to be arguing about salary levels). The relative ease with which the service moved from rehabilitation to diversion from custody as its justification for existence is troubling on at least two counts: first, proba-tion's dependence on government whim; and, second, the consequences in terms of more intensive probation work. Indeed, the Younger Report (ACPS 1974) can be seen as making the case for a more demanding, more controlling, more puni-tive probation service; while this path was not taken at the time, it can now be recognised as a significant pointer for the future. Despite what, on the surface, seemed to be a healthy, comfortable probation service that was busy growing and adapting to new demands, the various subterranean tensions that were present represented real threats that would soon emerge.

7 Alternatives to custody

The second half of the 1970s

If the 1960s were an exciting period (whether in a positive or negative sense), the second half of the 1970s saw the United Kingdom spiralling into a state of gloom. Inflation had begun to pose a problem at the beginning of the decade, leading to cuts in expenditure and efforts to impose wage controls, which in turn led to growing industrial relations difficulties and strikes. The so-called 'Troubles' in Northern Ireland increasingly began to impact upon mainland Britain, partly as a result of the deaths of British soldiers and partly because of mainland bombings. The brief Yom Kippur War between Israel and Egypt in 1973, which humiliated Egypt, led to the Arab oil-producing countries striking back by using oil as a weapon. They cut production and increased prices. At the same time, the miners demanded a considerable pay increase which was, predictably, turned down and a national strike was called. The oil cuts or a coal strike might have been manageable on their own, but together they represented a considerable threat and near-panic resulted:

> Plans were made for petrol rationing and coupons printed and distributed. The national speed limit was cut by 20 miles per hour to 50 miles per hour to save fuel. Then in January 1974 came the announcement of a three-day working week. Ministers solemnly urged citizens to share baths and brush their teeth in the bath. Television … was ended at 10.30 each evening.
>
> (Marr 2007: 340)

The minority Labour government that took office in February 1974 lasted until October when Labour won again, this time with an overall majority of three – not a significant improvement on the February result. Following Harold Wilson's resignation as Prime Minister in March 1976, he was succeeded by Jim Callaghan in April. By the autumn of that year, the economic situation had worsened to the point that the government sought help from the International Monetary Fund, with the resulting loan requiring major cuts in public expenditure. Early in 1977 Callaghan was forced to agree a pact with the Liberals in order for Labour to continue in government. With the government trying to hold pay down and increasing unrest among workers looking for wage rises above the government's 5 per cent level, several private sector strikes early in 1979 suddenly seemed to infect the public sector:

> On 22 January, 1.5 million public service workers began a 24-hour strike. Other regional stoppages had already occurred. Water workers, ambulance drivers, sewerage staff and dustmen were among those whose industrial action was causing widespread misery in a winter that seemed unending.
>
> (Sked and Cook 1984: 322)

Crime, while taking something of a backseat during this period of social, economic and political turmoil, continued to rise. In 1970 there were 1.5 million indictable offences known to the police; by 1979 the number had increased by almost 1 million. Prison numbers too increased, from an average daily population of 39,028 in 1970 to 42,220 in 1979. Indeed, 'In November 1979 the population of prison department establishments reached 43,036, higher than any previous level recorded this century' (Home Office 1980a: 9). On the surface at least there would seem to be little evidence that the new mission of probation and community service to act as alternatives to custody was having much effect upon prison numbers.

Table 7.1 shows the offences for which probation orders were made in 1970 and 1979, and those for which a community service order was imposed. With regard to probation orders, there is little evidence of these being used for more serious offences during the decade; indeed, their use for burglary halved. As for community service, while it was used for burglary rather more often than probation, it was also used almost as often as probation for summary offences – and this for a sentence that had been introduced with the objective of diverting offenders from custody.

Table 7.1 Offences for which probation orders were made in 1970 and 1979, and community service orders (CSOs) in 1979 (%)

Offence	Probation orders		CSOs
	1970	*1979*	*1979*
Violence	2	6	8
Sexual	2	3	–
Robbery	1	–	–
Burglary	28	13	19
Theft	46	51	47
Fraud/forgery	4	7	4
Criminal damage	–	2	2
Motoring	–	1	5
Other indictable	3	2	2
Summary offences	14	14	12
Total No.	53,432	27,541	15,356

Note: Numbers have been rounded and may not necessarily add up to 100%.

Community service was used more often in the Crown Court than probation: 21 per cent of CSOs were imposed in the Crown Court compared with only 13 per cent of probation orders. But it was used much less often for female offenders; in 1979 one-third of probation orders were imposed on females, while for CSOs the figure was 7 per cent. It is worth noting how quickly community service had become part of the sentencing scene: six experimental schemes had begun in 1973 and national roll-out followed from April 1975, although all probation areas only provided community service from 1976. There had also been a considerable decrease in the use of probation orders during the decade, largely as a result of the loss of those under 17: in 1970, 42 per cent of probation orders had been imposed on this age group. In the magistrates' courts the use of probation for indictable offences dropped from 13.5 per cent in 1970 to 5.7 per cent in 1979; while in the Crown Court the decrease was from 16.6 per cent to 5.5 per cent.

Research was not especially encouraging. Stephen Brody's (1976) *The Effectiveness of Sentencing* has usually been perceived as supporting Robert Martinson's (1974) 'conclusion' that 'Nothing Works'. But, as with Martinson, a closer look reveals that Brody's conclusions cannot be reduced to such a simple formula:

> Reviewers of research into the effectiveness of different sentences or ways of treating or training offenders have unanimously agreed that the results so far have offered little hope that a reliable and simple remedy for recidivism can be easily found. They have pointed out that studies which have produced positive results have been isolated, inconsistent in their evidence, and open to so much methodological criticism that they must remain unconvincing. The main criticisms, which are substantial ones, centre around questions as to the comparability of the samples (that is, whether influences other than the treatment are accounting for differences in outcome) and inconsistencies in standards of failure. It has seemed, therefore, that longer sentences are no more effective than short ones, that different types of institutions work about equally as well, that probationers on the whole do no better than if they were sent to prison, and that rehabilitative programmes ... have no predictably beneficial effects.
>
> (Brody 1976: 37)

As Brody goes on to point out, such findings encouraged questioning the use of reconviction rates as the sole criterion of success for a court sentence, and the possibility of arguing in favour of non-custodial disposals because they were likely to be less harmful than custody as well as less costly. It is also worth noting that half of the report is, in fact, a discussion of 'the failure of research' (Brody 1976: 39).

Following immediately after the publication of Brody's study, however, came the long-awaited results of the IMPACT (Intensive Matched Probation and After-Care Treatment) experiment and this report too has generally been seen as putting another nail in probation's coffin: 'The findings from the IMPACT experiment ... are consistent with Martinson's conclusion that no general effect from treatment can be demonstrated' (Folkard et al. 1976: 2). But the authors went on to note that they did find 'differential effects for different types of offender' (Folkard et al. 1976: 2) and they also argued that a major breakthrough in successful treatment of offenders was highly unlikely; small, piecemeal steps were much more likely to be achieved. Perhaps the problem was that expectations for a sudden solution were too high, and IMPACT was the culmination of a long programme of Home Office research that had been running since 1961. IMPACT has since been reassessed (Thornton 1987), but the initial impression of failure persists.

Even community service, despite being seen as a success story insofar as it had rapidly become nationally available with no real problems, was not effectively diverting offenders from custody. Yet another Home Office study (Pease et al. 1977) suggested that – at best – community service was responsible for diverting from custody around 45–50 per cent of those who were given orders, a result that was taken as disappointing, although we should not minimise the fact that half of those CSOs were alternatives to custody. But where had the remaining offenders come from?

> And the answer is clear: they are offenders who would not have been sentenced to custody and therefore had been pulled up-tariff to a more severe sentence than they would have received if the alternative had not existed. The implications of such a phenomenon are considerable, not just for the individuals who are involved in it, but for the process of justice as a whole.
>
> (Mair 2009: 174)

Net widening became a major preoccupation for probation officers as well as academics from this time onwards. And anxieties about net widening and efforts to alleviate it led to the development of one of the defining features of twenty-first-century probation: risk management (see Mair 2009). But despite the significance of the Home Office report in terms of raising the issues of net widening and risk, it marked virtually the end of probation research in the Home Office for a decade; a major programme of research had begun in the early 1960s with high hopes but the resources committed to this had failed to come up with any clear-cut evidence of effectiveness.

Given the economic difficulties facing the Labour government, it is no surprise that there was little sign of extra money being made available for probation. In 1975 'it became necessary for the first time, to place a specific limit on the net growth of the probation and after-care service' (Home Office 1976: 4), and this was happening at a time when increasing numbers of offenders were being dealt with by the courts. Constraints on resources meant not only limitations on what probation could do, but also pressure to make sure that what was being done was necessary and was carried out efficiently. Although the *Statement of National Objectives and Priorities* (Home Office 1984a) was almost ten years and a very different government away, it is clear that the Labour government was already thinking along such lines.

> There is no intention of imposing on the service significant new responsibilities of a mandatory nature before the necessary resources can be found, but a situation of relatively scarce resources requires that the service should itself give the closest possible consideration to the relative priorities that should be ascribed to particular functions. As resources for the probation and after-care service are certain to be limited for some years to come, the relative importance to be attached to the various tasks of the service and how to increase the effectiveness of professional manpower will be crucial matters of debate.
>
> (Home Office 1976: 4)

Yet at the same time, probation and after-care committees were being encouraged to introduce bail information schemes which might reduce the number of defendants remanded in custody.

Indeed, the reduction of the prison population was by the mid-1970s the main focus of criminal justice policy, as the *Review of Criminal Justice Policy 1976* (Home Office 1977) makes quite clear. The strain on probation (and the criminal justice system generally) as a result of developments since the mid-1960s was considerable: a rise in crime and consequent increase in numbers proceeded against in the courts, a decline in the proportionate use of probation, a rise in the prison population and a substantial increase in costs. Resources were not available to develop more alternatives to custody:

> For the time being ... it will not be possible as it has been previously to make the central feature of policies for the reduction of the prison population the development of facilities for the offender to be dealt with in the community, where fresh resources are required.
>
> (Home Office 1977: 7)

And probation was no longer assumed to have an effect upon recidivism. The overall picture was pessimistic, suggesting that a breakdown of the criminal justice system in the near future was possible:

> the increase in the level of reported crime – a matter of serious public concern in itself – taken together with ever tightening restrictions on resources may at some not too distant time produce acute delays in court business, ever worsening overcrowding in prison and burdens on the probation service which can no longer be sustained; indeed so far as the prison population is concerned the system is already under particularly severe strain.
>
> (Home Office 1977: 6)

The strain on prisons was such that the House of Commons Expenditure Committee devoted some time to the subject, publishing a three-volume report in 1978 that examined sentencing policy, the kinds of prisoners who did not necessarily require a custodial sentence, the conditions in which staff and inmates lived, and alternatives to custody (House of Commons 1978). With regard to alternatives to custody, the Committee's overall view was that they were a good thing and the more the better. There was no discussion in the report of the concept of net widening, and, while the Committee discussed nine existing alternatives to custody (probation, intensive probation, day training centres, day centres, supported work schemes, intermediate treatment for young offenders, community service, senior attendance centres and bail hostels), there was no analysis of how far each was contributing – or could contribute – to diverting offenders from custody. Its recommendations involving the probation service included:

- developing detoxification centres;
- extending community service to fine defaulters;
- further developing day training centres;
- providing more day centres;
- providing more bail hostels;
- providing accommodation for ex-prisoners and offenders;
- working in partnership with other agencies to develop crime prevention programmes.

Following the Expenditure Committee report, the government appointed an independent inquiry into the state of the prison service, chaired by Mr Justice May; once again, reducing the prison population was a key consideration (Home Office 1979). Certain categories of inmates might be dealt with elsewhere (mentally disordered offenders, fine defaulters, drunkenness offenders and petty persistent offenders), sentence lengths might be reduced, early release schemes could be extended, and non-custodial alternatives might be developed. But there was little optimism that any of these would alleviate prison overcrowding in the short term. With regard to non-custodial alternatives, resource constraints limited their potential contribution, they could make matters worse by leading to more custodial sentences (the suspended sentence being the prime example), and – more theoretically – caution was required about 'the long run effects of placing more mechanisms of social control in the community in the guise of alternatives to custody' (Home Office 1979: 60).

It is often claimed that Robert Martinson recanted his views in 1979, although modified seems a more appropriate term:

> contrary to my previous position, some treatment programs *do* have an appreciable effect on recidivism. Some programs are indeed beneficial; of equal or greater significance, some programs are harmful ... The most interesting general conclusion is that no treatment program now used in criminal justice

is inherently either substantially helpful or harmful. The critical fact seems to be the *conditions* under which the program is delivered.

(Martinson 1979: 244–54, emphasis in original)

Whether this might have helped probation is doubtful, but little note was taken of the article (which was published in an American law journal) and the probation service remained under pressure. One indication of this can be seen by the number of efforts made during this period to redefine the role of probation.

Redefining probation

The debates that had taken place about probation's position as a social work agency around the time of the Seebohm Report (Chapter 6), the introduction of community service, which had no pretensions to social work supervision, and of day training centres with their more intensive supervision, the subsequent refocusing of the probation service as providing alternatives to custody, and the Younger Report with its recommendation for a much more controlling order all suggested an atmosphere where the traditional foundations of probation were no longer firmly grounded. The titles of two collections of papers from Cropwood conferences held at the Institute of Criminology, University of Cambridge, in 1975 and 1978 give some idea of the issues facing probation: *Control Without Custody?* (King 1975) and *Pressures and Change in the Probation Service* (King 1978). And, as Tony Bottoms has argued, a powerful theoretical critique emanating from the US also served to undermine the probation mission: the justice model attacked the rehabilitative ideal as theoretically faulty, systematically discriminatory and inconsistent with justice (Bottoms 1980). Whether or not there was a coming penal crisis (Bottoms and Preston 1980), it certainly looked as if there was a crisis in probation. As one chief probation officer noted: 'The certainties of our traditional knowledge base have gone' (Thomas 1978: 30) and, if this was the case, the question was whether these might be replaced or rebuilt. During the second half of the 1970s a number of commentators discussed the problems facing probation and suggested possible solutions.

Most proposals centred around the care vs. control debate. Increasingly, probation officers were assumed to be moving (in a rather simplistic way) from the former to the latter, ignoring the historical evidence that probation had always been involved in control to some extent. But the debate had been sharpened by the attacks on rehabilitation and the emergence of diversion from custody as a major objective of probation. An early contributor saw the choice as being between 'becoming some form of correctional service linked to the penal system (a crime treatment service) or a less symptom-specific, more general social work agency linked to the courts (a court social work service)' (Murch 1969: 18). These were seen as mutually incompatible and the preferable option was, taking Seebohm into account, to become an independent, general social work service for the courts.

Robert Harris (1977) argued that probation was stuck in the past and had not developed an organisational structure that was fit for purpose. Harris was highly critical about how far probation could actually have any impact on crime:

> Whatever social work training does do, it does not give any expertise whatsoever in stopping people getting into trouble, and only when probation officers accept this, and only when the public know and accept this will the probation service be freed from a notional 'policing' activity, at which it persistently fails, and enabled to use the very considerable skills which it does have, and which all social workers should have, to the benefit of the client … The probation service is widely assumed to have, and does not deny that it has, some sort of magical power to prevent crime. That in reality it has no such power is indisputable, but what it is in a position to do is to provide a highly trained, caring and effective social work service to a disadvantaged section of the community: the offender. It can help him with accommodation, social security, jobs; it can give him counselling with many personal problems; it can teach him social skills; it can help with marital or family difficulties. In doing these things it may or may not enable a proportion of clients to steer clear of crime, but if it does, the proportion involved is apparently statistically insignificant.
>
> (Harris 1977: 435–6)

Harris's solution was simple and controversial: split social work with offenders apart from punishment by the courts. Probation officers would provide a social work service for offenders but would not carry out the supervision of court sentences. Harris (1980) expanded this vision: he set out the functions of his envisaged court-based social work service as crisis intervention, advocacy, marital and family work, extended social work, volunteer liaison and report writing.

Another suggestion was made by a group of senior probation managers. 'Sentenced to Social Work' (Bryant et al. 1978) also argued from the basis that there was a serious disjunction between the social work background of probation officers and their supervision of offenders. The answer for Bryant and his colleagues was for the court not just to make a probation order for a specific period for appropriate offenders but, in addition, to specify how often the offender would report. The court would, therefore, be defining the level of contact; this would not be the subject of arrangement between the probation officer and the offender. Those who were sentenced in this way would also be informed of the various kinds of help that were available through the probation service and they could avail themselves of these as and when they wished. The court order would be observed simply by reporting to the probation office and following any conditions that might have been imposed. One of the key individuals would be the receptionist who 'would need to be both sensitive and skilled in dealing with clients who may find it difficult on occasions to articulate their requests for assistance, whilst allowing those who simply wanted to report to do so without difficulty' (Bryant et al. 1978: 112). The scheme was intended to ensure that 'the supervisory and helping aspects of the [probation] service should run parallel to but separately from each other' (Bryant et al.1978: 113).

Working from the same kind of starting point as Harris and Bryant and his colleagues, but offering the most theoretically sophisticated of the various new models of probation suggested, was the Bottoms and McWilliams (1979) 'non-treatment paradigm'. The root of the problem here was 'treatment' which was (following Martinson, Brody and IMPACT) not only empirically failing but also (as the justice model argued) theoretically flawed. Bottoms and McWilliams began building their new model by setting out what they took as the four primary aims of probation work in relation to crime (Bottoms and McWilliams 1979: 168):

- Provision of appropriate help for offenders.
- Statutory supervision of offenders.
- Diversion of appropriate offenders from custodial sentences.
- Reduction of crime.

Help is substituted for treatment; the offender is allowed to define his or her problems or needs, these are agreed with the probation officer and strategies are planned together to address problems. The formal requirements of the order lie with the court; it is the authority of the court that forms the basis of the order, not the authority of the probation officer or the probation service. By abandoning treatment and avoiding recommending – directly or indirectly – custody in social enquiry reports, diversion from custody would be more likely to be achieved. And crime reduction would be possible by developing community work and crime prevention.

The models discussed so far have tended to privilege the social welfare side of probation work; they are aware of control, but wish to focus on the help that probation can offer offenders. At the Kent Control Unit, however, as the name suggests, control was the focus:

> probationers were required to attend six days a week for six months, includ-ing evenings, and to conform to curfew regulations when they went home to sleep. If they had jobs, they were to report to the unit straight after work. Before a day off (these were limited to Sundays and Bank Holidays) the probationer had the conditions of his order read out to him as a reminder.
>
> (Raynor 1985: 46)

This is a very different kind of animal from that proposed by Bryant and his colleagues, or Bottoms and McWilliams, and led to considerable criticism from many probation officers. A court case regarding attendance at a day centre that had not been designated as one of the four day training centres (*Cullen* v *Rogers* (1982)) raised legal objections to the kind of approach followed by the Control Unit; in the Criminal Justice Bill that was going through Parliament at the time the power to make requirements to attend at a particular place or take part in a specified activity for up to 60 days was included, and this halted the Control Unit's six-month requirement. But the concept of control was beginning to enter the vocabulary of chief probation officers: the chief of the Northern Ireland probation service accepted 'an unambiguously controlling role for probation officers' (Griffiths 1982: 99); and Colin Thomas, chief of the West Yorkshire service, noted the need for 'a re-examination of the concept of control in the community', arguing that the probation service 'tends to emphasise the negative aspects of simple oversight which it sees as inappropriate for a helping agency' (Thomas 1978: 29).

The most detailed discussion of a new model for probation was provided by David Haxby (1978) in his book *Probation: A Changing Service*. Haxby analysed and interpreted the various trends and developments that had taken place up to the mid-1970s and concluded that the answer was for probation to become a correctional service. The main priority would be to develop new non-custodial methods of working with offenders that would provide robust and effective alternatives to custody. The new service would need to have a much stronger base in the community, to get involved in crime prevention and to use volunteers and voluntary agencies more extensively. It would apply a wider range of methods, for example group work, community work, more intensive forms of supervision and specialised assessment. And it would work more closely with prisons in trying to develop an integrated approach to the through-care of prisoners.

A pressure group within Napo, the Napo Members' Action Group (NMAG) advocated a more radical reworking of probation and two of its members published a book containing a carefully constructed Marxist critique of the state and its role with regard to welfare in capitalist society, and relating this to the work of the probation service. Their way forward was to develop socialist probation practice which would involve the provision of realistic, practical and emotional help (rather similar to the client-defined help advocated by Bottoms and McWilliams); passing on knowledge and skills; developing services that were truly useful for clients; and working to build much closer links with local communities (Walker and Beaumont 1981).

Finally, and perhaps ironically given that it was published in the *Probation Journal*'s issue celebrating the centenary of the police court mission, it is worth noting a contribution from the then-Director of the National Association for the Care and Resettlement of Offenders (NACRO). Nicholas Hinton argued for a merger between prison and probation, despite all the administrative, structural and staffing difficulties that would be entailed: 'it is important that the combined resources of all or part of the Prison and probation services are deployed to develop and manage the necessary range of non-custodial facilities' (Hinton 1976: 91).

Reading the probation literature for the period around 1975–81 one is struck by how often certain similar terms occur: change, crisis, doubt, uncertainty, lack of confidence, confusion, loss of direction. Peter Raynor's (1985) *Social Work, Justice and Control* succinctly sums up the various models we have discussed as: separatism, controlism, radicalism, sentenced to social work and non-treatment. He provides an excellent account of these approaches and the context in which they developed, and also puts forward his own prescription for how probation should move forward (essentially balancing the care/help role alongside a recognition that greater control is necessary for some offenders). But, by the time his book was published, the probation service was deeply embroiled in its struggles to try to come to terms with the policies of a radical Conservative government.

Probation under Thatcherism

It was no surprise when the Conservatives won the general election of 1979, which followed on the heels of 'the winter of discontent'. The first Thatcher government was faced with a country in serious economic trouble and it was this matter that took up a great deal of its energies. But, in addition to trying to control government expenditure and reduce the role of the state, there was also a desire to curb the power of the trade unions which were perceived to be behind many of the economic problems and also to pose a threat to law and order. The Conservatives were pledged to restore the rule of law, which they claimed had been seriously undermined during the previous administration, and their election manifesto mentioned several law and order policies they would implement, thereby bringing 'law and order to the fore as a major election issue' (Downes and Morgan 1994:191). Only a couple of months after the election, the House of Commons voted on a motion to reintroduce the death penalty. And in November 1979 it was announced that tougher regimes would be introduced in two detention centres; the 'short, sharp shock' began in 1980 and was extended to a further two detention centres in 1981 (an evaluation found no effect on reconviction rates: Home Office 1984b).

Prisons, of course, were also a priority especially in the light of the *Report from the Expenditure Committee* (House of Commons 1978) and the May Report (Home Office 1979). The government response to these reports emphasised its commitment to law and order, noting that it would give 'priority to sustaining the law and order services at a time when other public services have had to be restricted' (Home Office 1980b: 1). Providing more prison places, cutting sentence lengths and using non-custodial sentences as alternatives to custody were all accepted as ways of tackling the problem of prison overcrowding. William Whitelaw, the new Home Secretary, pledged to

> continue to develop alternatives to imprisonment. The Government believe that the outside community must play an increasing part, whether through statutory or voluntary agencies, in the treatment and containment of offenders, particularly those who have not committed violent offences. We shall give full support to non-custodial methods, and we recognise the major contribution that the probation and after-care service must make to them.
>
> (Home Office 1980b: 31)

More specifically relevant to probation were the following responses to recommendations:

- The provision for using community service for fine and maintenance defaulters (contained in the Criminal Justice Act 1972) would not be implemented.
- No more day training centres would be set up because of their high costs.
- Further expansion of bail hostels was not necessary.
- More day centres should be provided by statutory as well as voluntary organisations.
- More senior attendance centres would be opened as soon as possible.

Only day centres were to be encouraged and, interestingly, there was no specific mention of probation in the discussion of how this was to be taken forward.

The 1982 Criminal Justice Act was heavily weighted towards dealing with young offenders (most importantly restricting the use of imprisonment for this group), but it also made some significant changes for probation. In Schedule 11 of the Act, the power to attach a requirement to attend a day centre or to participate in, or refrain from, specified activities for a maximum of 60 days was added. These two requirements played a key part in the subsequent development of probation. In addition, community service orders of between 40 and 120 hours were extended to 16-year-olds, social enquiry reports would have to be prepared for any offender who had not previously served a prison sentence, and the formal title of the service became the probation service, losing the 'After-Care' part but not the function. The Act marked a further stage in the development of probation, with the new requirements adding to the rigour of probation orders with the aim of making them more attractive as an alternative to custody.

Just as relevant to probation – though more indirectly at first – was the new government's obsession with the efficiency of the public sector. A key approach was to introduce private sector management techniques to public sector organisations; managerialism was, of course, not especially welcomed by the probation service – indeed McWilliams (1992: 4) talks of 'a degree of resistance remarkable in an agency previously noted for placid industrial relations'. The Financial Management Initiative (FMI) was launched by the government in May 1982, and, as Whitehead and Statham (2006: 87) point out,

> From this point onwards, the language of the 3Es (economy, efficiency and effectiveness); performance management; greater accountability; cash limits; value for money; the setting of clear objectives, priorities and targets; management information systems; becomes firmly established within government, the public sector, and of course the probation service was not left untouched.

But it took a few years and a second general election victory for the Conservatives in 1983 before they began to tackle the probation service. In 1984 they introduced a *Statement of National Objectives and Priorities* (SNOP) for probation and this marked the start of a decade of considerable change. We will examine briefly the most important of these developments in roughly chronological order, first focusing on those initiatives that originated from government and moving on to those that had their origins in professional developments even though they were taken up by the Home Office.

Statement of National Objectives and Priorities (SNOP)

The *Statement of National Objectives and Priorities* (Home Office 1984a) was a rather innocuous-looking document, scarcely six pages long. It set out, as its title suggests, to prescribe how the service should prioritise its work; not perhaps a particularly contentious issue today. But, at the time, probation officers saw SNOP as threatening the end of probation as they knew it, because their autonomy and discretion – key aspects of their professionalism – were being constrained. SNOP made it clear that the probation service was responsible for a wide range of tasks and that it had, therefore, to use its resources efficiently and effectively (a recurring theme of the government). New areas such as crime prevention, mediation and reparation were opening up and probation service involvement in these had resource implications. The need to work with other agencies – 'the courts, the police, the prison service, local authorities, local government services, educational institutions and a variety of voluntary organisations' (Home Office 1984a: 2) – was also emphasised. In terms of priorities, the supervision of offenders in the community, especially for those 'where custodial sentences would otherwise be imposed' (Home Office 1984a: 4), was deemed to be most important. Wider work in the community (crime prevention, victim support, work with voluntary agencies) was also judged to require increased attention. But the provision of reports for the courts, through-care and civil work were all considered to require either no increase in resources or 'a slightly reduced level of resources to better effect' (Home Office 1984a: 6).

SNOP's immediate significance may have been to pin down priorities, but the word 'national' in its title was hugely important. Probation areas were – essentially – local fiefdoms run by chief probation officers in conjunction with a committee made up mostly of magistrates. CPOs had a considerable degree of latitude in how they ran their local service, and from its beginnings probation had been a local service. By setting out *national* objectives and priorities, the Home Office was putting a symbolic marker down; while it is possible to make out the slow encroachment of central control (via the Home Office) over the years since the introduction of probation in 1907, from 1984 this is a development that becomes much more pronounced. Indeed, the responses of probation services to SNOP unwittingly demonstrated the need for a more concerted and consistent approach to probation work that might be encouraged by more central control. An analysis of these responses showed a wide variety of responses to SNOP on every possible dimension: 'the most notable feature of the local statements of objectives and priorities is their great diversity. They differ both in physical appearance and in theoretical structure and content' (Lloyd 1986).

PROBIS

The computerisation of probation began during the 1980s with a Home Office-driven project termed the Probation Information System (PROBIS), which began to shift the process of statistical data collection and transfer from a manual to a computer-based system. Obviously, data had to be collected in a standardised way and if different computer systems were used by different probation areas then incompatibilities might have led to all kinds of problems with the preparation of the annual Probation Statistics published by the Home Office. Probation services were, therefore, encouraged to follow the PROBIS system.

While there was, predictably, some opposition to the introduction of computers and to what was seen as yet more Home Office interference, on the whole computerisation seems to have proceeded with little serious resistance. Its significance, however, was immense as not only did the advent of computers change the old-fashioned ways of record-keeping and data collection, but they are another example of the Home Office 'encouraging' a national approach when – traditionally – probation services would have gone their own ways. Computerisation also offered scope for more sophisticated management systems (see below) and opened the way for databases to cover several agencies (e.g. probation, prisons and courts).

RMIS

As we noted above, the Financial Management Initiative began in 1982 but it was only in 1986 that it began to impinge on the probation service when management consultants were appointed to develop a financial management information system for the service (Humphrey 1991). SNOP had emphasised the need to use available resources effectively and efficiently and the Financial Management Information System was planned to help with this process. Work had begun soon after the publication of SNOP under the Probation Inspectorate but the complexities involved had hindered progress, and it was decided to bring in management consultants. The consultants had little knowledge of probation or the context in which it worked and they were expensive. Again, progress was slow and the scope of the FMIS was widened to become a RMIS (Resource Management Information System) with the lead being taken directly by the Home Office. Despite the difficulties, the Home Office remained keen, piloting a Case Management Classification System and looking at information needs from a more strategic perspective.

The significance of RMIS and its associated developments again shows the Home Office trying to exert control over probation this time by measuring its costs.

Performance indicators

The development and use of performance indicators was yet another example of government exercising control over probation and making it more accountable.

By setting out objectives for probation (SNOP) and trying to develop a more effective system of resource management, the development of performance indicators became almost inevitable. The cultural traditions of the probation service, however, were not exactly receptive to the idea of performance indicators (which were a key weapon in the Conservative government's drive to improve efficiency in the public sector). Indeed, it is unlikely that the staff of any organisation or agency would welcome the introduction of performance indicators, with their threat of greater accountability. Probation anxieties were exacerbated by the fact that performance indicators for the service were to be developed by the Probation Inspectorate – although representatives of the Association of Chief Officers of Probation (ACOP), the Central Council of Probation Committees (CCPC) and Napo were all on the working party – and used as part of their inspection programme. The professional relationship between probation staff and members of HMIP was always rather uneasy, but now the worry was that probation work was going to be judged (and resources allocated) on the basis of a set of quasi-scientific measures that had been devised by the Home Office. To make matters worse, the first set of indicators was based on the objectives set out in SNOP and, of course, area responses to SNOP had not followed these same objectives (Lloyd 1986). The first set of performance indicators was published in 1988 and subsequently used by HMIP in its inspections of probation work (HMIP 1988).

National standards

Partly as a result of the local nature of probation services and partly because individual probation officers had a great deal of discretion in how to carry on their work, a regular criticism of probation work in general was that it was all too often inconsistent, not just between areas but within areas. And such inconsistency can mean that offenders are treated differently, which is not compatible with justice. Community service had introduced a new set of inconsistencies, with probation areas differing in the kind of work they organised, the kinds of offender they dealt with, how hours of work were counted, how absences were dealt with, and so on. Ultimately, it was possible that sentencers might begin to lose confidence in the probation service if they felt that its sentences were bedevilled by inconsistencies. In April 1989 the Home Office introduced a set of National Standards for community service orders which covered such issues as:

- arrangement of work placements;
- assessment and referral of potential candidates for community service;
- length of time that should elapse between the court order and commencement of work;
- number of unacceptable absences before breach action should be taken;
- work rate.

This was followed in 1992 by a more comprehensive set of National Standards (Home Office et al. 1992), this time covering pre-sentence reports, probation orders, supervision orders, combination orders, the management of hostels, and supervision before and after release from custody, as well as a revision of the standards for community service. Subsequent revisions of the standards tightened them up and added new areas such as bail information schemes (see below).

Partnership

The probation service had always been encouraged to make use of local voluntary agencies as part of their work with offenders, but the use that different area services made of such agencies had never been monitored and it was likely that such use varied between areas. During the 1980s, the Home Office began to push the idea that the police could not deal with crime on their own: 'Preventing crime is a task for the whole community' (Home Office 1984c: 1). Crime prevention initiatives began with the Five Towns Initiative in 1986 and the more ambitious Safer Cities in 1988, and these relied on a multi-agency approach. Following the Green Paper *Punishment, Custody and the Community* (Home Office 1988a), a paper entitled *Tackling Offending: An Action Plan* (Home Office 1988b) was sent to all probation areas setting out the government's plans for dealing with young adult offenders. Part of this paper included a list of questions for reviewing local practice, one of which was 'To what extent does the probation service involve voluntary organisations in its work with offenders?' (Home Office 1988b: 8).

The use of voluntary organisations and other community services was further encouraged in the White Paper *Crime, Justice and Protecting the Public* (Home Office 1990a), a Green Paper devoted to the probation service, *Supervision and Punishment in the Community* (Home Office 1990b), and a discussion paper, *Partnership in Dealing with Offenders in the Community* (Home Office 1990c). The decision that emerged from this flurry of policy papers was that 'Each probation area should expect to spend a minimum of around 5% of its total revenue budget on partnership work run by the independent sector' (Home Office 1992: 5). Not only was this yet another step by central government to taking control of local probation, but it also meant that probation areas were being 'encouraged' to leave certain kinds of work that they might have tended to carry out themselves, to outside agencies (e.g. drugs work, help with employment).

Cash limits

All of the foregoing developments led, almost inevitably, to considerations about probation funding. Indeed, given the government's preoccupation with cutting the costs of the public sector, it was only a matter of time before probation funding would have been targeted in any case. The traditional model, as far as government was concerned, made little sense: a budget was prepared by individual probation areas and agreed with their local authorities who paid 20 per cent while the remaining 80 per cent was paid by the Home Office, which had no input into how the budget had been planned. If the Home Office wished to take a more controlling role with the probation service, one very clear method was to take greater control over its financing.

> Central government cannot continue to have an open-ended commitment to support whatever expenditure is agreed locally. The need to control government expenditure, together with considerations of efficiency, require that probation committees should, in common with the majority of public services, be subject to the discipline of cash limits. A system of cash limits will provide the means to achieve a fairer distribution of resources, but this apart, cash limits are not intended to affect the extent to which the service is coordinated and integrated with the rest of the criminal justice system. But their introduction could well alter the roles of probation committees and local authorities in deciding about overall spending levels.
>
> (Home Office 1990b: 25)

In 1992, cash limits were duly introduced on the government's contribution to probation funding, calculated according to a complex formula for each local service (Field and Hough 1993).

Reorganising the probation service

The preceding developments were taken forward separately, but it is very easy to examine them and see how closely related they all were. In addition, the government's plans for sentencing also had major implications for the probation service (see below), and with the publication of the *Victim's Charter* (Home Office 1990d) the service was given the new task of contacting the victims of serious offences with a view to keeping them informed of the sentence and taking account of any anxieties they might have about an offender's release. As a result, in 1990 a Green Paper was published proposing a major reorganisation of the probation service. *Supervision and Punishment in the Community* made it clear that probation was 'a criminal justice agency' (Home Office 1990b: 6) and that probation work was to be redefined (it is worth noting the repetition of 'must'):

- Probation officers are officers of the court, and must respond to the wishes of sentencers.
- They must supervise orders in a way envisaged by the courts, and enforce firmly any conditions attached to orders.
- In supervising offenders they must take full account of the need to protect the public.
- They must gear their work towards crime prevention in its broadest sense.
- They must work in closer co-operation with the police, local authorities and the rest of the community.
- Probation officers must see themselves less as exclusive providers of services and facilities, and more as managers of supervision programmes.

They must make greater use of the skills and experience of the voluntary and private sectors.
- Probation officers must show that they can produce results to justify the extra money being spent on the probation service.

(Home Office 1990b: iii)

In order to move towards this vision, significant structural changes were suggested: the amalgamation of smaller probation areas, making probation committees more like management boards, giving the Home Office more control over senior appointments, moving to 100 per cent funding by central government, changing the training system so that there would be greater emphasis on criminal justice issues and removing the need for probation officers to hold a social work qualification, and – perhaps most controversially – introducing a national probation service.

While there were few signs of these being taken forward in the short term, it is notable that within a decade a Labour government had moved to introduce these proposals.

Practice developments

At the same time as these more policy-oriented initiatives were taking place, at the level of practice probation officers were involved in a number of significant developments. Following the introduction of day centres (subsequently renamed probation centres) and specified activity requirements in the 1982 Criminal Justice Act, these two requirements proved popular with the courts. By the mid-1980s there were around 80 day centres in existence (Mair 1988) and just over 1,800 offenders commenced supervision in 1985 with a day centre requirement; in the same year, 850 individuals commenced supervision with a specified activity requirement. Ten years later, in 1995, the respective figures were 2,528 and 6,978 – increases of 40 per cent and over 700 per cent. Together these two requirements accounted for almost two-thirds of the requirements added to probation orders in 1995. Both had been introduced to stiffen up the probation order to try to make it more credible as an alternative to custody, and both tended to operate on group work principles rather than the traditional one-to-one model of probation supervision. Thus, probation officers were increasingly working in a rather different way, utilising a more rigorous and structured approach.

The probation organisations could see the direction in which probation was being moved and, in an effort to hold back the tide, came together to make the case for the probation service: 'over the next five years the probation service is the only organisation with experience, training and skills, which if adequately resourced can take on an increased role in ways which can relieve pressures on the prison system' (ACOP et al. 1987: 7). The argument was, essentially, more of the same; but it is perhaps indicative of the pressures faced by probation that the following year ACOP on its own published a paper arguing for a tougher and more demanding community sentence – a Community Restitution Order (ACOP 1988).

In the event, an even more demanding and rigorous form of supervision was introduced following *Tackling Offending: An Action Plan* which noted that 'The Home Office will also discuss, initially with the probation service, the possibility of "intensive probation" (IP) programmes being set up in selected areas' (Home Office 1988b: 6). Subsequently, nine probation areas agreed to set up IP projects which – unlike the IMPACT experiment in the 1970s – involved more intensive control rather than more intensive social work. The probation staff involved were, on the whole, keen on IP, and the schemes seemed to be reasonably successful at targeting offenders who were at risk of a custodial sentence, but with the introduction of the combination order in the 1991 Criminal Justice Act, Home Office interest in the IP project disappeared (Mair et al. 1994; Mair 1997).

Partly as a result of the development of day centres and the desire to target them effectively on those offenders who were at risk of a custodial sentence, predicting risk of custody became an important objective for probation officers. Statistical prediction instruments (more accurate than clinical prediction) were developed on an ad hoc basis by several probation officers – notably David Bale in Cambridgeshire – and the idea was taken up enthusiastically by the Home Office (Mair 1989; for a full discussion of the development of risk assessment in probation see Kemshall 1998). Risk prediction moved quickly from predicting risk of custody to sentence prediction and then to predicting risk of reconviction with the Offender Group Reconviction Scale (OGRS). Its significance is at least threefold: as an example of an initiative developed by practitioners that was taken up and taken over by the Home Office; as a move away from the traditional clinical prediction approach used by probation officers; and as an example of probation having to come to terms with new technology as OGRS was most easily calculated using a computer program.

Another example of technological innovation in dealing with offenders was the use of electronic monitoring to check on an individual's whereabouts. Predictably, the probation service was not impressed by tagging, seeing it as demeaning, infringing a person's human rights, and overly punitive. As a result, probation officers lost the opportunity to become responsible officers for those subject to electronic monitoring, and their involvement in the first two trials of tagging was minimal (Mair and Nee 1990; Mair and Mortimer 1996). Since then, probation officers seem to have accepted tagging, although how far this is a real change of heart or simply an acknowledgement of the inevitable is difficult to tell.

Probation was also widening its client group. There was an assumption that probation officers could only work with those who had been found guilty, as any discussion touching on whether or not an individual had carried out an offence would compromise the role of the probation officer. However, Inner London probation service had been involved in a project in the mid-1970s whereby probation officers interviewed defendants who had been held in police cells overnight and were considered to be at risk of a remand in custody with a view to them being granted bail. In the second half of the 1980s, with prison numbers a constant problem and around 20 per cent of the prison population at the time made up of remands in custody, and with ACOP keen to build a relationship with the Crown Prosecution Service which had begun operating in 1986, a new set of bail information schemes run by probation officers was underway. These schemes involved probation staff interviewing defendants who were deemed to be at risk of being remanded in custody in an effort to provide verifiable information that might instead lead to them being bailed. By 1992 more than 120 schemes were operating. Research suggested that the schemes were fairly successful at leading to bail for those who might otherwise have been remanded in custody (Lloyd 1992).

During this period, probation was also getting involved in community work in a more purposive way than had been the case previously. SNOP, ACOP, the Central Council of probation committees and Napo all appear to have been in favour of developing community probation work and, as Henderson and del Tufo (1991) show, the examples of community policing and crime prevention also encouraged such a move. Probation officers were involved, too, in crime prevention from its early days (see Geraghty 1991), and they played a part in panel assessment schemes designed to divert mentally disordered offenders away from the criminal justice process (Hedderman 1993).

The range and variety of practice developments probation was moving into might suggest a thriving and forward-looking organisation. But it might also suggest an organisation that was trying to cover too many bases in a desperate effort to demonstrate its importance and, in the process, forgetting its core business. Research carried out in 1987–8 showed that around half of probation officers saw themselves as specialists:

> The single most important finding from the survey of probation practice ... is that almost a half of all probation officers are employed in specialist duties; only 52 per cent describe themselves as field team POs working with a mixed caseload.
>
> (Boswell et al. 1993: 75)

The local nature of many practice developments meant that there was little evidence of consistency in day centre practice, for example, and there were dangers in a local risk of custody prediction instrument being taken over and used by another probation area where it had not been validated. The policy developments pointed towards objectives such as increasing consistency of practice, controlling costs, greater accountability – all to be achieved by a shift to more central control. And, although central control did not necessarily mean a national probation service, the two were certainly not incompatible.

The Criminal Justice Act 1991 and its aftermath

By far the greatest opportunity for probation at this time, as well as the greatest threat, was the 1991 Criminal Justice Act. While probation had many developments to come to terms with, and these tended to point the service in a certain direction, they were fragmented and not at all a consistent, clearly articulated initiative.

The 1991 Act, on the other hand, was carefully constructed, coherent and theoretically underpinned to a degree rarely seen in government legislation – and the probation service was fundamental to its successful realisation (for a detailed account of the background to the Act see Windlesham 1993). But probation would have to become more punitive because – as a senior civil servant made clear – only if the service was seen as offering credible and demanding sentences would the courts be willing to use community sentences instead of custody, thereby reducing the prison population:

> The extent to which the probation service can be used to divert more serious offenders from custody, is dependent on persuading the courts of the service's ability to hold and control serious offenders. An important issue for future consideration is whether more could and should be done to encourage the courts to have greater confidence in the service and the extent to which this might require a change in the probation service's attitude to offenders away from 'advising, assisting and befriending' towards controlling.
>
> (quoted in Windlesham 1993: 225–6)

From 1987 Home Office ministers and officials campaigned to persuade the probation service to move in the desired direction, and both the carrot and the stick were used: the service would be centre stage in the Home Office plans, but it would have to operate more restrictive and rigorous sentences and – if necessary – these could be organised by another agency entirely.

Punishment, Custody and the Community (Home Office 1988a) began the process by explicitly linking the two concepts of punishment and the community, whereas for most probation officers at the time punishment was probably something that occurred in prison while rehabilitation was carried out in the community. Both John Patten, Minister of State at the Home Office, and David Faulkner, Deputy Under-Secretary of State, argued that punishment and control were inescapable aspects of probation work (Windlesham 1993: 226–7; Faulkner 1989) and – as the Green Paper made clear – were necessary parts of punishment in the community if the use of custody was to be reduced (an objective that the great majority of probation officers would have been in favour of). The Green Paper floated various ideas:

- increasing probation involvement in mediation and reparation schemes;
- whether the minimum (40 hours) and maximum (240) hours for community service should be altered;
- lengthening the maximum of 60 days attendance at a day centre;
- using ancillary staff to track offenders;
- introducing a curfew order requiring an offender to remain at home;
- using electronic monitoring to enforce a curfew;
- introducing restrictions on an offender's liberty at weekends;
- programmes to deal with drug and alcohol abuse which might be monitored by urine tests.

Perhaps most significant, however, was the suggestion that a new sentence might be introduced – the supervision and restriction order – to pull together these proposals.

The proposals, by holding out the offer of more power, were clearly tempting – 'There are great opportunities for the probation service' (Home Office 1988a: 17) – but at the price of probation becoming more punitive and controlling. And there was a threat lurking at the end of the Green Paper hinting at what might happen if the service was not willing to cooperate:

> Another possibility would be to set up a new organisation to organise punishment in the community. It would not itself supervise offenders or provide facilities directly, but would contract with other services and organisations to do so.
>
> (Home Office 1988a: 17)

The probation service was subjected to further criticism the following year when both the Audit Commission (1989) and the National Audit Office (1989) published reports examining the economy, efficiency and effectiveness of the service. Probation was found to be wanting: increasing use of probation led, not to a reduction in custodial sentences, but to a reduction in the number of fines so better targeting was necessary; better management systems were needed; greater Home Office control was needed; there was not enough evaluation of probation projects. The National Audit Office report concluded:

> it is evident from the work of the National Audit Office and the Audit Commission that the full potential of the probation service is not yet fulfilled so that economy and efficiency suffer and ultimately the effectiveness of the effort is diminished.
>
> (National Audit Office 1989: 6)

And it was notable that while probation expenditure had increased from £186.8 million in 1985/6 to £286.7 million in 1990/91, and the number of probation officers had grown from 6,220 in 1985 to 7,153 in 1991, the average caseload per main grade officer had decreased during this period from 22.5 to 15.6 and the average number of reports completed by main grade officers dropped from 69.1 to 50.9 (Home Office 1993a).

The government's proposals for legislation (Home Office 1990a), which were based on a just deserts framework for sentencing, included making the probation order a sentence (a highly symbolic step), introducing two new community sentences – a combination order and a curfew order with the latter to be organised and run by an agency other than the probation service – making unit fines nationally available following a successful experiment (Moxon et al. 1990), and overhauling the parole system, which had significant implications for the probation service. In addition, national standards were to be extended and a major review of probation was to be carried out (see above).

The 1991 Criminal Justice Act was the most significant piece of legislation for probation since the 1948 Act. By setting the Act in a just deserts framework, whereby a sentence had to be proportionate to the seriousness of the offence, community sentences could no longer be considered as alternatives to custody and became sentences in their own right. It was ironic that, while the Act was to a large degree motivated by the need to cut prison numbers, it brought to an end (officially) the idea of probation or community service as alternatives to prison sentences.[1] The main provisions of the Act as far as probation was concerned were:

- The probation order would no longer be made *instead of* a sentence and became a sentence in its own right.
- The purposes of probation were threefold: to secure the rehabilitation of the offender; to protect the public from harm; and to prevent the commission of further offences.
- Pre-sentence reports (PSRs, previously social enquiry reports) became mandatory for most custodial or community sentences.
- New requirements which could be added to the probation order were introduced for treatment for those dependent on drugs or alcohol; and the 60-day limit for probation centre or specified activities was removed for sex offenders.
- The maximum number of hours for a person aged 16 sentenced to a community service order was raised from 120 to 240.
- The combination order was introduced, with a supervision element of between 12 and 36 months and community service of between 40 and 100 hours (and with availability of the requirements that could be added to the probation order).
- A curfew order which could be electronically monitored would be available for those aged 16 and over, and could be made for a period of up to six months and for between two and twelve hours a day.
- New arrangements for the early release of prisoners were introduced.

While these provisions certainly extended the reach of community sentences and made more work for the probation service, they also held warnings: the combination order had the potential to be a punitive sentence and probation officers were apprehensive about it being too demanding for some offenders; the curfew order was a threat to the probation monopoly of community sentences as private companies would be responsible for electronic monitoring (while there were by this time around 30 senior attendance centres, they represented no threat to probation); the boundaries between custody and community were blurred by the new arrangements for early release which envisaged a custodial sentence which continued in the community with supervision on licence. And, while it did not immediately concern the service, the Act also contained provisions for the privatisation of prisons, a highly significant step.

By the time the key provisions of the Act were implemented in October 1992, a full set of national standards for probation work had also been published (Home Office et al. 1992, see above). A survey of practitioners' views of the Act suggested that probation officers were, for the most part, reasonably satisfied with it (Mair and May 1995) but, within months of the survey being carried out and more than a year before its results were published, there was a sudden change of direction.

The two areas where sentencers had complained about the Act were unit fines and the admissibility of previous convictions. With regard to unit fines, there were press stories of huge fines for very minor offences such as dropping a crisp packet. In February 1993, James Bulger was murdered in Liverpool by two ten-year-old boys, a high-profile case with massive media coverage that resulted in increased nationwide anxiety about crime. Kenneth Clarke, Home Secretary at the time, had no commitment to the 1991 Act and, with little warning, decided to introduce legislation to change some of the elements of the Act. The 1993 Criminal Justice Act reintroduced the admissibility of previous convictions and scrapped unit fines, thereby undermining the foundations of the 1991 Act. While this had little impact upon the probation service, its brief moment at centre stage was about to come to an end with the arrival as Home Secretary of Michael Howard in May 1993.

Turbulent times

From the middle of the 1970s the probation service began to face a range of pressures that it had not had to grapple with seriously before: pressure on resources, questions about its effectiveness in rehabilitating offenders, increased government intervention, demands for it to be more accountable, the redefinition of its key task as the provision of alternatives to custody. The efficacy of probation work was no longer a matter of faith but something that had to be measured. New modes of practice were introduced, and the overall tendency of these was to make probation work more punitive than it had been in the past. While the various efforts by academics as well as practitioners to remake probation do suggest a healthy interest in the topic, they can also be seen as a sign of how troubled the service was. If all was well, why was there such a need to change things?

It would be difficult to argue against some of the changes. Probation practice had always had a certain vagueness, almost a mystical quality about its rehabilita-tive efforts. What was wrong with using the language of punishment a little more? There was little consistency in practice as each probation service had considerable freedom and this translated into probation officers having a good deal of discretion and autonomy in how they dealt with offenders. The way in which probation was financed – with government signing a blank cheque yet having little say in what was done by services – was, especially given the Conservatives, obsession with cutting costs, not something that could continue. And it would be hard to argue against the need to demonstrate effectiveness.

The problem was that too many initiatives were happening too quickly and were being imposed on an unreconstructed probation service; the existence of more than 50 local probation services with few strong links with central government made imposing the changes more difficult than they might have been.

But notwithstanding what were perceived as constant attacks by the Conservative government, there was still a belief that the probation service was needed; if the prison population was to be held down, then community sentences, and the probation service, were vital. To succeed in this, however, the received wisdom was that community sentences had to become more punitive and, while probation staff might not like moving in this direction, in reality they had little choice. The difficulty was that there was no evidence to suggest that community sentences were effective as alternatives to custody. The prison population had increased inexorably from 36,867 in 1974 to 43,349 in 1984 and then to 48,794 in 1994 (apart from a slight drop at the end of the 1980s which was probably due to sentencers anticipating the 1991 Act). The National Audit Office (1989) report had stated plainly that increased use of community sentences had not led to a drop in custody but to a decrease in the use of fines.

Table 7.2 shows the use of court sentences for indictable offences for the three years 1974, 1984 and 1994 and that the use of probation-run sentences for adults had more than tripled during the 20-year period (7 per cent for probation in 1974 to 24 per cent for probation, CSO and the combination order in 1994), while the use of custody had risen from 12 per cent to 17 per cent and use of the fine decreased by 20 per cent. In addition, community sentences were increasingly being used for summary offences: between 1984 and 1994 the use of the proba-tion order for summary offences had grown from 12 per cent to 31 per cent; for CS the figures were 12 per cent and 33 per cent; and despite the combination order being introduced as a high-level community sentence that might help to divert offenders from short-term custodial sentences, in 1994 – only two years

Table 7.2 Court sentences for indictable offences, 1974, 1984, 1994 (%)

Sentence	1974	1984	1994
Ab/Con Discharge	13	13	20
Fine	52	42	31
Probation	7	8	11
Supervision	5	3	2
CSO	–	7	10
ACO	2	3	2
Combination	–	–	3
Suspended	6	6	1
Custody	12	16	17
Other	3	1	2
Total No.	377,100	449,800	313,400

Note: Numbers have been rounded and may not necessarily add up to 100%.

since it had been available to the courts – 35 per cent of combination orders were used for summary offences.

Whichever way one looked at the matter, by the early 1990s probation did not look in good shape, and the punitive turn that occurred in 1993 meant that worse was to come.

8   The end of the road?

Prison works

Michael Howard's period as Home Secretary (1993–7) is often seen as being marked solely by his claim that 'Prison works'. While this assertion had very clear implications for the probation service and its work, various other developments took place while he was at Queen Anne's Gate that were just as significant for probation. But 'Prison works' symbolises the crucial turn towards a more punitive penal climate with which we have been living ever since. Prior to 1993, while the rehabilitation of offenders, community penalties and the probation service might not have been consistently encouraged by governments, they were at least tolerated and usually acknowledged as a useful approach to dealing with offenders. After 1993, a grudging toleration became the norm alongside persistent criticism and regular attempts to make changes to the service – changes which were all too easily seen as efforts to undermine its viability. The cross-party consensus about crime and how to deal with it may have looked shaky at various times since 1945, but it had – on the whole – held together reasonably well, until the Thatcher years. By 1993, however, the Conservatives were not doing well in the polls and a decision was made to make law and order a key policy issue:

> Alarmed by their deteriorating position in public opinion polls, both in general and on crime, the Conservatives rapidly cast their previous, and long-germinated penal policy to the winds and sought to reoccupy lost terrain. First Kenneth Clarke, then Michael Howard, as the new Conservative Home Secretaries after 1992, quickly dropped the key reforming clauses of the 1991 Act: unit fines (which linked the level of fines to disposable income) and the need normally to disregard previous convictions in sentencing. Michael Howard's notorious 'Prison Works' speech to the Tory Party Conference in 1993 was the climax to this somewhat panic-stricken shift.
>
> (Downes and Morgan 2002: 296)

This time the Labour party did not take the bait. Instead, a decision was made to match – and if possible to surpass – Conservative rhetoric so that for every criminal justice policy initiative announced by the Conservatives, Labour responded in kind. There was little to differentiate between the two parties in their new approaches to law and order and, ironically, a new bipartisan approach to law and order emerged, only this time it was based around being more punitive. Labour, it would appear, was determined never to be seen as soft on crime again – with significant consequences for the future.

At his first speech to the party conference as Home Secretary on 6 October 1993, Howard set out 27 proposals on law and order. Only two of these focused directly on the probation service – community service orders would be toughened up, and there would be a review of community sentences – neither of which looked too threatening. A number of other developments, however, began to put pressure on probation during Howard's time at the Home Office.

Probation was being held to account much more rigorously than it ever had been. Three-year plans (see Home Office 1993b, 1994, 1995a, 1996, 1997) became more detailed as performance indicators turned into key performance indicators (KPIs) and these in turn were informed by SMINs (supporting management information needs) as probation moved towards becoming an acronym-driven organisation. Cash limits, which had not been ungenerous when introduced in 1991 (partly in order to allay probation fears about loss of resources), began to be tightened with obvious implications for growth in probation (a glance at successive three-year plans for the service from that for 1994–7 to 1997–2000 is instructive). Partnership work was imposed by setting a target of 5 per cent of a probation service's budget to be spent on partnership schemes, although for 1995–6 this target was only half-way to being met (Home Office 1997). A review of probation training had been carried out in 1988–9 (Coleman 1989), but nothing had been done about its recommendations. A further review was carried out in 1994 (Dews and Watts 1994), recommending some major changes: repeal of the need for probation officers to hold a CQSW or DipSW; central control over the proposed new award of the Diploma in Probation Studies (DipPS); ending Home Office financial responsibility for training; and the new training programme to be practice-based. Those involved in delivering probation training were, of course, unhappy with the proposals (see Ward and Spencer 1994; Miller and Buchanan 1995), but the government went further and decided to suspend probation training completely from autumn 1996. Private prisons began operating with the opening of Wolds Remand Prison in the spring of 1992, with a further five private prisons either planned or starting to operate during the next few years. The implications for probation were only too clear and made even more transparent with the introduction of curfew orders, operated by private security organisations, as court sentences in 1995. The probation service had had such serious reservations about the first trials of electronic monitoring in 1989–90 that its members had only been involved on the periphery, and their reluctance to engage with tagging meant that they lost the chance to become the responsible officers for offenders who were tagged. Not only was privatisation a possibility for the probation service (and something very like it had been mentioned in the 1988 Green Paper; see Chapter 7), but other, private sector, organisations were moving into what had been assumed to be probation territory.

The Criminal Justice and Public Order Act of 1994 was a further step towards increasing punitiveness. Its only immediate relevance to probation was to permit the courts' greater discretion to dispense with a pre-sentence report for offenders aged 18 and above (thereby reversing a planned increase in the use of PSRs in the 1991 Criminal Justice Act). In addition, the Act introduced Secure Training Orders for 12–14 year olds, and by giving the police powers to restrict raves, new age travellers and hunt saboteurs was seen to be clamping down on the freedom of individuals to demonstrate and to enjoy themselves. Increased police powers in relation to stop and search and in the use of remand on bail were also introduced; and, following its introduction in the 1991 Act, curfew orders with electronic monitoring were implemented with trials beginning in three areas in July 1995.

Questions were also being asked about the way probation officers matched offenders to supervision programmes. A Home Office-funded study found little evidence of systematic assessment of offender needs and therefore very much a hit or miss approach to allocating offenders to programmes – which had implications for effectiveness. The conclusion was clear:

> The systematic assessment of offending-related needs is central to ensuring the accuracy of probation assessments, and the confidence sentencers have in them. One way of achieving this would be to ensure that every offender passed through an assessment programme before and/or after sentence.
>
> (Burnett 1996: xi)

By this time, a national risk of reconviction scale was available for use by probation. The Offender Group Reconviction Scale (OGRS) had been developed with Home Office funding by Professor John Copas, a leading statistician, but it was treated with considerable suspicion by many probation officers who distrusted what they saw as a mathematical approach to assessing offenders and felt that their judgement and professional autonomy were threatened (Mair 2001). Work was also undertaken at this time on testing out a needs assessment scale, concluding that while national implementation would have to be carried out carefully, there was 'an overwhelming case for collecting information in a structured and consistent manner on the extent to which offenders' needs have been addressed' (Aubrey and Hough 1997: 31). Probation services were experimenting with a variety of scales and there was an increasingly pressing question about how to impose national schemes and initiatives on more than 50 separate services.

At the same time as these threats, when the probation service badly needed support, there was a vacuum in probation policy at the Home Office; and nature, of course, abhors a vacuum. During the late 1980s and the first couple of years of the 1990s, the probation policy division (C6) had been led by Philippa Drew, who had very effectively given the probation service the impression that she had its best interests at heart while at the same time driving through government policy. Her immediate successor had only been in post a few months before moving on and his successor was not only disliked by the probation service but seen to be uninterested in supporting them. At around the same time, a new chief inspector of probation was appointed: Graham Smith had been chief of the Inner London Probation Service since 1980, responsible for the largest probation service in England and Wales and working closely with the Home Office. His appointment as HMCIP in 1992 meant that a powerful personality with strong views about the probation service was in charge of the Probation Inspectorate – traditionally and constitutionally a position that had no direct input to policy – at a time when the policy division responsible for probation seemed to be unable or unwilling to lead on probation policy.

The presence of Graham Smith in Queen Anne's Gate, however, did not help the probation service organisations in the face of the next Home Office publication. Traditionally, informal discussions took place with the probation organisations as new initiatives were planned, in order to take soundings as to how new ideas might be received, to try to minimise opposition, because that was how things were done. But neither ACOP, Napo or CCPC had any prior sight of the 1995 Green Paper *Strengthening Punishment in the Community* (Home Office 1995b), which came as something of a shock – partly because of its content but partly too because probation had not been party to its preparation, with all that that implied about the significance of the service to the government's plans. The key proposals (Home Office 1995b: 1–2) were:

- the introduction of a single integrated community sentence – which might be designated 'the community sentence' – replacing and incorporating all the current orders available in the adult courts;
- the matching of sentence elements to the three principal purposes of punishment in the community: restriction of liberty, reparation and prevention of reoffending;
- increased discretion for courts to determine the content of community sentences in individual cases and to decide what restrictions and compulsions should apply to offenders in pursuance of the three principal purposes;
- more consistent access for courts to information on the progress and outcome of community sentences;
- the removal of the present requirement that offenders consent to community orders.

A rationale, of course, lay behind the proposals, but as set out in the Green Paper the obvious question was why, if there were so many problems with community sentences, had it taken so long to notice these, especially as the 1988 Green Paper had stated that the existing community penalties were 'working well' (Home Office 1988a: 15). The government claimed that: community penalties had developed in a fragmented way and this had led to anomalies and incoherence (but development was surely down to government); community sentences were not well understood and did not have the confidence of the public (although no evidence was provided to support this claim); current orders lacked flexibility (again, surely a matter for government); they were used inconsistently and they could not be combined (except for the limited scope in the combination order);

and courts had very little knowledge about the content of a community sentence, although they were responsible for passing such sentences.

Interestingly, while the Green Paper implied throughout that the courts had little confidence in the probation service, it could not make such a claim in explicit terms. A Home Office Research Study published in the same year (May 1995) showed clearly that sentencers had considerable confidence in probation (89 per cent of magistrates said they were very or quite satisfied with the work of the service; 94 per cent said they had a very or quite good working relationship with the service; and 78 per cent were very or quite satisfied with the range of community disposals). The problem – as far as sentencers were concerned – seemed to be a serious lack of knowledge about the probation service: more than half of the sentencers questioned had not visited a probation office, a probation centre or a community service placement in the previous two years; around one-third of magistrates said they did not know how good the quality of supervision was for probation or community service orders; and more than one-quarter said they did not know about the quality of enforcement for probation or community service.

The proposed integrated community sentence would be made up of a number of options: supervision, attendance at a designated centre, community service, specified activities/treatment, financial compensation to victims, curfew and bans on attending specified places and undertaking specified activities. The 'potential for confusion and the overloading of sentences with unnecessary elements' (Home Office 1995b: 23) was acknowledged but brushed aside; although this, of course, had been the reason given for not taking this option in the 1988 Green Paper.

The two most contentious proposals were that sentencers should design the content of supervision programmes and that the requirement for consent before a community sentence was imposed should be removed. There was no evidence to suggest that sentencers wished to get involved in putting together supervision programmes, and, following the findings of May's (1995) study, a great deal of work would be required to bring them all up to speed on what was available given their relative lack of knowledge. With regard to consent, this was a key symbolic issue. Its removal was unlikely to have any real impact upon probation work, but consent had been a significant issue for probation since its beginnings; by agreeing to participate in a probation order, the emergence of a relationship between probation officer and offender was apparent and this constituted the basis of successful supervision. Worrall and Hoy (2005: 52) note:

> We know that the giving of consent to a probation order was no more than a residual ritual, but it may have meaning for some offenders and it was, in any case, a useful negotiating tool for probation officers at the pre-sentence report stage. Its removal, by contrast, was highly significant, for it demonstrated not only that the offender's consent does not matter but, yet again, that the probation officer's consent (to the wishes of the court) does not matter either.

The consent requirement was removed by the Crime (Sentences) Act 1997, except where a condition of drug/alcohol treatment or a mental health treatment requirement was proposed.

Following the Green Paper, the Home Office set up two sentencing exercises to test out how sentencers might use the proposed integrated sentence. The results were not encouraging: magistrates used custody more often and made less use of community sentences; more than half of the integrated sentences passed had between three and six elements; and nine out of ten elements of the sentence were classified as mandatory rather than desirable (meaning that failure to comply would lead to breach action and possible custody). The resource implications if such practice was to be replicated following the introduction of an integrated sentence were considerable (Mortimer and Mair 1996). In the end, the government decided not to legislate on the Green Paper but to carry out local demonstration projects which showed that better communication between probation and sentencers did lead to improved relations but did not 'lead to a significant increase in the use of community penalties and the question of whether new legislation is required must be revisited' (Hedderman et al. 1999: 69).

Certain trends in the use of community penalties were not conducive to optimism either. While overall the number of probation, community service and combination orders had increased from 100,700 in 1993 to 120,700 in 1997 (a rise of 20 per cent), the growth in use for indictable offences was 9 per cent but the growth for summary offences was 43 per cent. Community sentences – if they were to be taken seriously as penalties for serious offenders – were moving in the wrong direction. And this shift is confirmed by Tables 8.1and 8.2, which together suggest that the three main community sentences were moving rapidly down-tariff.

As is the case with the increased use for summary offences, community sentences were moving in the wrong direction: in the space of a few years the percentage of those starting a community service order who had previously served a custodial sentence fell by 10 per cent, while for the combination order (intended as a high-end community sentence for those who might otherwise have received a short custodial sentence) the decrease was 12 per cent; conversely, the use of community service for first offenders grew by 15 per cent, and combination orders almost doubled. Yet, as we noted earlier, sentencers seemed to have confidence in the probation service – although it may be that this confidence only related to probation officers' ability to deal effectively with low-level offenders.

Table 8.1 Commencements of community penalties with a previous custodial sentence, 1993–7 (%)

Community penalty	1993	1994	1995	1996	1997
Probation order	43	42	41	38	37
Community service	32	29	27	24	22
Combination order	49	48	42	39	37

Table 8.2 Commencements of community penalties with no previous convictions, 1993–7 (%)

Community penalty	1993	1994	1995	1996	1997
Probation order	12	15	16	18	19
Community service	19	25	28	32	34
Combination order	10	13	15	17	19

Whether or not it was solidly founded, there was certainly a feeling in probation circles that the very existence of the service was under threat. And it is this anxiety about probation's viability that can be seen to underpin the What Works initiative, which 'came to be represented as probation's only hope for organisational survival' (Oldfield 2002: 42). A range of factors lie behind the emergence of What Works (see Mair 2004a; Raynor and Vanstone 2002), but it is important to note that its origins did not lie with the Home Office; as with so many other policies, What Works began at a practice level and eventually was taken up by the Home Office. Research from Canada and England and Wales, the energy and belief of several probation services in organising conferences for a number of years, and Graham Smith, the chief probation inspector, who following a paper written by Andrew Underdown (an assistant chief probation office with Greater Manchester Probation Service; Underdown 1995) commissioned him to carry out a much more extensive study examining the extent of programme evaluation in probation services in England and Wales (Underdown 1998) were all significant. Just what impact this activity would have had on a Michael Howard-led Home Office is a matter for speculation. In 1997 a general election was held resulting in a win for the Labour party which returned to power after 18 years in opposition. For many, and certainly in the probation service, there was an expectation that things could only get better.

A national service

Following the Labour election victory it quickly became clear that the new government was unlikely to reverse the tough approach to law and order taken by the Conservatives. Indeed, given its obsession with modernisation and an evidence-based approach to policy and practice, it quickly became clear that the speed and scope of change as far as the probation service was concerned were increasing and deepening. In July 1997 a prisons–probation review was announced 'to look at ways in which better integration could improve their efficiency and performance' (Home Office 1998: 4). Closer liaison between the two services working with adult offenders would have been difficult to argue against, but the problem for the probation service was that the proposals went somewhat further than this:

- probation had to become more accountable and more cost-effective;
- there were too many probation services leading to inconsistent performance;

- probation had to embrace new technologies (meaning, essentially, electronic monitoring);
- a national leadership was needed;
- a unified probation service should be set up as a Next Steps Agency with 100 per cent central funding and probation staff becoming civil servants;
- the service should be renamed as should the various community sentences.

As far as probation officers were concerned, the only positive note in the document was that a merger with the prison service was firmly ruled out as 'a bridge too far' (Home Office 1998: 12). This did not, however, preclude a number of measures that were expected to lead to improvements in the *joint* performance of the two services: better integrated and coordinated policy and planning; shared aims and objectives; shared performance indicators; National Standards for probation work with offenders in custody; information sharing; a common system of programme accreditation; the adoption of a single risk/need assessment tool by both services; moving towards more integrated staff training; closer liaison between the Probation and the Prisons Inspectorates. Given the difference in size between the two services, there was an understandable fear amongst probation staff that any coming together of the two organisations risked probation being swamped by the prison service.

But it was not just major structural change that was approaching. 1998 also saw the publication of the HMIP report on the What Works project (Underdown 1998) which, despite the claims made by it in terms of identifying the factors necessary for effective probation work (targeting, programme delivery, appropriate organisational structures, etc.), in fact could only find four programmes out of a total of 267 where there was some reasonably convincing evidence of effectiveness – and none of the four was wholly convincing. This did not stop the What Works (or Effective Practice) initiative being rolled out nationally, raising interesting questions about just how far the government's enthusiasm for evidence-based policy actually went. A further publication (Chapman and Hough 1998) claimed to translate the results of the first one into practical guidance, but essentially was a glossy, well-designed handbook with pages of bullet points. There was little to explain how such soundbite advice could be woven into a coherent framework for practice. The third part of this trilogy was a Home Office Research Study that took advantage of the new government's interest in evidence by examining how various research studies demonstrated how crime could be reduced (Goldblatt and Lewis 1998). Once again, the chapter on 'Effective interventions with offenders' promised much more than it actually delivered.

Yet, as we have noted, the Effective Practice initiative was implemented nationally with considerable fanfare, despite the fact that it was based on surprisingly little evidence. If this was meant to save the probation service, then it was a high-risk strategy. The initial thrust of the initiative lay in cognitive behavioural programmes which, according to meta-analyses, were the most promising approach to reducing offending. But the meta-analyses were almost wholly based around research from North America, their relevance to the UK was untested, and they tended to focus on juveniles. One of the most influential and ambitious was carried out by Mark Lipsey (1992) who examined 443 studies, but a close reading of his work raised a number of problematic issues that had a bearing upon how his results could be interpreted. For example, how much faith could be placed on conclusions about the effectiveness of treatments for juvenile offenders when the following limitations were present in the data?

> For the primary delinquency measure (which is not always recidivism) half of the follow-up studies have follow-up periods of less than six months. Almost half of the studies were coded as having low treatment integrity (43.8 per cent), and approximately 75 per cent were either low or moderate on this rating (79.5 per cent). Twenty per cent of the studies covered institution-alized juveniles and 50 per cent covered non-juvenile justice interventions. Almost two-thirds of the programmes were less than two years old, which raises questions about the lasting impact of an initially enthusiastic response to a programme. Finally, one-quarter of the programmes were administered by criminal justice personnel, one-quarter by mental health personnel, and 20 per cent by lay persons.
>
> (Mair 1995a: 462)

The Effective Practice initiative as rolled out in June 1998 was heavily driven by programmes based upon cognitive behavioural approaches to working with offenders. But, again, there was little direct evidence from the UK that these were effective – although they were encouraged by the two Inspectorate reports. A Home Office study had noted the 'inconclusive findings' (Vennard et al. 1997: 35) associated with evaluations of cognitive behavioural programmes, and although almost 200 such programmes were being run by probation services in England and Wales there was little evidence about effectiveness, monitoring was rare, there was a 'lack of commitment to programme integrity' (Hedderman and Sugg 1997: 51) and offenders were not well matched to appropriate programmes.

Both the prisons–probation review and the HMIP *What Works?* report had noted the need for the accreditation of programmes. Traditionally, probation services had been free to set up programmes with little or no Home Office input, which, it has been argued, had serious disadvantages in that it led to 'uncontrolled discretion, lack of accountability, reinvention of the wheel, "flavour of the monthism" ... inefficiency and ineffectiveness and ... a poor service to courts and offenders' (Mair 1995b: 254). A more centralised and planned approach to programme development was likely to reduce such disadvantages, and two such panels had been running in respect of the prison service since 1996 (Joint Prison/ Probation Accreditation Panel 2000). A Joint Prison/Probation Accreditation Panel was established in July 1999 as part of the government's Crime Reduction Programme (CRP), with a membership consisting of Home Office officials, the Probation Inspectorate, ACOP, the prison service and a dozen 'independent' experts.

The Panel (renamed the Correctional Services Accreditation Panel in 2002) began its work slowly, fully accrediting only one programme in its first year (a prison sex offender programme). Its initial focus, not surprisingly, was heavily biased towards cognitive behavioural approaches and a number of the Pathfinder programmes launched under the Effective Practice initiative were considered for accreditation at its first two meetings, none of which were fully accredited. The Panel has had its critics (see Maguire et al. 2010; Rex et al. 2003; Mair 2000) and there will always be problems with such a bureaucratic and cumbersome approach to programme development, but perhaps most significant was the fact that, with its existence, there was now central control over the way in which the probation service worked with offenders.

The Effective Practice initiative was overtaken by the CRP that was introduced in 1999; effectively an attempt to put into practice the claims made in the Home Office *Reducing Offending* report (Goldblatt and Lewis 1998). This was a huge and very costly undertaking, and represented

> the most comprehensive, systematic and far-sighted initiative ever undertaken by a British government to develop strategies for tackling crime. The government also backed up its stated aim of promoting 'evidence-based' policy and practice by allocating 10 per cent of the original budget of £250 million to evaluations undertaken by external researchers – an unprecedented amount of research money in the UK crime and justice field (indeed, an early plan was to evaluate *every* project). If the visions of its original designers and champions had been realized, we would by now be in possession of a library of dependable knowledge about the effectiveness and cost-effectiveness of a wide array of interventions, and would be witnessing a systematic 'roll-out' across the country of those strategies and methods found to work 'best' among the 1500 projects funded under the CRP.
>
> (Maguire 2004: 214)

Four key areas became Pathfinder programmes for probation under the CRP: general offending behaviour programmes, basic skills programmes, enhanced community service and resettlement projects for short-term prisoners. If national implementation of What Works had been risky, then the Pathfinder programmes – part of an ambitious effort to show that crime could be reduced, and with substantial research to evaluate their impact built in – added to the risk. Probation was about to be evaluated more comprehensively than ever before.

The service was also extending its responsibilities as a result of the 1998 Crime and Disorder Act. The Act led to the introduction in every local authority of Crime and Disorder Reduction Partnerships (CDRPs) which would work together to reduce crime. Local probation services were statutorily obliged to participate in CDRPs, which, if there were several local authorities in a probation service area, meant that considerable resources might have to be used. The Act also introduced the Drug Treatment and Testing Order (DTTO), a new community penalty that could last for between six months and three years, and where the offender's consent was necessary. Much of the thinking behind DTTOs had come from the example of US drug courts which were perceived as having led to reductions in offending (Turnbull et al. 2000).

The DTTO was significant for several reasons. First, with regard to the 'testing' part of the order, an offender was required to permit drug testing (usually via a urine sample) and this was a major development for probation staff. Given Napo's opposition to electronic monitoring, it is no surprise that they had also been opposed to the idea of drug testing individuals (invasion of privacy, attacking human rights). But it is a sign of just how far the probation service had moved on from its traditional welfare role – partly in recognition of the importance of drugs as drivers of crime – that there was no serious opposition to DTTOs (a more cynical explanation might be that in general most of the actual drug testing for DTTOs was not carried out by probation officers). The second significant aspect of the order was that it incorporated a review, whereby the offender would attend the court which had made the order so that his or her progress could be assessed. Sentence review was a novel development in England and Wales and would obviously lead to increased demands on probation officers.

Alongside this increase in work, it should be remembered that since 1996 no new probation officers had been recruited and trained. How far the vacuum in probation training and recruitment would have lasted under the Conservatives is an interesting question, but Jack Straw, the Labour Home Secretary, announced that probation training would begin again in 1998. There was, however, to be a key difference between the old training scheme and the new one. Previously probation officers had been trained as social workers, whereas the new training scheme (leading to a Diploma in Probation Studies) broke the link with social work and was much more oriented towards criminal justice. As Whitehead and Statham (2006: 162) rightly state: 'if you want to change the culture of an organisation you need to change the staff within it' and taking control of training was one vital way of affecting culture. Central control over three fundamental aspects of probation work – funding (with the imposition of cash limits), programme development (via the Accreditation Panel) and training – had thus been imposed by the end of the century, and that is not taking account of *national* standards. The local nature of probation was being remodelled.

The (quasi-official) role of community penalties as alternatives to custody had been officially ended as a result of the 1991 Act, although the combination order was certainly aimed at offenders who might have received a short custodial sentence. Following Michael Howard's assertion that 'Prison works' and the deliberate decision to follow a more punitive policy, prison numbers had increased since 1993 and – as the Labour government took a similar approach – showed no signs of decreasing. The average prison population in 1993 had been 44,500; by 1997, when Labour came to power it was 61,100 (an increase of 37 per cent) and by 2000 it was 64,600 (a 45 per cent increase in seven years). Shortly after Labour had won the 1997 election, the House of Commons Home Affairs Committee launched an inquiry into the growing prison population, which they saw as 'unsustainable. Unless halted – and in due course reversed – it will end badly' (House of Commons 1998: lxii). The Committee did not attempt to carry out any analysis of the reasons for the growing use of prison (which was due to a considerable growth in short custodial sentences and the increased use of community penalties for summary offences) and its conclusions were simplistic: alternatives to custody must be used more often. In other words, community sentences should return to the place they had held prior to the 1991 Criminal Justice Act – not perhaps a particularly helpful conclusion, but one that demonstrated the lack of clarity about how community sentences should be used. While the Committee's inquiry was underway, so was the prisons–probation review, and while the idea of a national service was not discussed to any great extent by the Home Affairs Committee, it is interesting to note that Napo was in favour of a national service but Graham Smith – the chief probation inspector – was more cautious (House of Commons 1998: xxxv).

One fascinating indicator of just how far the image of probation had moved came with the BBC1 series *Jack of Hearts*, which was shown in August/September 1999. The drama, about a probation officer, focused on the hero's personal life as well as his work, and the main character wore a leather jacket, appeared unshaven and looked – and acted – rather more like a tough detective than a traditional probation officer. Jack Denby was played by Keith Allen, an actor with an edgy reputation, so while the probation work had not changed much the look of the probation officer had (clearly the drama was not a success as it only ran for six episodes).

The culmination of 15 years of fragmented initiatives and changes that had tended to point in the same overall direction came with the 2000 Criminal Justice and Court Services Act, which created a National Probation Service (NPS). This was a profoundly important development; probation had been, since its beginnings, a local service with a great deal of local autonomy. Admittedly, this had been reduced – slowly and indirectly at first and rather more rapidly since 1984 – but the local nature of probation was held up by most probation officers, and certainly by ACOP (whose members probably had most to lose), as one of its defining characteristics. Centralisation did have some advantages as Martin Wargent, an ex-CPO who became chief executive of the Probation Boards' Association, recognised, although he also noted potential tensions:

> The creation of the National Probation Service constitutes a major change of governance, a definitive act of centralisation. It certainly gives the service a stronger and much needed national voice, a higher political profile and hopefully, the benefit of some consistency in practice. But how well might the balance between local and central be struck? What cognisance will be given to the need for independent judgement about the crime reduction needs of local areas, and the availability of local knowledge?
>
> (Wargent 2002: 190)

And although Napo welcomed in principle the development of a national service, its Chair was concerned that 'the "straitjacketing" of the probation service, for political reasons, will do long-term damage to the traditional independence, creativity, and free-thinking which lies at the heart of the Service's effectiveness in working with offenders and protecting local communities' (Ledger 2001: 213).

The NPS came into being in April 2001. Amalgamations meant that the previous 54 local services were reduced to 42 local probation areas, which were co-terminus with police force and CPS area boundaries in order to facilitate cross-agency work (but not with Youth Offending Teams which were local authority-based). The chief officers for each area were employed and appointed by the Home Office, and many of these were new appointments as around half of the CPOs who had been in post prior to April 2001 left the probation service (encouraged perhaps by a substantial redundancy package). The NPS as a whole would be led by a national director (the first was Eithne Wallis who had been CPO of the Oxfordshire and Buckinghamshire probation service before taking up a post in the Home Office to manage the change process to a national service), and would be 100 per cent funded by government. Each local probation area was to be governed by a Probation Board (the chief officer would be a member) whose members would have to be approved by the Home Office. Boards were, in a sense, a fig leaf to retain some sense of local input to how area services were run; in fact, Boards had very little scope to develop their own policies, essentially they looked after the rowing while the National Directorate and the Home Office did the steering. With a national director running the National Probation Service, there would be far less difficulty in government imposing its wishes on a number of different, 'independent' probation services (remember the inconsistent response to SNOP), policies could be driven through more effectively, and direct accountability could be strengthened.

The 2000 Act also turned the NPS into a fully fledged criminal justice agency as it ended probation's responsibility for family court welfare services by hiving off this part of the service's work into the new Children and Family Court Advisory and Support Service (CAFCASS). Although civil work had been moving towards the margins for some years, it had been part of probation since its beginnings and accounted for perhaps 10–15 per cent of all probation work. The names of the three main community orders were clumsily changed, as the prisons–probation review had suggested: the probation order became the community rehabilitation order (CRO); the community service order became the community punishment order (CPO); and the combination order, with considerable ingenuity, became the community punishment and rehabilitation order (CPRO). A new order was introduced by the Act: the exclusion order, whereby an offender could be ordered not to enter a certain area for up to 12 months. And a drug abstinence order became another requirement that could be added to a CRO or CPRO. By 2001, therefore, there were more than half a dozen community penalties with more than 15 separate specified requirements that could be added to the CRO or CPRO.

In addition, the Act introduced Multi-Agency Public Protection Panels (MAPPPs) whereby the police and the probation service had to work together to manage the risks posed by sexual and other high-risk offenders. This was another significant step for probation; in the past, probation officers and police officers would not have mixed well professionally, but MAPPPs seem to have been a success story (Kemshall et al. 2005) as the police came to acknowledge the expertise of probation in risk assessment and probation learnt to understand how the police can help keep high-risk offenders in the community.

Victim contact work, too, was extended by the Act. Prior to this, victim contact work had not been a statutory part of probation work and had been restricted for the most part to those cases where the offender had been sentenced to four years or longer. The Act made victim contact work statutory from April 2001 in cases where the offender had been sentenced to 12 months imprisonment or longer.

Following such a major change in organisation and operation, a period of calm might have been expected to permit the changes time to bed down.

From the NPS to NOMS

While it might have been expected that the NPS was headed in a new direction, semantics suggested something more confusing. *A New Choreography* (Home Office 2001a), which set out the strategic framework for the NPS for its first three years, was certainly replete with managerial terms such as 'strategic imperatives' and 'stretch objectives' which were alien to the probation service, but it is also worth bearing in mind that a dance (new or otherwise) does not tend to lead in a new direction; dancing sees the dancers moving around an area, changing partners perhaps, but ultimately ending up where they began. The nine stretch objectives set out for the NPS were:

- more accurate and effective assessment and management of risk and dangerousness;
- more contact and involvement with the victims of serious sexual and other violent crime;
- the production and delivery of offender programmes which have a proven track record in reducing reoffending;
- intervening early to take young people away from crime;
- enforcement (despite being acknowledged as having the 'highest priority' (Home Office 2001a: 29), this had the least attention paid to it);
- providing courts with good information and pre-trial services;
- valuing and achieving diversity in the NPS and the services it provides;
- building an excellent organisation that is fit for purpose;
- building an effective performance management framework.

Only the last two of these objectives could be said to be new, and they were a welcome recognition that for an organisation to be effective it has to pay attention to its structures, procedures and processes. Overall, however, the objectives had a series of challenging targets to be met within a specified timescale, and these were linked to 'a financial inducement in the cash limit formula to encourage local Probation Boards to improve performance and contribute to the national targets' (Home Office 2001a: 49). Payment by results was not something that probation officers had encountered previously and it could not be said to fit comfortably with traditional probation culture.

By 2001, then, the NPS was building a new organisation, heavily involved in the development of Pathfinder programmes that were being evaluated, getting up to speed with DTTOs and MAPPPs, and facing targets that were designed to be demanding with the threat of cuts in budget and the loss of government support if successful delivery was not achieved. This combination of demands was asking a lot of an organisation that had been under real pressure for almost a decade and the NPS struggled.

Regular performance reports were sent to all probation areas by the National Directorate and these made for worrying reading. The report for the year ending 2001/2, for example, shows what can only be described as serious failure on several key measures: in enforcement, only one area was above target; for accredited programme completions (and this had implications for the evaluations of Pathfinder programmes), only four areas were at or above target; and only three areas hit the target for PSR timeliness (National Probation Service 2002). Two years later, while the situation had improved, it was still the case that the majority of areas were failing to hit targets: for enforcement 13 areas hit the target; for accredited programme completions a total of 20 areas achieved the target; and for PSR timeliness no area hit the target, a drop in performance that may have something to do with this measure being cash-linked in 2001/2 but not in 2003/4 (National Probation Service 2004). How far these failures can be related to challenging targets and a number of demanding initiatives resulting in a sick and demoralised workforce is an interesting question. In 2001/2, eight areas met the sickness absence measure of 10 days (the average days absence from July 2001 to March 2002 was 12.59 days), while in 2003/4 only five areas achieved this target (average days absence for April 2003 to March 2004 was 12.3 days).[1]

The results of the Pathfinder projects did not live up to expectations, although one of the problems here was that expectations were much too high in the first place. Rightly or wrongly, there was a feeling from all the activity emanating from the What Works initiative that programmes based on cognitive behavioural therapy offered the answer to offending, although Rod Morgan, the new chief inspector of probation, sounded a warning note when in his first annual report he cautioned against 'programme fetishism' (Morgan 2002: 8). It would be hard to deny probation staff the right to feel positive after all of the difficulties of the previous decade, but it was clear from the academic debates that swirled around What Works that its prescriptions were not as clear-cut as might have been desirable – or even possible. No matter where an individual was located on the What Works debate, there was substantial agreement that the Pathfinder projects had not really delivered:

> Overall, it is fair to conclude that the Pathfinder studies carried out in the probation service have not delivered the unambiguous endorsement of

the methods and processes of the 'What Works' project which its leaders, drawing on the international research, originally expected.

(Raynor 2004: 314)

the evidence from rigorously conducted reconviction studies suggests that we are unlikely to see a major impact on reoffending rates, as promised by the 'What Works' literature, from programmes alone.

(Merrington and Stanley 2004: 18)

While it must be emphasised that the full results of the What Works programmes have yet to appear, the indicators ... are not especially encouraging.

(Mair 2004a: 28)

The obstacles to success had been present from the beginning, but were much easier to recognise with hindsight. The political demand for clear, positive find-ings within a relatively short time scale was much too ambitious. There were many implementation problems with the projects themselves. Staffing difficulties meant that projects were not always fully staffed with properly trained workers. As we have already noted, the introduction of the NPS and new tasks for the probation service meant that resources were stretched in too many directions. The need to get offenders on to programmes (and hit targets) had implications for successful completion as inappropriate allocation could lead to a lower likelihood of successful completion. There was also a tension between getting offenders on to programmes and the need for rigorous enforcement, and this too had implica-tions for completion (and the one reasonably consistent – though not surprising – finding from the Pathfinder evaluations was that successful completion meant a lower chance of reconviction). Even some of the researchers realised that they had some responsibility for what had happened: 'a valid criticism that can be laid at the door of most evaluators, myself included, is that they did too little (in the early days at least) to warn the Home Office that too much was being expected of the research it was commissioning' (Maguire 2004: 228). Nor were matters helped by the Home Office decision to publish the results of the evaluations in a haphazard and fragmented fashion in a range of formats, or even not to publish at all (Mair 2008).[2] Perhaps fortunately for the NPS, the Home Office tended to blame the research, despite the fact that, as Peter Raynor (2008) has pointed out, many of the methodological decisions had been decided in advance by the Home Office.

Even if the What Works initiative had been a failure in terms of its intended outcome of reduced reconviction rates, however, it was acknowledged by chief probation officers that it might have other, significant positive outcomes:

It had given the probation service a public profile and offered increased credibility that had been conspicuously absent in the past. It would help to change the culture of the probation service from a welfare-oriented, 'soft' organisation to one where staff were fully accountable and fully committed to being part of a criminal justice agency. It would help to unify the service nationally and lead to greater consistency in work with offenders. Even if the accredited programmes did not succeed, the basic idea behind What Works of monitoring and rigorously evaluating practice, and replacing less effective programmes with more effective ones, was a major step forward.

(Mair 2004b: 275)

From this point of view, What Works becomes the key to a radical change in probation culture.

One of the difficulties that hindered the What Works initiative was the delay in preparing a new risk/needs assessment tool. OASys (the Offender Assessment System) was a key factor in several developments: first, as a national assessment tool it was intimately related to a national service; second, it was intended for use by both the prison and probation services, thereby linking both organisations more closely; and, third, it was considered important for What Works as accurate, systematic assessment of offenders and matching them to appropriate programmes was agreed to be a key factor in effective outcomes (see Robinson 1999, 2001, 2002 for a detailed discussion of the relationship between What Works and risk/ needs assessment). OASys, however, was not rolled out electronically to probation areas until 2003 and probation officers were not universally happy with it. Using a statistical tool to predict risk of custody had led to some worries; OGRS had increased anxieties about loss of autonomy and deskilling, and OASys – coming on the back of so many other developments – was not likely to be welcomed uncritically. However, a survey of probation officers' views about OASys carried out between March and December 2004 suggested that most probation officers recognised it had advantages as well as some disadvantages; on the one hand it was 'comprehensive, detailed, good for risk assessment, and helpful in focusing on factors that might have been overlooked in the past ... it was [also] time-consuming, too detailed and too inflexible' (Mair et al. 2006). Despite the potential for difficulties, OASys seems to have become established as part of probation practice remarkably quickly.

Even before the NPS had officially begun work, the government had made it clear that further changes were on the way. In *Criminal Justice: The Way Ahead* (Home Office 2001b) various reforms of the criminal justice system were mooted. In general, there was a great deal of emphasis on joined-up working so that the various criminal justice agencies would work more closely together to greater effect. More specifically, with regard to probation, there were plans to introduce 'a more flexible community sentence [which] would provide courts with a menu of options to choose from, providing elements of punishment, crime reduction and reparation, to fit both the offender and the offence' (Home Office 2001b: 42). The new sentence would be considered as part of a major review of the sentencing framework that was underway and that reported in July 2001. *Making Punishments Work* (Halliday 2001) started from the premise that improvements in the sentencing framework were necessary; the present situation was muddled, inconsistent, narrowly conceived, inflexible, did not inspire confidence and lacked transparency. The What Works initiative was seen – rather prematurely – as offering new opportunities.

The sentencing review emphasised the need to consider community sentences as alternatives to custody, thereby harking back to a pre-1991 position for the service:

- Courts should have clear discretion to pass a non-custodial sentence of sufficient severity, even when a short prison sentence could have been justified, bearing in mind their ability to resentence in the event of repeated breach of conditions.
- Unless only a prison sentence of 12 months or more would meet the needs for punishment, sentencers should consider the scope for a community sentence to meet the needs of punishment, crime reduction and reparation.

(Halliday 2001: 21)

At the same time, it argued for a new sentence of 'custody plus', whereby any custodial sentence of less than 12 months would consist of a period in prison (a maximum of 3 months) and a period of supervision in the community lasting a minimum of 6 months. Intermittent custody was also discussed, as was the possibility of a new form of suspended sentence. The implementation of such ideas had implications for probation as they would lead to more work for the service. But such increased resources would come with a price in terms of increased punitiveness:

> Wider recognition that, for imprisonable offences, non-custodial sentences are, in effect, 'conditional' prison sentences should enhance their credibility and effectiveness. A new framework could make this even clearer, through the way it was expressed. A visible sanction of imprisonment for breach of conditions, if absolutely necessary backed up by closer monitoring and tougher enforcement, could justify increased use of non-custodial sentences.

(Halliday 2001: 37)

A new community punishment order was recommended which would replace the existing community sentences, and which would have a range of requirements. Pre-sentence reports were considered to be a vital part of Halliday's proposals, but these were intended to become focused upon the assessment and management of risk, using OASys. Just as significant as the proposals in the report was the language used: Halliday popularised such terms as 'sentence management' and 'the seamless sentence', both of which came with cool, detached, technocratic connotations.

A White Paper (Home Office 2002) endorsed the Halliday report and legislation followed. The Criminal Justice Act 2003 introduced the community order, the suspended sentence order (SSO), the intermittent custody order (piloted for a short time and then quietly dropped) and a custody plus order (implementation of which has been delayed indefinitely). The community order replaced existing community sentences and attempted to rationalise the various requirements that were available to the community rehabilitation order and the community rehabilitation and punishment order. The new order consisted of at least one of 12 possible requirements: supervision, unpaid work, accredited programme, drug rehabilitation, alcohol treatment, mental health treatment, residence, specified activity, prohibited activity, exclusion, curfew and attendance centre. It could last for between two hours (if the shortest requirement, a curfew, was imposed for the minimum period possible) and three years. Guidelines prepared by the Sentencing Guidelines Council (2004) made it clear that the community order could act as an alternative to custody. But so could the suspended sentence order.

The SSO is made up of the same requirements as the community order, but it is a custodial sentence, even though it should be served in the community if all goes well. It should be used when the court is minded to pass a sentence of imprisonment of less than 12 months, so the custody threshold has been passed. The SSO can run for between 6 months and two years. The two orders differ in how breach is dealt with, with the expectation for the SSO being that breach will lead to activation of the suspension. And the requirements for the SSO should be 'less onerous' (Sentencing Guidelines Council 2004: 25) than for the community order, as the punitive nature of the SSO carries with it the threat of custody in case of breach.

Despite the Criminal Justice Act 1991 making community penalties sentences in their own right, and thereby officially ruling out their use as alternatives to custody, the theme of diversion from custody remained significant as the prison population continued to rise. Between June 1994 and June 2004, the prison population had increased from 48,929 to 74,488 (a rise of 52 per cent). Numbers had been reasonably steady between 1998 and 2001, but between 2001 and 2003 there had been an increase of 11 per cent, most of it accounted for by an increase in the number of sentences for four years or longer (excluding life) and by remands in custody. A detailed study accounting for the growth in the prison population despite crime falling noted that:

> There are two main reasons why the prison population has grown. Sentencers are now imposing longer prison sentences for serious crimes, and they are more likely to imprison offenders who 10 years ago would have received a community penalty or even a fine.
>
> Tougher sentencing practice has come about through the interplay of several factors: an increasingly punitive climate of political and media debate about punishment; legislative changes and new guideline judgements; and sentencers' perceptions of changes in patterns of offending.
>
> (Hough et al. 2003: ix)

An independent inquiry into alternatives to prison was set up in 2002, chaired by Lord Coulsfield, a recently retired Scottish judge, and reported two years later (Coulsfield 2004). This report and its companion research volume

(Bottoms et al. 2004) explored in considerable detail the various sentences available to the courts, how far they were used as alternatives to custody, and whether they could be so used more effectively. Community penalties were, therefore, being defined back into the diversion from custody space they had inhabited quasi-officially from roughly 1973 until 1991.

This was confirmed by the Carter Report (Carter 2003) which had been set up to review the correctional services, and it should be noted that the use of this term was highly significant; indeed it had been prefigured by the Joint Prison/Probation Accreditation Panel being renamed the Correctional Services Accreditation Panel in 2002. Carter argued that both prison and probation were dealing with far too many low-level offenders; in Morgan's (2003: 15) phrase, probation caseloads were 'silting up ... with less serious offenders'. Sentencing had to be targeted more effectively so that probation would deal with more of those who were currently being sentenced to short terms of imprisonment, and fines would deal with those who currently were receiving community penalties. Thus, diversion from prosecution should be encouraged (again), day fines should be introduced (again), community sentences should be more demanding (a perennial recommendation), electronic monitoring should be used more widely, persistent offenders should be both punished and helped more, and prison should be reserved for the most serious offenders (again). None of these recommendations was novel, but the report's insistence upon effective end-to-end management of offenders and the inefficiencies of having two different organisations dealing with offenders, led to the first of its two radical proposals: 'The establishment of a National Offender Management Service – replacing the Prison and Probation Services, with a single Chief Executive, accountable to Ministers for punishing offenders and reducing re-offending' (Carter 2003: 43). With hindsight, this had been on the cards for at least a few years – certainly since it had been floated in *Joining Forces to Protect the Public* (Home Office 1998) – but it was surprising that it had happened so soon after the restructuring of probation into a national service only a couple of years earlier. The NPS had been given little chance to settle down and be fully evaluated, but its time was running out.

The second radical proposal was what was termed 'contestability', essentially competition from the private and voluntary sectors, which was intended to improve the provision of services for offenders, make them more target-driven, effective and efficient, and provide better value for money. Again, a probation worry for some years about the possibility of partnership leading to outside agencies taking over probation work was now becoming a reality. Further, a purchaser/provider split was built into the new structure so that 'The Regional Offender Managers would not line manage the providers of prisons, community punishments and interventions. They would have a purely contractual relationship [with providers]' (Carter 2003: 36). This proposed separation between offender management and interventions, was an almost incomprehensible development as far as the probation service was concerned.

The government response (Home Office 2004) to Carter was suspiciously fast: Carter's report was published in December 2003, while the Home Office response appeared the following month. Carter's proposals for targeted sentences, a national offender management service (NOMS) and contestability, were all accepted and NOMS was planned to begin on 1 June 2004.

100 years of probation

Napo fought hard against the proposed changes and identified a number of potentially serious risks in the government's plans:

- the risk of effectively dismantling the probation service by splitting it into two to create the purchaser/provider model;
- the risk of introducing contestability based on competition rather than on co-operation, which would lead to more and stronger separate silos rather than breaking them down;
- the risk of losing probation's historic relationship with the local community;
- the risk associated with introducing a confused governance model;
- the risk of hurried and badly prepared administrative change.

In addition, they noted further layers of bureaucracy and expenditure would be added as a result of the plans to commission services from a variety of providers, and that the proposals demonstrated a fundamental misunderstanding of the nature of the voluntary sector, which was composed to a large degree of small, flexible groups which might be disadvantaged in competing in the marketplace and whose strengths might be eroded by such competition. Ultimately, of course, if such risks were to be realised then the aim of reducing offending would be unlikely to be met (Napo 2004).

The planned legislation was seen as bringing an end to the probation service, but the Bill had to be dropped as a result of the forthcoming election. Debates about exactly what form NOMS would take rumbled on for some time (Morgan 2007). Late in 2005, two proposals in the consultation paper *Restructuring Probation to Reduce Re-offending* (Home Office 2005) were highly significant:

- to give the Secretary of State the statutory duty to make arrangements with others to provide probation services; and
- to create new bodies [trusts], replacing local probation boards, with whom he may contract.

The use of the term 'probation services' made it quite clear that services for offenders would no longer be supplied by a local probation service but by a number of agencies which might include probation as well as other public, private and community organisations. It was notable that, in 2005, the Probation Boards' Association Annual Lecture was delivered by the Director-General of the Confederation of British Industry, Sir Digby Jones, who spoke on 'Offender rehabilitation: business as a deliverer of criminal justice' (Jones 2005). A trust could conceivably, as a result of contestability, end up providing little or no interventions for offenders and would thus 'cease to exist' (Home Office 2005: 7). Responses to *Restructuring Probation to Reduce Re-offending* were by no means positive and even the government admitted that its proposals were seen as 'contentious' (Home Office 2006a: 3). Probation staff continued to worry that the government's plans meant the end for the national probation service. Despite the claims that the changes would lead to more effective targeting of interventions, improved sentence planning, better value for money – all leading to reduced reoffending – there was no evidence to support such claims; indeed, the potential for confusion, for cultural tensions between probation staff and those from private and voluntary agencies, for increased fragmentation of the probation service, for greater costs, for poor staff morale – all leading to less effective work with offenders – were ignored by government. Indeed no aspect of probation work was ruled out of the contestability process (Home Office 2006a). The first tasks that were to be subjected to contestability were expected to be unpaid work and work with victims (Home Office 2006b).

The community order and the suspended sentence order became available to the courts on 4 April 2005 for offences committed on or after that date (offences committed prior to 4 April remained subject to the CRO, CPO, CPRO, DTTO, etc.). Early research (Mair et al. 2007) suggested that there was no sign of requirement overload in either order, although the use of the SSO was double that expected by the Home Office. Half of the 12 requirements available were rarely used, and there was wide variation between probation areas in terms of the number and type of requirements used. There was no evidence to suggest that either of the orders was acting as an alternative to custody, something that the government had also concluded:

> Early evidence also suggests the new Suspended Sentence Order may be being used in cases where a community order would be appropriate … The evidence so far is that the courts are not using community orders as fully as they might. The anticipated switch to these new community sentences from short terms of imprisonment that was envisaged has not happened but is a crucial part of the package of sentencing reform we wish to achieve.
>
> (Home Office 2006c: 6–7)

The government's anxiety about the use of both orders for lower-level offenders (the reverse of what had been hoped for) was reflected in their proposal to legislate to make community orders unavailable for either all or some non-imprisonable offences (Home Office 2006c), and SSOs unavailable for summary offences (Ministry of Justice 2007a). Neither proposal was taken forward, although plans for a Higher Intensity Community Order were implemented (Ministry of Justice 2008a) despite sentencers being scornful of the idea (Mair et al. 2008).

The probation service had always remained somewhat in the background of the criminal justice system with little publicity; research suggested that the general public had little knowledge of the service and what it did, but were not necessarily unsupportive (Allen and Hough 2007; Maruna and King 2004). By 2006, however, there was considerable publicity of the wrong kind for probation; the murders of John Monckton and Robert Symons (in 2004) and Mary-Ann Leneghan and Naomi Bryant (both in 2005) led to sustained criticism of the service for failing to supervise effectively those responsible for the murders. Although the pressures under which probation officers were working were rightly condemned and mistakes had been made (Bridges 2006a, 2006b), to hold the probation service wholly responsible for the deaths was unjustified. However, the Home Secretary at the beginning of 2006 (Charles Clarke) had been quoted as considering the probation service as 'the dagger at the heart of the criminal justice system, undermining public confidence in criminal justice as a whole' (Allen and Hough 2007: 566) and his successor John Reid later the same year claimed that 'the probation service is not working as well as it should' (BBC News 2006). Perhaps this explains the tone of *Improving Prison and Probation Services* (Home Office 2006b) and the Ministry of Justice[3] paper published to present the new department to the public where the need to introduce other providers of services for offenders than the probation service is very evident:

> At the heart of our vision is end-to-end case management for offenders, and a strong focus on commissioning the most effective interventions for men and women which will best support the management and rehabilitation of offenders. This includes the systematic identification of which interventions work best, encouraging providers to innovate to improve the effectiveness of interventions, *making use of the fullest range of providers – including public, private and voluntary sectors* – and the strategic management of providers with a strong focus on delivering outcomes.
>
> (Ministry of Justice 2007b: 12, emphasis added)

On 26 July 2007, the Offender Management Act received Royal Assent. Napo had campaigned vigorously against several of its key proposals and had achieved some success, but the Act radically changed the position of the probation service. The Act set out the new arrangements for the provision of 'probation services' (and we have already noted the significance of this term) which could be provided by a variety of providers – public, private or voluntary. The probation service as (effectively) monopoly provider of community interventions for offenders – a situation that had lasted for 100 years notwithstanding the introduction of senior attendance centres and electronic monitoring – was gone in the same year that the service celebrated its 100th birthday.

The Act also replaced probation boards with trusts which were to be more business-oriented than their predecessors. Trusts were expected to be the primary providers of probation services for an area, but the commissioning of services could take place at local, regional or national level. The Justice Secretary became ultimately responsible for the provision of probation services and could use prison staff for this purpose if appropriate. While this opened up any aspect of probation work to competition, the Act did state that core offender management work would remain with the probation service until at least 2010, and that court work would not be awarded to any non-public sector provider (although this restriction could be repealed by both Houses of Parliament).

At the same time, the structure of NOMS was continuing to undergo repeated tinkering, leading in the end to probation becoming, according to a NOMS official, 'just a small community wing of the prison service' (McKnight 2009: 337). Prison numbers continued to grow so that by 2006 the average population in custody was 78,100, an increase of more than 10,000 since 2001. The situation was becoming serious and once again the government turned to Patrick Carter to report on ways of resolving the pressures on the prison system. Carter's new report (Carter 2007) scarcely mentioned the possibility of trying to use community sentences as alternatives to custody; it was almost as if he had given up on this as a realistic response to the problem. Instead, he focused on the need to start building new prisons so that up to 6,500 additional places would be in place by the end of 2010. The House of Commons Justice Committee (2008) also addressed the issue of prison numbers, although in the wider context of sentencing policy, and it did return to the theme of using community sentences to divert from custody. The Committee did not mince matters: 'A key element of the coherent sentencing strategy envisaged under the Criminal Justice Act 2003 was to deal with low level offenders by community punishments rather than short custodial sentences. It is clear that this strategy has not worked' (House of Commons Justice Committee 2008: 34). The government was urged to ensure that non-custodial sentences were adequately funded, that they were more effectively targeted (the Committee argued that the new orders were displacing fines), that the availability of requirements needed to be audited, and that while the government had allocated an extra £40 million for probation in 2008/9 this might not be adequate as

> The probation service does not know with any certainty how many Community Orders it has the potential capacity to deliver within its resources, nor has it determined the full cost of delivering Community Orders; we recommend that this [sic] data be collated as a matter of urgency.
>
> (House of Commons Justice Committee 2008: 47)

The Committee made use of a study carried out into community orders by the National Audit Office (2008) which pointed to inconsistencies in the use of the order, a lack of certain requirements resulting in long waiting lists, a lack of data on completion of requirements, and a lack of knowledge on the part of the probation service about capacity and resources. The NAO report was also behind a critical report on community orders by the House of Commons Committee of Public Accounts (2008). Yet in 2008 127,600 community orders were made by the courts and the new sentence was liked by sentencers; in the same year, 41,100 suspended sentence orders were passed, although sentencers were not quite so positive about them as they were thought to have been used too often and not as appropriately as they should be (Mair et al. 2008). The government response to the Justice Select Committee report was anodyne and failed to provide convincing arguments to rebut the Committee's criticism (Ministry of Justice 2008b).

There was yet more criticism of the community order in the report prepared for the Cabinet Office by Louise Casey (2008). The focus of this study was on how the 'community' might be more involved in the fight against crime, and the low public profile of community orders was noted as was their use: 'the increase in the number of offenders getting community sentences when they might in the past have been fined has placed a greater strain on the capacity of probation services to manage community orders that punish offenders effectively' (Casey 2008: 49). Casey was keen on pushing the profile of unpaid work (one of the 12 requirements available for community orders and SSOs) and proposed that it be made more visible to the community, renamed (again) as Community Payback, contracted out from probation, made more demanding by making offenders work more frequently and for longer periods, and that PSRs should no longer be necessary to assess suitability for work. Unpaid work was the most commonly used requirement for both community orders and SSOs, and in December 2008 high visibility vests were introduced for those starting Community Payback – a development that many probation officers considered to be unnecessarily humiliating and possibly dangerous for offenders. The government response to Casey was positive with plans to give the public a chance to suggest what work might be done as Community Payback, make it more timely so that offenders could start work within five days instead of ten, and expand the use of Intensive Community Payback schemes (Office for Criminal Justice Reform 2009).

By 2008 it looked as if the probation service was in the middle of a perfect storm: the government approach to criminal justice meant that the service was attacked as being too soft (not that this was an unusual claim); it was being swallowed up in the NOMS monster by the prison service; it was held to be responsible for several high-profile murders; its new community order was not achieving what had been hoped and the prison population continued to rise; and its work was about to be put out to competitive tender. These were very much local to probation. The biggest threat, however, was on a global scale as the financial crisis of 2008 began to bite into government spending plans. Major cuts to the Ministry of Justice budget were reported at the end of 2007 (Napo 2007/8) and 12 months later this had become a 25 per cent cut in the probation budget (Napo 2008/9). By the end of 2009, the situation had improved slightly:

> The probation service faces a cut of 4% in real terms to its budget in the financial year 2010/11. Further cuts of at least a similar amount are thought certain to occur in financial year 2011/12. These cuts are bound to lead to the loss of posts, a curtailment and a reduction in the number of offender programmes that the probation service currently provides. The Probation budget will be cut by £24 million in the financial year 2010/11, from an outturn in the previous financial year of £894 million. However this is an improvement on the indicative budget which was issued in October.

That anticipated a cut of £50 million in the financial year 2010/11 and a similar cut in 2011/12.

(Napo 2009/10b: 2)

By 2009, the average prison population was 83,500 and plans were underway to increase the capacity of prisons to 96,000 places by 2014; competition was to be the way forward in improving efficiency and innovation for both prisons and probation because

> Competition is a proven mechanism to improve performance and price, whether it be in the previously nationalised utilities, such as electricity or telephones, or in public services such as refuse collection, or offender services and prison provision.

(Ministry of Justice 2009a: 7)

Unfortunately, dealing with offenders is not the same as providing electricity, telephones or refuse collection; and there was no conclusive evidence to show that competition had improved offender services and prison provision, despite the government's claims. But Best Value reviews for Community Payback and Victim Contact were planned for 2009/10, and Probation Trusts were expected to replace Boards. If Boards failed to show that they met the standards required of Trusts then they might be merged with 'successful neighbouring Trusts, or alternatively, its services will be competed in the open market' (Ministry of Justice 2009a: 12).

The probation statistics for 2009 provided a mixed message. The service was preparing more PSRs than ever – in 2009 a total of 217,858 reports were prepared, an increase of 4 per cent from 2006 – but the number of traditional PSRs (known as standard PSRs) decreased by 35 per cent while fast delivery reports increased by 87 per cent (indeed written fast delivery reports grew by 47 per cent while oral FDRs grew by a remarkable 1,000 per cent). While the numbers starting supervision as a result of court orders increased by 7 per cent between 2006 and 2009 (from 155,614 to 166,387), the caseload decreased by 4 per cent (from 146,532 to 140,951) because the average length of a community order dropped from 17.6 months to 13 months during these years. Over the same period, the average length of an SSO remained stable (17.4 months in 2006 and 17.1 months in 2009). Almost half of community orders were made for summary offences (48 per cent compared with 50 per cent in 2006) while for SSOs the figure was 34 per cent (42 per cent in 2006). With regard to supervision tiers, both orders seemed to be moving towards less serious offenders: in 2007, 27 per cent of those starting community orders were classified as Tier 1 (requiring least intervention) while the figure for 2009 was 37 per cent; for SSOs the figures were 14 per cent in 2006 and 25 per cent in 2009. There was also some evidence that the more rehabilitative requirements were being used less often for both orders: for the community order, the use of the supervision requirement fell from 36 per cent in 2006 to 34 per cent in 2009, while use of the accredited programme requirement (in many ways the backbone of the What Works initiative) dropped from 16 per cent to 10 per cent; in the case of the SSO, supervision fell from 42 per cent to 37 per cent and accredited programmes from 20 per cent to 14 per cent. On the other hand, more punitive requirements appeared to be becoming more popular as the use of unpaid work and the curfew requirement had increased for both orders. Both orders were more likely to be completed successfully, although in both cases more than one-third of orders were terminated early as a result of failure.

All of this suggests that the service is working harder than ever in terms of reports and court orders, but that there is less time available for work. The traditional skills of probation officers in spending time with offenders and getting to know their problems are disappearing (the huge increase in oral fast delivery reports is particularly significant). And there is evidence that orders are becoming more punitive while a considerable proportion of orders are made on those convicted of summary offences. In addition, there is little sign that either of the new orders is having any impact as an alternative to custody (Mair and Mills 2009).

Labour plans to cut probation expenditure were justified on the grounds that funding had risen considerably since 2001, but two recent publications have questioned such claims (Centre for Crime and Justice Studies 2010; Mills et al. 2010). While expenditure did increase significantly for the first five years of this decade, most of this increase resulted from two developments: the creation of the NPS and the implementation of the new sentencing framework following the 2003 Criminal Justice Act. Since 2005/6 increases in expenditure have been much more modest. Staff numbers seem to have kept pace with the increases in caseload, but this is only when the total number of staff is considered: senior managers increased by 78 per cent between 1998 and 2008; qualified probation officers, however, have increased by only 7 per cent; probation service officers (PSOs, who are not fully qualified), however, have increased by 177 per cent. Indeed, there are now more PSOs than qualified POs in the probation service (Mills et al. 2010). The possible implications of this situation where less-qualified staff are working with increasing numbers of offenders are considerable: compliance with orders may be less likely and further offending more likely. Indeed, the situation may worsen. The new Probation Qualifications Framework (Ministry of Justice 2009b) introduced in 2010 means that those appointed to supervisory roles are now all initially employed as probation service officers, only some of whom will go on to become fully qualified POs. This is likely to result in the PSO/PO balance shifting even further towards the former, with PSOs becoming involved in an even wider range of responsibilities that traditionally had been part of a PO's work, even if only as a result of financial considerations.

The organisation of the community order and the SSO may be doing the service no favours either. At the heart of effective probation work lies a good relationship between offender and supervisor, but the new orders do not encourage such a relationship: the various requirements may be supervised by different individuals; the offender manager who is expected to make the order a coherent whole may rarely see the offender (indeed, a leaked document has recently suggested that offender managers spend only 24 per cent of their time in direct contact with offenders, either face-to-face or by telephone: Napo 2009/10a); and some requirements may be supervised not by probation staff but by members of a voluntary or private agency. Thus the coherence of the old probation order is fragmented and offenders may perceive two or three requirements as different sentences.

As we write, a new government has been in power for six months. In the first few months ministers had little to say about the probation service, being far too preoccupied with the serious financial problems facing the country, but the troubles facing the service are only likely to worsen. The Ministry of Justice, like all government departments, was instructed to plan for cuts of at least 25 per cent and possibly 40 per cent. It is difficult to see how any organisation could continue to function effectively if one-quarter of its resources are cut and the consequences for the probation service can scarcely be contemplated. Ken Clarke, in his first major speech as Justice Secretary (Clarke 2010), talked of a rehabilitation revolution, but as he conspicuously failed to mention the probation service it was all too easy to imagine the worst. He was critical of imprisonment: 'Too often prison has proved a costly and ineffectual approach that fails to turn criminals into law-abiding citizens' (Clarke 2010: 6). One might be forgiven for speculating how far this is a pragmatic response to the continuing rise in the prison population and a need to save money, rather than an article of faith. What was needed was

> a far more constructive approach. This means prisons that are places of punishment, but also of education, hard work and change. It means rigorously enforced community sentences that punish offenders, but also get them off drugs and alcohol abuse and into employment. The voluntary and private sectors will be crucial to our success. We want to make far better use of their enthusiasm and expertise to get offenders away from the revolving door of crime and prison. The most radical part of our new approach ... will involve paying independent organisations by results in reducing reoffending.
>
> (Clarke 2010: 7)

To a certain extent, this was depressingly familiar; prison numbers mean that community sentences must be made more demanding so that they will be used more often to divert offenders from custody. How much more demanding can community sentences become before they lose their 'community' orientation? Already the SSO has not just blurred the boundaries between community and custody but has erased them. And there is no evidence from the past that making such sentences more rigorous has had any impact on the numbers being sentenced to imprisonment. The difference this time is that the probation service does not appear to be part of the 'solution'; Clarke puts his faith in the private and voluntary sectors and the fragmented nature of the community order and the SSO would appear to be perfectly suited to such a piecemeal policy. The Green Paper published in December 2010 (Ministry of Justice 2010) built on Clarke's speech, promising decentralisation and greater freedom for those working with offenders, which could lead to probation staff regaining some of the discretion they have lost but could also mean less accountability and greater inconsistency. It also promises to open up the market for rehabilitation services to new providers from the private, voluntary and community sectors and makes it clear that such services will no longer be provided 'directly without testing where the private, voluntary or community sectors can provide it more effectively and efficiently' (Ministry of Justice 2010: 41).

After more than one hundred years of work with offenders, often with little encouragement or recognition for their efforts, a small island of decency and humanity in the criminal justice system may be disappearing. There have been times when the probation service has looked to be in trouble, but this time the future looks bleak indeed.

9   Concluding reflections

There could be little argument with the claim that the probation service has changed considerably during its 100 years of existence. Starting with the size of the service, it has grown from a few hundred officers in 1908 to more than 21,000 staff, including administrative and support staff, in 2008 (the most recent estimate; see Mills et al. 2010). This may seem like a large increase in numbers, but it has taken place over the course of a century, other criminal justice agencies have experienced similar – if not greater – levels of growth, and that compared with the police (with more than 200,000 staff) and the prison service (with around 50,000), the probation service is a small organisation.

One of the consequences of such growth is a need for structure and bureaucracy and the service now has a hierarchy of roles, a defined organisational structure, and probably around 25 per cent of its staff involved in what might be termed as bureaucratic tasks (administration and management) which involve no significant work with offenders. It is important to acknowledge, however, that such developments are a normal concomitant to the growth of an organisation, and that they have been developing over 100 years. What is seen – usually pejoratively – as managerialism is only another step in forms of organising and managing probation work that have taken place since its beginnings. And despite what – in the 1980s and 1990s – seemed like a wish to return to a romanticised past where management had no significant place in its work, there is no doubt that with the growth of the organisation and the increase in its responsibilities, probation needed good management. With the considerable autonomy permitted to probation officers for most of the history of the service, and the relative freedom of principal (and then chief) probation officers to manage as they saw fit, there was wide scope for very different styles of management – poor as well as effective. In the long run, this could only have led to inconsistent work with offenders and weak representation of the service to government. Whatever the quality of probation management today, chief executives are aware of the need to lead and manage their staff to achieve clear objectives, which was not the case for much of probation's history.

Of course, no matter how well chief executives manage their staff, a crucial difference is that probation is no longer subject to local control. Originally managed by local justices of the peace, then by principal (chief) probation officers, probation services were defined by the fact that they were local agencies; if they were accountable, they were accountable to local magistrates and to local authorities. Despite occasional visits by probation inspectors, chief probation officers were – to a large extent – free to run their services as they saw fit. As we have shown, slowly and without any conscious plans about taking overall control, the Home Office intruded step by step onto probation's domain. For much of the time this was welcomed (or at least not opposed) by probation staff as it increased their responsibilities and power. But from the second half of the 1980s when, relatively quickly, what probation did, how it did it, its financing and its training all became directly controlled by the Home Office, relationships with government became seriously strained. Probation is now centrally directed, although there is little evidence to suggest that the Ministry of Justice (or its predecessor, the Home Office) has any idea about how to run a probation service. In theory, a national service directed by a government department could have strengthened probation as its three national organisations (ACOP, CCPC and Napo) rarely acted together and had little power. A place at the centre of government should have given probation a more powerful voice. In practice, probation seems to have even less credibility and authority since it became a national service as it has been overwhelmed by its partner in NOMS, the prison service.

Along with the growth of the service, there have been changes in its responsibilities. For more than half of its existence, probation's clientele was characterised by its youthfulness; as late as 1970, almost half (47 per cent) of those placed on probation for indictable offences were under the age of 17 (Home Office 1972). By 1981, only 9 per cent of those receiving criminal supervision by the probation service were under the age of 17, while, today, probation only deals with offenders under court orders aged 18 and above, and only 1 per cent of its 2009 caseload was aged under 18. So juveniles are no longer a probation responsibility and it is worth recalling that only a few years ago the Youth Justice Board attempted to take responsibility for young adults in addition to juveniles. As well as losing juveniles, probation has also lost civil work – a small but significant part of probation work for almost 100 years. And it has lost the myriad of miscellaneous tasks such as advice about difficult children and neighbours' quarrels that the Morison Committee still considered to be appropriate for the probation service to carry out in 1962 (see Chapter 6).

Major tasks were taken on too, or minor ones grew to become a significant part of probation work. Perhaps the most important addition to probation's responsibilities was the introduction of community service (now known as Community Payback, its fourth title). The popularity of community service meant that within ten years almost two-fifths (38 per cent) of those commencing criminal supervision were made up of community service commencements; the figure for probation was 45 per cent. Today, Community Payback is the most popular form of community orders and SSOs (suspended sentence orders), making up one-third of the former and one-fifth of the latter passed by the courts (a supervision requirement makes up 12 per cent of community orders and 11 per cent of SSOs). Community service meant the arrival of staff working with offenders who were not trained probation officers; their expertise might be in painting and decorating, gardening, woodwork, or working with old people, but they were not trained social workers and brought a new ethos into traditional probation culture. Community service also meant a shift from probation's focus on rehabilitation, as reparation and punishment – although not perhaps as clearly articulated as they might have been – entered the probation repertoire.

Probation also has a presence in prisons, working with inmates to prepare them for resettlement in the community, and supervises a large number of released prisoners every year. At the end of 2009, more than 102,000 individuals were subject to pre- and post-release supervision by the probation service, compared with 141,000 subject to court orders. Working with prisoners – whether in custody or after release – has meant that probation's community focus has become blurred and that it has had to deal with higher-risk offenders. The introduction of the suspended sentence order in 2005 has now erased the boundary between custody and community completely, as probation staff routinely supervise offenders who have been given a custodial sentence (albeit one that is served in the community if all goes well).

From a relatively informal role, reports for the courts have grown to become a crucial part of probation work and in 2009 a total of around 230,000 reports were prepared (including those prepared for breach hearings and following a deferred sentence). PSRs (pre-sentence reports) are aimed at helping sentencers to decide upon the most appropriate sentence, but they also act as a showcase for probation expertise and offer a chance to encourage use of its services. PSRs are perhaps the key nexus where probation officers and sentencers can meet, and it is notable that court reports are one probation task that has not been immediately considered for contestability (although this situation could, of course, easily change).

Over the years, an increasing number of requirements have been introduced as conditions that could be added onto the traditional probation order (and subsequently to the combination order). By 1992 there were 14 separate specific requirements listed in the Probation Statistics (along with an 'Other' category) and by 2004 half of community rehabilitation orders had an added requirement. Requirements had several consequences: first, they made probation orders more rigorous and demanding; second, they often required the expertise of non-probation staff (e.g. drugs workers, mental health professionals); and third, they fragmented the simplicity of the traditional order. Their inexorable growth led to the introduction of the community order and the suspended sentence order in 2005, sentences which are defined by their requirements.

In addition, the service has also taken on various tasks that would not have been considered appropriate 30 years ago:

• The Drug Treatment and Testing Order (DTTO) was not welcomed universally by probation officers as the idea of drug testing offenders was abhorrent to many of them. It was considered demeaning to offenders and an infringement of their civil liberties. Yet within four years of its introduction in October 2000, almost 8,500 offenders started a DTTO, and in 2009 more than 16,000 drug rehabilitation requirements were commenced (12,000 under community orders and 4,000 on SSOs).

- Contacting victims of crime was not culturally problematic in the way that DTTOs might have been, but probation officers were apprehensive that their primary task of working with offenders – and being perceived all too often as being on the offender's side – precluded them from being able to offer meaningful face-to-face work with victims of crime. Between April 2006 and March 2007, probation staff contacted 15,500 victims.

- A final example is bail information schemes, which were at first opposed by many in the probation service because they involved probation officers dealing with individuals who had not been found guilty and therefore whose offence could not be discussed (see Lloyd 1992; Mair and Lloyd 1996). But as the schemes aimed to divert individuals from a remand in custody, they spread rapidly across probation services. At their height, there were probably around 200 bail information schemes running in England and Wales, but as resources were squeezed and Home Office interest in diversion lessened following Michael Howard's arrival as Home Secretary, their numbers decreased and many of those running today are organised by partnership agencies.

Increasing and shifting responsibilities have been associated with the growth of partnership work and the de-professionalisation of probation. Since its beginnings, probation has been encouraged to use the potential of local voluntary groups to assist in its work with offenders but for most of the time any such 'partnership' work was dominated by probation; outside agencies were very much the junior partner with their services purchased as necessary. Contestability meant that any outside agency could take over an aspect of probation work, so that probation becomes simply one provider of services for offenders among many, and this policy is set to continue – if not develop further – under the new Conservative/Liberal Democratic government. For much of its history, the probation service has worked hard to achieve recognition as a professional organisation based around its social work expertise, but this specialist knowledge is no longer the foundation of probation work and no other expertise has replaced it. Specialist knowledge is now located just as easily in voluntary, private or other public sector organisations.

As Maurice Vanstone (2004a) has shown, probation work has never been defined by a single method throughout its history. Probation officers have had considerable autonomy to utilise whatever theory or method seemed most appropriate to them; rehabilitation could be effected by a number of approaches. But rehabilitation is no longer the immediate aim of probation work; risk management and control are the objectives now, irrespective of the latest talk of a rehabilitation revolution. But it is not just the aims of probation that have changed: the methods utilised to attain the aims have become tightly controlled by the Accreditation Panel, although it will be interesting to find out if the Panel has any place in the new government's plans as outlined in *Breaking the Cycle*

(Ministry of Justice 2010). Probation officers' discretion to use whichever method felt to be appropriate has been constrained and thus their professionalism has been diminished, although again changes may be on the way.

Deprofessionalisation has developed in other ways too. First, it is highly significant that since 2002 probation service officers have outnumbered qualified probation officers; indeed, in the decade from 1998 the number of PSOs has increased by 177 per cent, compared with a 7 per cent increase in POs (Mills et al. 2010). And traditional PSRs, requiring the skills and experience of a qualified PO, have been decreasing in number during the course of the decade; in 2000 they made up 93 per cent of all court reports, while in 2009 the figure was 53 per cent. Indeed, fast delivery oral PSRs, which require a brief discussion with the offender while the court adjourns, have increased by over 1,000 per cent since their introduction in 2005 (they now make up one in five of all reports in the magistrates' courts). Whatever the merits or demerits of fast delivery oral PSRs, they do not require the expertise of a qualified social worker that was brought to the preparation of a traditional PSR.

Although evidence is hard to come by, it is likely that public perceptions of probation are lower than they were. For much of its history, the probation officer has been seen as the person to contact for many minor neighbourhood problems, which suggests a degree of confidence in the service. As far as the media are concerned, the probation service was – until recently – virtually invisible. Recent data from the British Crime Survey show that fewer than one in four (23 per cent) of the public think probation is doing a good or excellent job; only the Youth Court was thought to be doing less well, and probation was the only criminal justice agency whose rating had decreased since 2002/3 (Smith 2010). Probation has received a great deal of damaging media coverage in the past few years for its alleged failures in a number of high-profile murder cases: John Monckton, Robert Symons (2004), Mary-Ann Leneghan, Naomi Bryant (2005), Laurent Bonomo and Gabriel Ferez (2008). Such a level of publicity, as well as its negativity, is not something that probation has been used to and it is difficult to respond positively.

It is important to emphasise three things about these changes we have discussed. First, they do not always represent radical discontinuities with the past. Many are simply developments that have grown significantly over time, for example work with released prisoners, reports for the courts, the use of requirements, partnership work. Even governmental control did not suddenly happen overnight; as we have shown, almost as soon as probation was introduced with the 1907 Act, the Home Office began to intervene slowly and without any signs of consistency of approach or coherent planning to guide and direct and – eventually – control the work of the service. Second, probation has always been subject to change – this is not something that has just begun to happen in the last couple of decades, although the scope, speed and depth of change are now very different. What is different has been the way in which change has come about. For most of its history, developments in probation were rooted in the practical everyday work of the service. Today, change is driven from the top down.

And, third, we would argue that similar levels and kinds of change could be found if the last hundred years of any criminal justice agency or any major social policy issues were to be examined. We must try to avoid thinking about probation simply as a unique case. It is, in many ways, just another example of what David Marquand (2004) has termed the 'decline of the public' which he sums up thus:

> The single most important element of the New Right project of the 1980s and 1990s was a relentless *kulturkampf* designed to root out the culture of service and citizenship which had become part of the social fabric. De-regulation, privatization, so-called public–private partnerships, proxy markets, performance indicators mimicking those of the private corporate sector, and a systematic assault on professional autonomy narrowed the public domain and blurred the distinction between it and the market domain.
>
> (Marquand 2004: 2)

Focusing more particularly on criminal justice, David Garland (2001: 6) has famously listed 12 'indices of change' that overall characterise the developments that have taken place in crime control and criminal justice since the 1970s. One might argue how far police, prisons and probation have been affected by each of these 12 developments, but as far as probation is concerned the following would seem to be most important: the decline of the rehabilitative ideal, the re-emergence of punitive sanctions, the return of the victim, protection of the public, politicisation, new management styles, and a perpetual sense of crisis.

Garland has also summed up a number of 'social and historical conditions that underpinned criminological modernism and the penal-welfare compromise' and the significance of these for the growth of probation hardly requires comment (Garland 2001: 48–51):

- a specific style of governance that was 'associated with a social democratic form of politics and a civic narrative of inclusion';
- high levels of informal social control that were imposed by families, communities, schools and places of employment;
- an economic context that was founded upon Keynesianism;
- the authority of social expertise such as that provided by social workers and psychiatrists;
- the support of social elites for the '*ethos* of penal-welfarism';
- perceived validity and effectiveness which meant that hard questions were either not asked about failure or explained away;
- a distinct absence of any active public or political opposition.

As these conditions changed in the last quarter or so of the twentieth century, so penal-welfare approaches generally and, for our purposes, probation specifically became weakened and more open to attack.

In a similar way, Paul Senior and his colleagues (2007) have examined how far different criminal justice agencies have responded to the demands of modernisation, which – following Newman (2001) – they see as a key New Labour project. They break modernisation down into nine dimensions (a mixed economy of provision, contestability, performance management, deconcentration and regionalisation, audit and inspection, penal populism and risk management, pluralisation, joined-up justice and responsibilisation) and, while all the agencies they discuss have not been affected equally by these dimensions, they have all, including probation, been touched by them to a greater or lesser extent.

While the changes that have taken place in probation are a part of much wider social, economic and cultural shifts and must be seen in this context, there is little doubt that probation has changed in profoundly important ways. Whether or not social work was the appropriate basic qualification for a probation officer, it did offer the professionalisation that was so desired by Napo in its early days and provided a solid foundation on which to carry out work with offenders. Without such a foundation, probation has lost a language, a distinct theoretical model (or models) and perhaps a justification for its existence. Becoming a fully fledged criminal justice agency may have been necessary – even desirable – but it has left probation rootless.

The service is now under the control of the Ministry of Justice. Whatever the advantages of being a local service might have been – and probation staff have often appeared to think that this was the only possible way to organise the service – the local approach meant that probation staff at all levels had a great deal of autonomy. This relative freedom was a double-edged sword as on the one hand it encouraged innovation, but on the other it led to duplication of effort and limited accountability both within local probation services and to central government. And, as efficiency, cost-effectiveness, performance indicators and targets became significant aspects of government policy from the early 1980s onwards, probation's autonomy and lack of accountability were recognised as weaknesses that required action.

While control was always a part of probation work, it would be difficult to deny that there has been a shift in its significance. For the first half of probation's history, control was tacitly understood to be part of the supervision process, but this was mainly about helping offenders and control lurked in the background. The care v. control debates that characterised much probation writing from the 1960s on demonstrated that control was becoming acknowledged as part of supervision, albeit a not particularly welcome part. The balance has now shifted to control being the primary task of supervision with care left as something that may be done but is most often left unstated. Thus probation work has become more punitive, and this can be seen in various developments: the loss of juveniles, the introduction of new sentences such as community service and the combination order, the increasing use of requirements, the large percentage of those convicted of summary offences who receive a community order (almost half in 2009), and the popularity of the suspended sentence order which is – legally speaking – a custodial sentence.

The service is no longer a monopoly provider of supervisory sentences to the courts. The introduction of attendance centres following the 1948 Criminal

Justice Act was the first threat to this monopoly, but there were never enough centres to challenge seriously probation's dominant role. The arrival of curfew orders posed a much more significant threat and probation failed to recognise it as such; curfew requirements are currently the fourth most popular requirement for both the community order and the SSO. The presence of partnership agencies in many of the requirements that make up the orders (e.g. the drug treatment, alcohol treatment and mental health requirements) also weakens probation's position. While the service has lost its monopoly position, it still has a dominant role but contestability and the plans of the new government could challenge that. The more other agencies or organisations become providers of probation services, the more the probation service will become just another provider among many.

Another crucial change has been the incorporation of the probation service into the National Offender Management Service. It is not difficult to understand the logic of such a development, and prisons and probation work together effectively in both Norway and Sweden. However, Patrick Carter's (2003) report proposing the introduction of NOMS was very vague on detail, was accepted and acted upon remarkably quickly by government, and since then NOMS has gone through various structural changes which have weakened the position of probation. Given the much larger size of the prison service, probation was always going to have to struggle to make sure its voice was heard in NOMS and with the overwhelming dominance of prison staff at senior management levels it looks as if the struggle has been lost. The implications of this marginalisation of probation are serious:

> The lack of a loud and powerful probation voice must inevitably impact on criminal justice policy as it affects the advice Ministers receive. The lack of a probation voice at the centre also impacts on many aspects of the Service itself, including resources, professional standards and value and diversity and inevitably the very nature of the future of the Service ... The lack of a probation voice at the centre of NOMS, inevitably questions who speaks for the Service when it comes to the regular negotiations with the Treasury over resource allocation.
>
> (McKnight 2009: 338)

It is worth emphasising that, on their own, each of these key changes did not necessarily pose a threat to the existence of the probation service. There is no reason why each, on its own, could not have led to a stronger, more powerful service. Yet, taken together, and alongside the persistent sniping that the service has had to endure from governments since at least 1974 and 'Nothing Works', probation is now under real threat. Each of the changes represents a loss: the loss of social work, of the local, of welfare work with offenders, of a monopoly position, of independence. It is this overarching narrative of loss that characterises probation today, not the confident words of Radzinowicz (Cambridge Department of Criminal Science 1958: x) writing as probation celebrated 50 years in existence and acclaiming probation as 'the most significant contribution made by this country to the new penological theory and practice which struck root in the twentieth century'.

This is not to underestimate the significance of the considerable amount of academic work that has recently been carried out into the rehabilitation of offenders. This is a subject that has, following the 'What Works' initiative of 1998, been flourishing. The research and writing of Fergus McNeill, Peter Raynor, Gwen Robinson and Shadd Maruna, for example, all advocate models of rehabilitation for the probation service in the twenty-first century. This neo-rehabilitationism, or perhaps more accurately retro-rehabilitationism – in spite of its surface innovations its substance is rooted in the past (it may be worth adding that we do not use the term disparagingly) – makes a strong case for the continuing importance of probation. And this is a case with which we have every sympathy.

There are, however, two factors that would inhibit the rejuvenation of the probation service by retro-rehabilitationism. First is the fact that the rehabilitation of an offender utilising the skills of a qualified probation officer is no longer the primary task of the service. As we have noted, much of the service's work with offenders is already carried out by probation service officers. The structure of the community order and the SSO is such that it requires the input of more than one supervisor, thereby militating against the offender–supervisor relationship that is a crucial part of rehabilitation. The more rehabilitative requirements of the orders are decreasing in use, and community payback is now by far the most commonly used type of community order and SSO. In addition, workers from other agencies can be involved in the supervision of offenders; with regard to stand-alone curfew requirements the probation service has no involvement, and contestability could lead to greater moves in this direction. All of this would suggest that a rehabilitation renaissance (not a rehabilitation revolution) would be very difficult to nurture and grow in practice.

The second factor is even more of an obstacle. It would be difficult to deny that certain aspects within probation itself can be blamed for its current woes. The service was always a small organisation without the clout of the police or the prison service; indeed, it was not even a unified service until 2001. It never had a single body to speak for it, and ACOP, CCPC and Napo rarely spoke with a single voice. The service was perhaps politically naïve with too much faith in its own inherent goodness to grasp fully the punitive nature of late-twentieth-century crime-control policies. It was uninterested in demonstrating its effectiveness for far too long, and its longstanding image of being soft on crime was – eventually – damaging. But, despite these failings, probation's narrative of loss has been driven by government not by the service.

It is hard to escape the conclusion that, with respect to probation policy, government has had little idea of what it has been doing for the past 25 years. For the first 40 years of its existence, relations between the Home Office and the probation service were largely harmonious and policy followed suit. Following the Second World War, and up to 1979, penal policy was driven – to a considerable degree – by the advice of the Advisory Council on the Treatment of

Offenders and subsequently by the Advisory Council on the Penal System, both of which were nominally independent of government and whose members had a wide knowledge of the criminal justice system. Crucially, for most of this period, rehabilitation was accepted as what probation did, and, as Bottoms and Stevenson (1992) argue persuasively, probation was largely unharmed by the problems that were caused for police and prisons by rising crime, staffing problems and uncomfortable research results.

While the service was strengthened by the introduction of community service in 1973, it was also – in hindsight – weakened: a more punitive sentence competed with the probation order; a new group of staff were recruited who had little in common with traditional probation ideals; the diversion of offenders from custody became a probation objective. With the arrival of the Conservative government in 1979 advocating a more punitive approach to law and order, and a cavalier attitude to the application of ideological principles such as the privatisation of the public sector and the use of private sector managerial techniques in the public sector, probation's position worsened. Many of the developments in probation from 1984 to 1993, while perhaps desirable in themselves, led inexorably to increasing governmental control. And after Michael Howard became Home Secretary any empathy with the probation service or understanding of the difficulties it faced disappeared. Probation was an easy target for advocates of a punitive approach to crime control and the service was stripped of the assets that made it what it was. The process continued under the Labour governments from 1997 and looks set to carry on under the Conservative/Liberal Democrat coalition.

It is not so much that the key changes imposed on probation were mistakes in themselves. Probation needed to change and was reluctant to do so. It was that the full, long-term, cumulative impact of the changes was not thought through. Thus, becoming a fully fledged criminal justice agency was a sensible development, but having to lose completely its social work foundations meant that probation lost its unique nature. There were certainly many problems with having separate probation areas, but moving to a fully centralised service based in the Home Office was not the only solution to these problems. Community penalties in general needed to be seen as more rigorous, but consistently making the service more punitive was a wasted effort as it could never compete with prison in these terms, and it meant the marginalisation of rehabilitation which – however difficult it may be to evidence consistently – does work in reducing offending, is less harmful to offenders and cheaper than custody. Probation had been working successfully with voluntary agencies since its earliest days, and perhaps encouraging more and more consistent use was a positive development; to open probation work up to competition, however, means not only a myriad of difficulties of regulation, control and accountability, but risks thrusting probation into a market-place where it could easily lose its way. Finally, closer working with the prison service could only have been beneficial for offenders, but the form that NOMS has taken was not necessarily the way to achieve that and the many structural changes that NOMS has had to endure since 2004 are, at the very least, suggestive of government unease.

At best, the probation service – despite the many changes it has come through – still exists and for that we should be grateful. At worst, the service has lost its roots, its traditions, its culture, its professionalism. Its political masters seem to have lost faith in its abilities and it is about to lose a significant part of its funding as the decisions of the coalition's Spending Review begin to be implemented. Community penalties may well have a future, even if it is only as an alternative to custody, but whether this is the case for the probation service is another matter entirely.

Notes

1 Origins

1 Superannuated warships began to be introduced as floating prisons following the outbreak of the American War of Independence in 1775 when transportation came to a halt.
2 Interestingly, Page (1992: 35) argues that Section 4 of the Youthful Offenders Act of 1901 was a 'step in the direction of probation'. This part of the Act was to do with remands in custody of young people and proposes that the person may be committed into the custody of any fit person who is willing to receive him or her.

2 The first decade

1 It is worth noting that the Home Office did decide to appoint two women as special children's probation officers for London. Page (1992) notes that they seem to have had very few cases until the Children Act of 1908 was implemented on 1 April 1909, introducing juvenile courts. These two officers were paid a salary, unlike their colleagues who were paid by fees.
2 Gard (2007) discusses a further, confidential Home Office review of probation in London that was produced in 1913 and primarily examined pay, although Gard also suggests that the review acknowledged differences 'in working methods and social backgrounds' between Home Office appointed probation officers and missionaries.

3 Consolidation

1 This figure of 711 is rather less than the 784 mentioned in the 1922 Committee report, but is probably accounted for by an increase in the number of full-time officers and by the amalgamation of areas that had taken place following the 1925 Act.
2 Totals of 15,949, 15,973 and 15,989 can all be found in the report (see Home Office 1928: Tables IIIA, IIIB, IIIC, IIID and IV).
3 It is interesting to note that Page (1992) comments that in 1931 two veterans of the London Police Court Mission retired, each of whom had been working as missionaries for about 40 years. The descriptions of them that he provides are fondly complimentary, but could never be said to suggest that they were professional diagnosticians.
4 It seems likely that by this time at least one chief probation officer had been appointed – in Liverpool as early as 1920.

5 1950–62: A golden age?

1 Interestingly, one of us (GM) was told by a member of the Probation Inspectorate in the late 1980s that the film had been used in the training of probation officers.

2 The first PWO was Frank Dawtry who was appointed to Wakefield in 1937; in 1948 he became the general secretary of Napo until his retirement in 1967.
3 St John was a full-time writer whose account is rooted in journalism, while Todd had worked as a journalist, becoming a probation officer in her mid-forties.

6 From Morison to Martinson, 1962–74

1 In Scotland the Kilbrandon Committee (Scottish Home and Health Department and Scottish Education Department 1964) had gone down a similar road and a system of children's hearings was instituted following the Social Work (Scotland) Act 1968. Kilbrandon also led (via the same Act) to the disbanding of a separate Scottish probation service and its integration in generic social work departments, a development that was regarded with considerable anxiety by probation officers south of the border (for an overview of the development of probation in Scotland see McIvor and McNeill 2007).
2 In 1966 the National Association of Discharged Prisoners' Aid Societies (NADPAS) was reconstituted as the National Association for the Care and Resettlement of Offenders (NACRO), which became a highly significant voluntary organisation working with offenders.
3 To her credit, some years later Baroness Wootton admitted that she felt 'slightly ashamed' about the way community service was made to appeal to all shades of penal opinion (Wootton 1978: 128).

7 Alternatives to custody

1 The near-obsession with alternatives to custody during this period can be seen by such publications as *Alternatives to Prison* (Stanley and Baginsky 1984), *Alternatives to Custody* (Pointing 1986), *Probation as an Alternative to Custody* (Raynor 1988), *The Real Alternative* (NACRO 1989) and *Alternatives to Prison* (Vass 1990).

8 The end of the road?

1 The performance target had decreased from 10 days for 2001/2 to nine days for 2003/4, but the 10-day target can be calculated from the Performance Report (National Probation Service 2004).
2 For an excellent series of papers discussing the Crime Reduction Programme, see the special issue of *Criminal Justice* edited by Mike Hough (2004).
3 Following criticism by John Reid that that the Home Office was not fit for purpose, it was split into two separate government departments, with the Home Office retaining responsibility for policing, counter-terrorism, drugs policy and immigration, while the new Ministry of Justice took responsibility for the courts, prisons and probation.

References

ACOP (1988) *More Demanding than Prison: A Discussion Paper*. London: Association of Chief Officers of Probation.

ACOP, CCPC and Napo (1987) *Probation: The Next Five Years*. London: Napo, ACOP and CCPC.

ACPS (1970) *Non-Custodial and Semi-Custodial Penalties*. Advisory Council on the Penal System (the Wootton Report). London: HMSO.

—— (1974) *Young Adult Offenders* (The Younger Report). London: HMSO.

ACTO (1957) *Alternatives to Short Terms of Imprisonment*. Advisory Council on the Treatment of Offenders. London: HMSO.

—— (1958) *The After-Care and Supervision of Discharged Offenders*. London: HMSO.

—— (1959) *The Treatment of Young Offenders*. London: HMSO.

—— (1960) *Corporal Punishment*. London: HMSO.

—— (1962) *Non-Residential Treatment of Offenders under 21*. London: HMSO.

—— (1963) *The Organisation of After-Care*. London: HMSO.

Advisory Committee on Drug Dependence (1968) *The Rehabilitation of Drug Addicts*. London: HMSO.

Allard, J.W. (2005) *The Logical Foundations of Bradley's Metaphysics: Judgement, Inference and Truth*. Cambridge: Cambridge University Press.

Allen, R. and Hough, M. (2007) 'Community penalties, sentencers, the media and public opinion', in L. Gelsthorpe and R. Morgan (eds) *Handbook of Probation*. Cullompton: Willan.

Andrews, D. (1995) 'The psychology of criminal conduct and effective treatment', in J. McGuire (ed.) *What Works: Reducing Reoffending*. Chichester: John Wiley & Sons.

Anon. (1929a) 'Editorial notes', *Probation* 1(2): 19–20.

—— (1929b) 'Chief probation officers', *Probation* 1(2): 25.

—— (1930) 'Failures in probation', *Probation* 1(3): 40–42.

—— (1936) 'Summary Courts (Social Services) committee report', *Probation* 2(4): 49–52.

—— (1937/8) 'Review of "Probation: a Sheaf of Memories"', *Probation* 2(11): 170.

—— (1949) ' "Probation Officer": a film', *Probation* 5(21): 274.

Aubrey, R. and Hough, M. (1997) *Assessing Offenders' Needs: Assessment Scales for the Probation Service*. Home Office Research Study 166. London: Home Office.

Audit Commission (1989) *The Probation Service: Promoting Value For Money*. London: HMSO.

Bailey, V. (1987) *Delinquency and Citizenship: Reclaiming the Young Offender, 1914–1948*. Oxford: Clarendon Press.

Barr, H. (1966) *A Survey of Group Work in the Probation Service*. Studies in the Causes of Delinquency and the Treatment of Offenders 9. London: HMSO.

BBC News (2006) 'Reid proposes probation overhaul', 7 November. Available at http://news.bbc.co.uk/1/hi/uk/6123966.stm (accessed 13 April 2011).

Blair, T. (2010) *A Journey*. London: Hutchinson.

Bochel, D. (1976) *Probation and After-Care: Its Development in England and Wales*. Edinburgh: Scottish Academic Press.

Booth, C. (1892–97) *Life and Labour of the People in London*, 9 vols. London.

Boswell, G., Davies, M. and Wright, A. (1993) *Contemporary Probation Practice*. Aldershot: Avebury.

Bottoms, A.E. (1980) 'An introduction to "The Coming Crisis"', in A.E. Bottoms and R.H. Preston (eds) *The Coming Penal Crisis: A Criminological and Theological Exploration*. Edinburgh: Scottish Academic Press.

Bottoms, A.E. and McWilliams, W. (1979) 'A non-treatment paradigm for probation practice', *British Journal of Social Work* 9(2): 159–202.

Bottoms, A.E. and Preston, R.H. (eds) (1980) *The Coming Penal Crisis: A Criminological and Theological Exploration*. Edinburgh: Scottish Academic Press.

Bottoms, A.E. and Stevenson, S. (1992) 'What Went Wrong?: criminal justice policy in England and Wales 1945–70', in D. Downes (ed.) *Unravelling Criminal Justice: Eleven British Studies*. London: Macmillan.

Bottoms, A.E., Rex, S. and Robinson, G. (eds) (2004) *Alternatives to Prison: Options for an Insecure Society*. Cullompton: Willan.

Bowpitt, G. (2007) 'Review of F. Prochaska "Christianity and Social Service in Modern Britain"', *Social Policy and Administration* 41(1): 105–7.

Bridges, A. (2006a) *An Independent Review of a Serious Further Offence Case: Anthony Rice*. London: HM Inspectorate of Probation.

—— (2006b) *An Independent Review of a Serious Further Offence Case: Damien Hanson and Elliott White*. London: HM Inspectorate of Probation.

Brody, S. (1976) *The Effectiveness of Sentencing*. Home Office Research Study No.35. London: HMSO.

Bruggen, M. (1974) 'Napo's response to the report so far', *Probation* 21(4): 117–18.

Burnett, R. (1996) *Fitting Supervision to Offenders: Assessment and Allocation Decisions in the Probation Service*. Home Office Research Study 153. London: Home Office.

Burt, C.L. (1925) *The Young Delinquent*. London: University of London.

Bryant, M., Coker, J., Estlea, B., Himmel, S. and Knapp, T. (1978) 'Sentenced to social work?', *Probation Journal* 25(4): 110–14.

Burns, Dr (1930) 'The psychology of the criminal', *Probation Journal* 1(3): 38–40.

Calvert, E.R. and Calvert, T. (1933) *The Lawbreaker: A Critical Study of the Modern Treatment of Crime*. London: George Routledge & Sons.

Cambridge Department of Criminal Science (1958) *The Results of Probation*. London: Macmillan.

Carr-Saunders, A.M., Mannheim, H. and Rhodes, E.C. (1943) *Young Offenders: An Enquiry into Juvenile Delinquency*. Cambridge: Cambridge University Press.

Carter, P. (2003) *Managing Offenders, Reducing Crime*. London: Strategy Unit.

—— (2007) *Securing the Future: Proposals for the Efficient and Sustainable Use of Custody in England and Wales*. London: Cabinet Office.

Casey, L. (2008) *Engaging Communities in Fighting Crime*. London: Cabinet Office.

Centre for Crime and Justice Studies (2010) *Probation Resources, Staffing and Workloads 2001–2008*. Revised edition. London: Centre for Crime and Justice Studies.

Chapman, T. and Hough, M. (1998) *Evidence-Based Practice: A Guide to Effective Practice*. London: HMIP.

Chinn, H. (1929) 'Juvenile courts in America', *Probation* 1(2): 27–9.

Chuter Ede, J. (1949) 'The Home Secretary's speech to Conference', *Probation* 5(21): 269–72.

Clarke, K. (2010) 'The government's vision for criminal justice reform'. Speech presented at the Centre for Crime and Justice Studies 30 June 2010. Available at: http://www.justice.gov.uk/news/sp300610a.htm (accessed 19 April 2011).

Clarke Hall, W. (1917) *The State and the Child*. London: Headley Bros.

—— (1929) 'The training and appointment of probation officers', *Probation* 1(1): 7–8.

—— (1933) 'The extent and practice of probation in England', in S. Glueck (ed.) *Probation and Criminal Justice: Essays in Honour of Herbert C. Parsons*. New York: Macmillan.

Coleman, D.A. (1989) *Home Office Review of Probation Training: Final Report*. London: Home Office.

Corden, J. (1980) 'Review of W. Young "Community Service Orders"', *British Journal of Social Work* 10(2): 260–62.

Coulsfield, Lord (2004) *Crime, Courts and Confidence: Report of an Independent Inquiry into Alternatives to Prison*. London: The Stationery Office.

Craig, M.J. (1945) 'Relationships in case work', *Probation* 4(10): 103–8.

Creighton-Miller, H. (1929) 'The unconscious motive of the juvenile delinquent', *Probation* 1(1): 12–14.

Davies, M. (1969) *Probationers in their Social Environment*. Home Office Research Studies 2. London: HMSO.

—— (1973) *An Index of Social Environment*. Home Office Research Studies 17. London: HMSO.

—— (1974) *Social Work in the Environment*. Home Office Research Studies 21. London: HMSO.

Davies, M. and Knopf, A. (1973) *Social Enquiry Reports and the Probation Service*. Home Office Research Studies 18. London: HMSO.

Dawtry, F. (1958) 'Whither probation?', *British Journal of Delinquency* 8(3): 180–87.

Department of Employment (1972) *Report of the Butterworth Inquiry into the Work and Pay of Probation Officers and Social Workers*. London: HMSO.

Dews, V. and Watts, J. (1994) *Review of Probation Officer Recruitment and Qualifying Training*. London: Home Office.

Downes, D. and Morgan, R. (1994) ' "Hostages to Fortune?" The politics of law and order in post-war Britain', in M. Maguire, R. Morgan and R. Reiner (eds) *The Oxford Handbook of Criminology*, 1st edn. Oxford: Clarendon Press.

—— (2002) 'The skeletons in the cupboard: the politics of law and order at the turn of the millennium', in M. Maguire, R. Morgan and R. Reiner (eds) *The Oxford Handbook of Criminology*, 3rd edn. Oxford: Oxford University Press.

Ellison, M. (1934) *Sparks Beneath the Ashes: Experiences of a London Probation Officer*. London: John Murray.

Faulkner, D. (1989) 'The future of the probation service: a view from government', in R. Shaw and K. Haines (eds) *The Criminal Justice System: A Central Role for the Probation Service*. Cambridge: Institute of Criminology.

Feversham, Lord (1929a) 'Foreword', *Probation* 1(1): 3–4.

—— (1929b) 'Opening Remarks', *Probation* 1(1): 7.

Field, S. and Hough, M. (1993) *Cash-Limiting the Probation Service: A Case Study in Resource Allocation*. Research and Planning Unit Paper 77. London: Home Office.

Folkard, M.S., Fowles, A.J., McWilliams, B.C., McWilliams, W., Smith, D.D., Smith, D.E. and Walmsley, G.R. (1974) *IMPACT: Intensive Matched Probation and After-Care Treatment*. Home Office Research Studies 24. London: HMSO.

——, Smith, D.E. and Smith, D.D. (1976) *IMPACT Intensive Matched Probation and After-Care Treatment, Vol. 2: The Results of the Experiment*. Home Office Research Study No.36. London: HMSO.

Forsythe, W.J. (1991) *Penal Discipline, Reformatory Projects and the English Prison Commission 1895–1939*. Exeter: University of Exeter Press.

Gamon, H.R.P. (1907) *The London Police Court: Today and Tomorrow*. London: J.M. Dent.

Gard, R. (2007) 'The first probation officers in England and Wales 1906–14', *British Journal of Criminology* 47(6): 938–54.

Garland, D. (1985) *Punishment and Welfare: A History of Penal Strategies*. Aldershot: Gower.

—— (2001) *The Culture of Control: Crime and Social Order in Contemporary Society*. Oxford: Oxford University Press.

Gelsthorpe, L. and Morgan, R. (eds) (2007) *Handbook of Probation*. Cullompton: Willan.

Gelsthorpe, L. and Morris, A. (1994) 'Juvenile justice 1945–92', in M. Maguire, R. Morgan and R. Reiner (eds) *The Oxford Handbook of Criminology*. 1st edn. Oxford: Clarendon Press.

Geraghty, J. (1991) *Probation Practice in Crime Prevention*. Crime Prevention Paper 24. London: Home Office.

Gibbens, T.C.N. (1959) 'Supervision and probation of adolescent girls', *British Journal of Delinquency* 10(2): 84–103.

Glover, E.R. (1949) *Probation and Re-education*. London: Routledge & Kegan Paul.

Goldblatt, P. and Lewis, C. (eds) (1998) *Reducing Offending: An Assessment of Research Evidence on Ways of Dealing with Offending Behaviour*. Home Office Research Study 187. London: Home Office.

Griffiths, W.A. (1982) 'A new Probation Service', *Probation Journal* 29(3): 98–9.

Grunhut, M. (1948) *Penal Reform: A Comparative Study*. Oxford: Clarendon Press.

—— (1952) 'Probation as a research field', *British Journal of Delinquency* 2(4): 287–302.

—— (1956) *Juvenile Offenders before the Courts*. Oxford: Clarendon Press.

—— (1963) *Probation and Mental Treatment*. London: Tavistock.

Halliday, J. (2001) *Making Punishments Work: Report of a Review of the Sentencing Framework for England and Wales*. London: Home Office.

Harding, C., Hines, B., Ireland, R. and Rawlings, P. (1985) *Imprisonment in England and Wales: A Concise History*. London: Croom Helm.

Harris, J. (1937) *Probation – A Sheaf of Memories: 34 Years Work in a Local Police Court*. Lowestoft: The Library Press.

Harris, R.J. (1977) 'The probation officer as social worker', *British Journal of Social Work* 7(4): 433–42.

—— (1980) 'A changing service: the case for separating "care" and "control" in probation practice', *British Journal of Social Work* 10(2): 163–84.

Harris, S.W. (1936) 'Summary Courts (Social Services) committee report', *Probation* 2(5): 69–79.

——— (1937) *Probation and Other Social Work of the Courts: The Third Clarke Hall Lecture*. Rochester: Stanhope Press.

Hartley, L.P. (1953) *The Go-Between*. London: Hamish Hamilton.

Haxby, D. (1978) *Probation: A Changing Service*. London: Constable.

Hedderman, C. (1993) *Panel Assessment Schemes for Mentally Disordered Offenders*. Research and Planning Unit Paper 76. London: Home Office.

Hedderman, C. and Sugg, D. (1997) 'The influence of cognitive approaches: a survey of probation programmes', in C. Hedderman, D. Sugg and J. Vennard *Changing Offenders' Attitudes and Behaviour: What Works?* Home Office Research Study 171. London: Home Office.

Hedderman, C., Ellis, T. and Sugg, D. (1999) *Increasing Confidence in Community Sentences: The Results of Two Demonstration Projects*. Home Office Research Study 194. London: Home Office.

Henderson, P. and del Tufo, S. (1991) *Community Work and the Probation Service*. London: Home Office.

Hennessy, P. (2006) *Never Again: Britain 1945–1951*. London: Penguin.

——— (2007) *Having It So Good: Britain in the Fifties*. London: Penguin.

Hinde, R.S.E. (1951) *The British Penal* System *1773–1950*. London: Duckworth and Co.

Hinton, N. (1976) 'Developments in the Probation Service: a personal view', *Probation Journal* 23(3): 90–92.

HMIP (1988) *Performance Indicators for the Probation Service*. Her Majesty's Inspectorate of Probation. London: Home Office.

Hodges, D.J. (1953) 'Some problems of probation work arising from seasonal employment in a coastal holiday resort', *British Journal of Delinquency* 3(4): 281–8.

Home Office (1895) *Report of the Departmental Committee on Prisons*. London: HMSO.

——— (1907) *Memorandum on the Probation System as at Present in Force in the United States of America*. London: HMSO.

——— (1910a) *Report of the Departmental Committee on the Probation of Offenders Act, 1907: Report*. London: HMSO.

——— (1910b) *Report of the Departmental Committee on the Probation of Offenders Act, 1907: Minutes of Evidence and Appendices*. London: HMSO.

——— (1922) *Report of the Departmental Committee on the Training, Appointment and Payment of Probation Officers*. London: HMSO.

——— (1923) *Report on the Work of the Children's Branch*. London: HMSO.

——— (1924) *Second Report on the Work of the Children's Branch*. London: HMSO.

——— (1925) *Third Report on the Work of the Children's Branch*. London: HMSO.

——— (1926a) *Report of the Committee on the Superannuation of Probation Officers*. London: HMSO.

——— (1926b) *The Probation Rules 1926*. London: Home Office.

——— (1927) *Report of the Departmental Committee on the Treatment of Young Offenders*. London: HMSO.

——— (1928) *Fourth Report on the Work of the Children's Branch*. London: HMSO.

——— (1932) *Report of the Departmental Committee on Persistent Offenders*. London: HMSO.

——— (1934) *Report of the Departmental Committee on Imprisonment by Courts of Summary Jurisdiction in Default of Payment of Fines and Other Sums of Money*. London: HMSO.

—— (1936) *Report of the Departmental Committee on the Social Services in Courts of Summary Jurisdiction*. London: HMSO.

—— (1938a) *The Probation Service: Its Objects and Its Organisation*. London: HMSO.

—— (1938b) *Report of the Departmental Committee on Corporal Punishment*. London: HMSO.

—— (1940) *Criminal Statistics England and Wales 1938*. London: HMSO.

—— (1948) *Report of the Departmental Committee on Grants for the Development of Marriage Guidance*. London: HMSO.

—— (1952) *Probation as a Career*. London: HMSO.

—— (1953) *Report of the Committee on Discharged Prisoners' Aid Societies*. London: HMSO.

—— (1959) *Penal Practice in a Changing Society*. London: HMSO.

—— (1960) *Report of the Committee on Children and Young Persons*. London: HMSO.

—— (1961) *Report of the Interdepartmental Committee on the Business of the Criminal Courts*. London: HMSO.

—— (1962a) *Report of the Departmental Committee on the Probation Service* (The Morison Report). London: HMSO.

—— (1962b) *Second Report of the Departmental Committee on the Probation Service*. London: HMSO.

—— (1964) *The War Against Crime in England and Wales 1959–1964*. London: Home Office.

—— (1965a) *The Child, the Family and the Young Offender*. London: HMSO.

—— (1965b) *The Adult Offender*. London: HMSO.

—— (1966a) *Report on the Work of the Probation and After-Care Department 1962 to 1965*. London: HMSO.

—— (1966b) *First Report of the Working Party on the Place of Voluntary Service in After-Care: Residential Provision for the Homeless Discharged Prisoner*. London: HMSO.

—— (1967) *Second Report of the Working Party on the Place of Voluntary Service in After-Care: The Place of Voluntary Service in After-Care*. London: HMSO.

—— (1968) *Children in Trouble*. London: Home Office.

—— (1969a) *Report on the Work of the Probation and After-Care Department 1966 to 1968*. London: HMSO.

—— (1969b) *People in Prison (England and Wales)*. London: HMSO.

—— (1969c) *The Sentence of the Court: A Handbook for Courts on the Treatment of Offenders*, 2nd edn. London: HMSO.

—— (1972) *Report on the Work of the Probation and After-Care Department 1969 to 1971*. London: HMSO.

—— (1976) *Report on the Work of the Probation and After-Care Department 1972 to 1975*. London: HMSO.

—— (1977) *A Review of Criminal Justice Policy 1976*. London: HMSO.

—— (1979) *Committee of Inquiry into the United Kingdom Prison Services: Report* (The May Report). London: HMSO.

—— (1980a) *Prison Statistics England and Wales 1979*. London: HMSO.

—— (1980b) *The Reduction of Pressure on the Prison System: Observations on the Fifteenth Report from the Expenditure Committee*. London: HMSO.

—— (1984a) *Probation Service in England and Wales: Statement of National Objectives and Priorities*. London: Home Office.

—— (1984b) *Tougher Regimes in Detention Centres*. London: HMSO.

—— (1984c) *Criminal Justice: A Working Paper*. London: Home Office.

—— (1988a) *Punishment, Custody and the Community*. London: HMSO.

—— (1988b) *Tackling Offending: An Action Plan*. London: Home Office.

—— (1990a) *Crime, Justice and Protecting the Public*. London: HMSO.

—— (1990b) *Supervision and Punishment in the Community*. London: HMSO.

—— (1990c) *Partnership in Dealing with Offenders in the Community*. London: Home Office.

—— (1990d) *Victim's Charter: A Statement of the Rights of Victims of Crime*. London: Home Office.

—— (1992) *Partnership in Dealing with Offenders in the Community: A Decision Document*. London: Home Office.

—— (1993a) *Probation Statistics England and Wales 1991*. London: Home Office.

—— (1993b) *The Probation Service: Three-Year Plan for the Probation Service 1993–1996*. London: Home Office.

—— (1994) *The Probation Service: Three-Year Plan for the Probation Service 1994–1997*. London: Home Office.

—— (1995a) *The Probation Service: Three-Year Plan for the Probation Service 1995–1998*. London: Home Office.

—— (1995b) *Strengthening Punishment in the Community*. London: HMSO.

—— (1996) *The Probation Service: Three-Year Plan for the Probation Service 1996–1999*. London: Home Office.

—— (1997) *The Probation Service: Three-Year Plan for the Probation Service 1997–2000*. London: Home Office.

—— (1998) *Joining Forces to Protect the Public: Prisons–Probation. A Consultation Document*. London: Home Office.

—— (2001a) *A New Choreography: An Integrated Strategy for the National Probation Service for England and Wales*. London: National Probation Service.

—— (2001b) *Criminal Justice: The Way Ahead*. London: The Stationery Office.

—— (2002) *Justice for All*. London: The Stationery Office.

—— (2004) *Reducing Crime – Changing Lives: The Government's Plans for Transforming the Management of Offenders*. London: Home Office.

—— (2005) *Restructuring Probation to Reduce Re-offending*. London: Home Office.

—— (2006a) *Working with Probation to Protect the Public and Reduce Re-offending: Summary of Responses to Restructuring Probation to Reduce Re-offending*. London: Home Office.

—— (2006b) *Improving Prison and Probation Services: Public Value Partnerships*. London: Home Office.

—— (2006c) *Making Sentencing Clearer*. London: Home Office.

—— Department of Education and Science, Department of Housing and Local Government and Department of Health (1968) *Report of the Committee on Local Authority and Allied Social Services*. (The Seebohm Report). London: HMSO.

—— Department of Health and Welsh Office (1992) *National Standards for the Supervision of Offenders in the Community*. London: Home Office.

Hood, R. (1966) 'A study of the effectiveness of pre-sentence investigations in reducing recidivism', *British Journal of Criminology* 6(3): 303–10.

Hood, R. and Sparks, R. (1970) *Key Issues in Criminology*. London: Weidenfeld and Nicolson.

Hood, R. and Taylor, I. (1968) 'Second report of the study of the effectiveness of pre-sentence investigations in reducing recidivism', *British Journal of Criminology* 8(4): 431–4.

Hough, M. (ed.) (2004) 'Evaluating the crime reduction programme in England and Wales', *Criminal Justice* (Special Issue) 4(3).

Hough, M., Jacobson, J. and Millie, A. (2003) *The Decision to Imprison: Sentencing and the Prison Population*. London: Prison Reform Trust.

House of Commons (1971) *First Report from the Expenditure Committee: Probation and After-Care*. London: HMSO.

—— (1978) *Fifteenth Report from the Expenditure Committee: The Reduction of Pressure on the Prison System, Vol. 1: Report*. London: HMSO.

—— (1998) *Home Affairs Committee Third Report: Alternatives to Prison Sentences, Vol.1*. London: The Stationery Office.

House of Commons Committee of Public Accounts (2008) *The Supervision of Community Orders in England and Wales: Forty-Eighth Report of Session 2007–8*. London: The Stationery Office.

House of Commons Justice Committee (2008) *Towards Effective Sentencing: Fifth Report of Session 2007–08, Vol. 1*. London: The Stationery Office.

Howard League (1927) *The Treatment of Young Offenders*. London: Howard League for Penal Reform.

Hughes, E.W. (1945) 'An analysis of the records of some 750 probationers', *British Journal of Educational Psychology* 35: 113–25.

Humphrey, C. (1991) 'Calling on the experts: the Financial Management Initiative (FMI), private sector management consultants and the Probation Service', *Howard Journal* 30(1): 1–18.

Ignatieff, M. (1978) *A Just Measure of Pain: The Penitentiary in the Industrial Revolution 1750–1850*. London: Macmillan.

Jarman, D. (1974) 'Younger – or better?', *Probation* 21(4): 105–7.

Joint Prison/Probation Accreditation Panel (2000) *What Works: First Report from the Joint Prison/Probation Accreditation Panel*. London: JPPAP.

Jones, Sir Digby. (2005) 'Offender rehabilitation: business as a deliverer of criminal justice'. The PBA Annual Lecture 2005. London: Probation Boards' Association.

Jones, T. and Newburn, T. (2007) *Policy Transfer and Criminal Justice: Exploring US Influence over British Crime Control Policy*. Maidenhead: Open University Press.

Kemshall, H. (1998) *Risk in Probation Practice*. Aldershot: Ashgate.

Kemshall, H., Mackenzie, G., Wood, J., Bailey, R. and Yates, J. (2005) *Strengthening the Multi-Agency Public Protection Arrangements*. Home Office Development and Practice Report 45. London: Home Office.

King, J.F.S. (ed.) (1958) *The Probation Service*. London: Butterworths.

—— (ed.) (1969) *The Probation and After-Care Service*, 3rd edn. London: Butterworths.

—— (ed.) (1975) *Control Without Custody? Papers Presented to the Cropwood Roundtable Conference December 1975*. Cambridge: Institute of Criminology.

—— (ed.) (1978) *Pressures and Change in the Probation Service: Papers Presented to the Cropwood Roundtable Conference December 1978*. Cambridge: Institute of Criminology.

Kynaston, D. (2007) *Austerity Britain 1945–51*. London: Bloomsbury.

—— (2009) *Family Britain, 1951–1957*. London: Bloomsbury.

Labour Party Study Group (1964) *Crime: A Challenge To Us All* (The Longford Report). London: Labour Party.

Le Mesurier, L. (ed.) (1935) *A Handbook of Probation and Social Work of the Courts*. London: National Association of Probation Officers.

Ledger, J. (2001) 'The National Probation Service: dancing to its own tune?', *Probation Journal* 48(3): 211–13.

Leeson, C. (1914) *The Probation System*. London: P.S. King and Son.

—— (1917) *The Child and the War: Being Notes on Juvenile Delinquency*. London: P.S. King and Son.

Lipsey, M. (1992) 'Juvenile delinquency treatment: a meta-analytic inquiry into the variability of effects', in T.D. Cook et al. (eds) *Meta-Analysis for Explanation*. New York: Russell Sage Foundation.

Lloyd, C. (1986) *Response to SNOP*. Cambridge: Institute of Criminology.

—— (1992) *Bail Information Schemes: Practice and Effect*. Research and Planning Unit Paper 69. London: Home Office.

Lloyd, C., Mair, G. and Hough, M. (1994) *Explaining Reconviction Rates: A Critical Analysis*. Home Office Research Study 136. London: HMSO.

Lord Chancellor's Department (1947) *Final Report of the Committee on Procedure in Matrimonial Causes*. London: HMSO.

McClintock, F.H. and Avison, N.H. (1968) *Crime in England and Wales*. London: Heinemann.

McConville, S. (1981) *A History of English Prison Administration, Vol. 1: 1750–1877*. London: Routledge and Kegan Paul.

—— (1995) 'The Victorian Prison: England 1865–1965', in N. Morris and D.J. Rothman (eds) *The Oxford History of the Prison: The Practice of Punishment in Western Society*. New York: Oxford University Press.

McIvor, G. and McNeill, F. (2007) 'Probation in Scotland: past, present and future', in L. Gelsthorpe and R. Morgan (eds) *Handbook of Probation*. Cullompton: Willan.

MacKenzie, D. (1979) 'Eugenics and the rise of mathematical statistics in Britain', in J. Irvine, I. Miles and J. Evans (eds) *Demystifying Social Statistics*. London: Pluto Press.

McKnight, J. (2009) 'Speaking up for probation', *Howard Journal* 48(4): 327–43.

Macrae, F.J. (1958) 'The English probation training system', *British Journal of Delinquency* 8(3): 210–15.

McWilliams, W. (1983) 'The mission to the English police courts 1876–1936', *Howard Journal* 23(3): 129–47.

—— (1985) 'The mission transformed: professionalism of probation between the wars', *Howard Journal* 24(4): 257–74.

—— (1986) 'The English probation system and the diagnostic ideal', *Howard Journal* 25(4): 241–60.

—— (1987) 'Probation, pragmatism and policy', *Howard Journal* 26(2): 97–121.

—— (1992) 'The rise and development of management thought in the English probation system', in R. Statham and P. Whitehead (eds) *Managing the Probation Service: Issues for the 1990s*. Harlow: Longman.

Maguire, M. (2004) 'The crime reduction programme in England and Wales: reflections on the vision and the reality', *Criminal Justice* 4(3): 213–37.

Maguire, M., Grubin, D., Losel, F. and Raynor, P. (2010) 'What Works and the Correctional Services Accreditation Panel: taking stock from an inside perspective', *Criminology and Criminal Justice* 10(1): 37–58.

Mair, G. (1988) *Probation Day Centres*. Home Office Research Study 100. London: HMSO.

—— (ed.) (1989) *Risk Prediction and Probation: Papers from a Research and Planning Unit Workshop*. Research and Planning Unit Paper 56. London: Home Office.

—— (1991) *Part Time Punishment? The Origins and Development of Senior Attendance Centres*. London: HMSO.

—— (1995a) 'Evaluating the impact of community penalties', *University of Chicago Roundtable* 2(2): 455–74.

—— (1995b) 'Specialist activities in probation: "confusion worse confounded"', in L. Noaks, M. Levi and M. Maguire (eds) *Contemporary Issues in Criminology*. Cardiff: University of Wales Press.

—— (1997) 'Evaluating intensive probation', in G. Mair (ed.) *Evaluating the Effectiveness of Community Penalties*. Aldershot: Avebury.

—— (2000) 'Credible accreditation?', *Probation Journal* 47(4): 268–71.

—— (2001) 'Technology and the future of community penalties', in A. Bottoms, L. Gelsthorpe and S. Rex (eds) *Community Penalties: Change and Challenges*. Cullompton: Willan.

—— (2004a) 'The origins of What Works in England and Wales: a house built on sand?', in G. Mair (ed.) *What Matters in Probation*. Cullompton: Willan.

—— (2004b) 'What Works: a view from the chiefs', in G. Mair (ed.) *What Matters in Probation*. Cullompton: Willan.

—— (2008) 'Research on Community Penalties', in R.D. King and E. Wincup (eds) *Doing Research on Crime and Justice*, 2nd edn. Oxford: Oxford University Press.

—— (2009) 'Community Sentences', in A. Hucklesby and A. Wahidin (eds) *Criminal Justice*. Oxford: Oxford University Press.

Mair, G. and Lloyd, C. (1996) 'Policy and progress in the development of bail schemes in England and Wales', in F. Paterson (ed.) *Understanding Bail in Britain*. Edinburgh: HMSO.

Mair, G. and May, C. (1995) *Practitioners' Views of the Criminal Justice Act: A Survey of Criminal Justice Agencies*. Research and Planning Unit Paper 91. London: Home Office.

Mair, G. and Mills, H. (2009) *The Community Order and the Suspended Sentence Order Three Years On: The Views and Experiences of Probation Officers and Offenders*. London: Centre for Crime and Justice Studies.

Mair, G. and Mortimer, E. (1996) *Curfew Orders with Electronic Monitoring*. Home Office Research Study 163. London: Home Office.

Mair, G. and Nee, C. (1990) *Electronic Monitoring: The Trials and their Results*. Home Office Research Study 120. London: HMSO.

Mair, G., Lloyd, C., Nee, C. and Sibbitt, R. (1994) *Intensive Probation in England and Wales: An Evaluation*. Home Office Research Study 133. London: HMSO.

Mair, G., Burke, L. and Taylor, S. (2006) '"The worst tax form you've ever seen?" Probation officers' views about OASys', *Probation Journal* 53(1): 7–23.

Mair, G., Cross, N. and Taylor, S. (2007) *The Use and Impact of the Community Order and the Suspended Sentence Order*. London: Centre for Crime and Justice Studies.

Mair, G., Cross, N. and Taylor, S. (2008) *The Community Order and the Suspended Sentence Order: The Views and Attitudes of Sentencers*. London: Centre for Crime and Justice Studies.

Major, J. (1999) *The Autobiography*. London: HarperCollins.

Mannheim, H. (1955) *Group Problems in Crime and Punishment and Other Studies in Criminology and Criminal Law*. London: Routledge and Kegan Paul.

Mannheim, H. and Wilkins, L. (1955) *Prediction Methods in Relation to Borstal Training*. London: HMSO.

Marquand, D. (2004) *The Decline of the Public: The Hollowing-Out of Citizenship*. Cambridge: Polity Press.

Marr, A. (2007) *A History of Modern Britain*. London: Macmillan.

Martinson, R. (1974) 'What Works? Questions and answers about prison reform', *The Public Interest* 35: 22–54.

—— (1979) 'New findings, new views: a note of caution regarding sentencing reform', *Hofstra Law Review* 7(2): 243–58.

Maruna, S. and King, A. (2004) 'Public opinion and community penalties', in A. Bottoms, S. Rex and G. Robinson (eds) *Alternatives to Prison: Options for an Insecure Society*. Cullompton: Willan.

Marwick, A. (1982) *British Society since 1945*. Harmondsworth: Penguin.

—— (1998) *The Sixties: Cultural Revolution in Britain, France, Italy and the United States, c.1958–1974*. Oxford: Oxford University Press.

May, C. (1995) *Measuring the Satisfaction of Courts with the Probation Service*. Home Office Research Study 144. London: Home Office.

Mayhew, H. (1851) *London Labour and the London Poor,* 3 vols. London.

—— (1862) *The Criminal Prisons of London*. London.

Merrington, S. and Stanley, S. (2004) 'What Works? Revisiting the evidence in England and Wales', *Probation Journal* 51(1): 7–20.

Miller, M. and Buchanan, J. (1995) 'Probation: a crisis of identity and purpose', *Probation Journal* 42(4): 195–8.

Mills, H., Silvestri, A. and Grimshaw, R. with Silberhorn-Armantrading, F. (2010) *Prison and Probation Expenditure 1999–2009*. London: Centre for Crime and Justice Studies.

Ministry of Health/Scottish Home and Health Department (1965) *Drug Addiction: The Second Report of the Interdepartmental Committee on Drug Addiction*. London: HMSO.

Ministry of Justice (2007a) *Penal Policy: A Background Paper*. London: Ministry of Justice.

—— (2007b) *Justice: A New Approach*. London: Ministry of Justice.

—— (2008a) *Prison Policy Update: Briefing Paper*. London: Ministry of Justice.

—— (2008b) *Government's Response to the Justice Select Committee's Report: Towards Effective Sentencing*. London: The Stationery Office.

—— (2009a) *Capacity and Competition Policy for Prisons and Probation*. London: Ministry of Justice.

—— (2009b) *Probation Qualifications Framework Review*. London: Ministry of Justice.

—— (2010) *Breaking the Cycle: Effective Punishment, Rehabilitation and Sentencing of Offenders*. London: The Stationery Office.

Minn, W.G. (1948) 'Training for the work of a probation officer in England and Wales', *Journal of Criminal Science* 1: 165–72.

Morgan, R. (2002) 'Foreword', in HM Inspectorate of Probation, *Annual Report 2001–2002*. London: Home Office.

—— (2003) 'Thinking about the demand for probation services', *Probation Journal* 50(1): 7–19.

—— (2007) 'Probation, governance and accountability', in L. Gelsthorpe and R. Morgan (eds) *Handbook of Probation*. Cullompton: Willan.

Morrison, W.D. (1896) *Juvenile Offenders*. London: T. Fisher Unwin.

Mortimer, E. and Mair, G. (1996) 'Integrating community sentences: results from the Green Paper sentencing exercises'. Unpublished report to the Home Office.

Moxon, D., Sutton, M. and Hedderman, C. (1990) *Unit Fines: Experiments in Four Courts*. Research and Planning Unit Paper 59. London: Home Office.

Murch, M. (1969) 'Seebohm: a painful dilemma for probation', *Probation Journal* 15(1): 18–23.

NACRO (1989) *The Real Alternative: Strategies to Promote Community Based Penalties*. London: NACRO.

Napo (1965) 'The child, the family and the young offender: observations by the National Association of Probation Officers', *Probation* 11(3): 83–91.

—— (1966) 'Local authority and allied personal social services', *Probation* 12(3): 102–10.

—— (2004) 'NOMS organisational design: a risk too far'. *Napo News* Issue 161 (July/August).

—— (2007) *Changing Lives: An Oral History of Probation*. London: Napo.

—— (2007/8) 'Ministry of Justice faces massive cuts'. *Napo News* Issue 195 (December/January).

—— (2008/9) 'Probation meltdown and crime crisis'. *Napo News* Issue 205 (December/January).

—— (2009/10a) 'Only 24% direct contact time – it's official'. *Napo News* Issue 215 (December/January).

—— (2009/10b) 'Probation budget cut falls to 4%'. *Napo News* Issue 215 (December/January).

National Audit Office (1989) *Home Office: Control and Management of Probation Services in England and Wales*. London: HMSO.

—— (2008) *National Probation Service: The Supervision of Community Orders in England and Wales*. London: The Stationery Office.

National Probation Service (2002) *Performance Report 4 Year Ending 2001/2*. London: NPS.

—— (2004) *Performance Report 12 and Weighted Scorecard 2003/4*. London: NPS.

—— (2007) *A Century of Cutting Crime 1907–2007*. London: NPS.

Nellis, M. (2007) 'Humanising justice: the English probation service up to 1972', in L. Gelsthorpe and R. Morgan (eds) *Handbook of Probation*. Cullompton: Willan.

Newman, J. (2001) *Modernising Governance: New Labour, Policy and Society*. London: Sage.

Newton, G. (1956) 'Trends in probation training', *British Journal of Delinquency* 7(2): 123–35.

Norman, H.E. (1939) 'The Criminal Justice Bill', *Probation* 3(4): 52.

Office for Criminal Justice Reform (2009) *Engaging Communities in Criminal Justice*. London: The Stationery Office.

Oldfield, M. (2002) *From Welfare to Risk: Discourse, Power and Politics in the Probation Service*. Issues in Community and Criminal Justice Monograph 1. London: Napo.

O'Mahony, D. and Chapman, T. (2007) 'Probation, the state and community: delivering probation services in Northern Ireland', in L. Gelsthorpe and R. Morgan (eds) *Handbook of Probation*. Cullompton: Willan.

Page, M. (1974) 'Reflections on the Report', *Probation* 21(4): 107–13.

—— (1992) *Crimefighters of London: A History of the Origins and Development of the London Probation Service 1876–1965*. London: Inner London Probation Service.

Pearson, H. (1929) 'London police court mission', *Probation* 1(2): 21.

Pease, K., Billingham, S. and Earnshaw, I. (1977) *Community Service Assessed in 1976*. Home Office Research Study No. 39. London: HMSO.

Peden, G. (2000) *The Treasury and British Public Policy 1906–1959*. Oxford: Oxford University Press.

Pepler, D. (1915) *Justice and the Child*. London: Constable.

Pinchbeck, I. and Hewitt, M. (1969) *Children in English Society, Vol. 1: From Tudor Times to the Eighteenth Century*. London: Routledge and Kegan Paul.

References 207

—— (1973) *Children in English Society, Vol. 2: From the Nineteenth Century to the Children Act 1948*. London: Routledge and Kegan Paul.
Pointing, J. (ed.) (1986) *Alternatives to Custody*. Oxford: Basil Blackwell.
Radzinowicz, L. (1999) *Adventures in Criminology*. London: Routledge.
Radzinowicz, L. and Hood, R. (1986) *A History of English Criminal Law, Vol. 5: The Emergence of Penal Policy*. London: Stevens & Sons.
Rawlings, P. (1999) *Crime and Power: A History of Criminal Justice 1688–1998*. Harlow: Longman.
Raynor, P. (1985) *Social Work, Justice and Control*. Oxford: Basil Blackwell.
—— (1988) *Probation as an Alternative to Custody*. Aldershot: Avebury.
—— (2002) 'Community penalties: probation, punishment, and What Works', in M. Maguire, R. Morgan and R. Reiner (eds) *The Oxford Handbook of Criminology*, 3rd edn. Oxford: Oxford University Press.
—— (2004) 'The Probation Service "Pathfinders": finding the path and losing the way', *Criminal Justice* 4(3): 309–25.
—— (2007) 'Community penalties: probation, "What Works" and offender management', in M. Maguire, R. Morgan and R. Reiner (eds) *The Oxford Handbook of Criminology*, 4th edn. Oxford: Oxford University Press.
—— (2008) 'Community penalties and research: on the way back to "nothing works"?', *Criminology and Criminal Justice* 8(1): 73–87.
Raynor, P. and Vanstone, M. (2002) *Understanding Community Penalties: Probation, Policy and Social Change*. Buckingham: Open University Press.
Reiner, R. (2000) *The Politics of the Police*, 3rd edn. Oxford: Oxford University Press.
Rex, S., Lieb, R., Bottoms, A. and Wilson, L. (2003) *Accrediting Offender Programmes: A Process-based Evaluation of the Joint Prison/Probation Services Accreditation Panel*. Home Office Research Study 273. London: Home Office.
Reynolds, B.J. (1943) 'Thirty-First National Conference Proceedings', *Probation* 4(5): 53–6.
Roberts, J. (1980) 'Strands in the development of community service: reflections and suggestions', in K. Pease and W. McWilliams (eds) *Community Service by Order*. Edinburgh: Scottish Academic Press.
Robinson, G. (1999) 'Risk management and rehabilitation in the probation service: collision and collusion', *Howard Journal* 38(4): 421–33.
—— (2001) 'Power, knowledge and "What Works" in probation', *Howard Journal* 40(3): 235–54.
—— (2002) 'Exploring risk management in probation practice: contemporary developments in England and Wales', *Punishment and Society* 4(1): 5–25.
Rose, A.G. (1947) 'What kind of probation officers do we need?', *Probation* 5(12): 166–7.
—— (1961) *The Struggle for Penal Reform*. London: Stevens and Sons.
Royal Commission on Marriage and Divorce (1956) *Report 1951–1955*. London: HMSO.
Royal Commission on the Penal System (1967a) *Written Evidence from Government Departments, Miscellaneous Bodies and Individual Witnesses, Vol. 3: Miscellaneous Bodies (Part 2)*. London: HMSO.
—— (1967b) *Minutes of Evidence taken before the Royal Commission*. London: HMSO.
Russell, C.E.B. and Rigby, L. (1906) *The Making of the Criminal*. London: Macmillan and Co.

Rutherford, A. (1984) *Prisons and the Process of Justice*. Oxford: Oxford University Press.

—— (1986) *Growing Out of Crime*. Harmondsworth: Penguin.

St John, J. (1961) *Probation: The Second Chance*. London: Vista Books.

Sandbrook, D. (2006) *Never Had It So Good: A History of Britain from Suez to the Beatles*. London: Abacus.

—— (2007) *White Heat: A History of Britain in the Swinging Sixties*. London: Abacus.

—— (2010) *State of Emergency: The Way We Were: Britain 1970–1974*. London: Allen Lane.

Sander, L.F. (1932) 'Children and Young Persons Bill: an address to the 20th annual conference of the National Association of Probation Officers', *Probation* 1(13): 194–6.

Sanders, H. (1962) 'A turning point: in which direction?', *Probation* 10(2): 21–4.

Scottish Home and Health Department and Scottish Education Department (1964) *Children and Young Persons (Scotland)*. Edinburgh: HMSO.

Senior, P., Crowther-Dowey, C. and Long, M. (2007) *Understanding Modernisation in Criminal Justice*. Maidenhead: Open University Press.

Sentencing Guidelines Council (2004) *New Sentences: Criminal Justice Act 2003 Guideline*. London: Sentencing Guidelines Council.

Shaw, M. (1974) *Social Work in Prison*. Home Office Research Studies 22. London: HMSO.

Silberman, M., Chapman, B., Sinclair, I., Snow, D., and Leissner, A. (1971) *Explorations in After-Care*. Home Office Research Studies 9. London: HMSO.

Simon, F.H. (1971) *Prediction Methods in Criminology*. Home Office Research Studies 7. London: HMSO.

Sinclair, I. (1971) *Hostels for Probationers*. Home Office Research Studies 6. London: HMSO.

Sked, A. and Cook, C. (1984) *Post-War Britain: A Political History*, 2nd edn. Harmondsworth: Penguin.

Smith, D. (2006) 'Making sense of psychoanalysis in criminological theory and probation practice', *Probation Journal* 53(4): 361–76.

—— (2010) *Public Confidence in the Criminal Justice System: Findings from the BCS 2002/03 to 2007/08*. Ministry of Justice Research Series 16/10. London: Ministry of Justice.

Sparks, R.F. (1971) 'The use of suspended sentences', *Criminal Law Review*, July: 384–401.

Stanley, S. and Baginsky, M. (1984) *Alternatives to Prison: An Examination of Non-custodial Sentencing of Offenders*. London: Peter Owen.

Stevenson, J. (1984) *British Society 1914–45*. Harmondsworth: Penguin Books.

Stokes, S. (1950) *Court Circular*. London: Michael Joseph.

Tallerman, M.H. (1933) 'The Policy of NAPO for the New Children Act', *Probation* 1(16): 251–3.

Templewood, Viscount (1954) *Nine Troubled Years*. London: Collins.

Thatcher, M. (1993) *The Downing Street Years*. London: HarperCollins.

Thomas, C. (1978) 'Supervision in the community', *Howard Journal* 17(1): 23–31.

Thornton, D.M. (1987) 'Treatment effects on recidivism', in B.J. McGurk, D.M. Thornton and M. Williams (eds) *Applying Psychology to Imprisonment: Theory and Practice*. London: HMSO.

Todd, M. (1964) *Ever Such a Nice Lady*. London: Victor Gollancz.

Tuckwell, G. (1936) 'Chairman's address to 24th annual conference', *Probation* 2(5): 67–8.

Turnbull, P.J., McSweeney, T., Webster, R., Edmunds, M. and Hough, M. (2000) *Drug Treatment and Testing Orders: Final Evaluation Report.* Home Office Research Study 212. London: Home Office.

Underdown, A. (1995) *Effectiveness of Community Supervision: Performance and Potential.* Manchester: Greater Manchester Probation Service.

—— (1998) *Strategies for Effective Supervision: Report of the HMIP What Works Project.* London: HMIP.

Vanstone, M. (2003) 'A history of the use of groups in probation work, part one: from "clubbing the unclubbables" to therapeutic intervention', *Howard Journal* 42(1): 69–86.

—— (2004a) *Supervising Offenders in the Community: A History of Probation Theory and Practice.* Aldershot: Ashgate.

—— (2004b) 'A history of the use of groups in probation work, part two: from negotiated treatment to evidence-based practice in an accountable service', *Howard Journal* 43(2): 180–202.

Vass, A.A. (1990) *Alternatives to Prison: Punishment, Custody and the Community.* London: Sage.

Vennard, J., Sugg, D. and Hedderman, C. (1997) 'The use of cognitive-behavioural approaches with offenders: messages from research', in C. Hedderman, D. Sugg and J. Vennard *Changing Offenders' Attitudes and Behaviour: What Works?* Home Office Research Study 171. London: Home Office.

Walker, H. and Beaumont, B. (1981) *Probation Work: Critical Theory and Socialist Practice.* Oxford: Basil Blackwell.

Ward, D. and Spencer, J. (1994) 'The future of probation qualifying training', *Probation Journal* 41(2): 95–8.

Wargent, M. (2002) 'The new governance of probation', *Howard Journal* 41(2): 182–200.

Warner, Miss (1929) 'The technique of probation', *Probation* 1(1): 10–12.

Waugh, B. (1873) *The Gaol Cradle: Who Rocks It?* London: Strahan & Co.

Whitehead, P. and Statham, R. (2006) *The History of Probation: Politics, Power and Cultural Change 1876–2005.* Crayford: Shaw and Sons.

Wiener, M.J. (1990) *Reconstructing the Criminal: Culture, Law and Policy in England, 1830–1914.* Cambridge: Cambridge University Press.

Wilkins, L.T. (1958) 'A small comparative study of the results of probation', *British Journal of Delinquency* 8(3): 201–9.

Windlesham, Lord (1993) *Responses to Crime, Vol. 2: Penal Policy in the Making.* Oxford: Clarendon Press.

Wootton, B. (1978) *Crime and Penal Policy: Reflections on Fifty Years Experience.* London: Allen and Unwin.

Worrall, A. and Hoy, C. (2005) *Punishment in the Community: Managing Offenders, Making Choices*, 2nd edn. Cullompton: Willan.

Young, P. (1976) 'A sociological analysis of the early history of probation', *British Journal of Law and Society* 3: 44–58.

Young, W. (1979) *Community Service Orders: The Development and Use of a New Penal Measure.* London: Heinemann.

Younger, Sir K. (1974) 'Introducing the Report', *Probation* 21(4): 98–9.

Index

Note: Page numbers in **bold** indicate tables

juvenile courts **40**, **51**, 64, 96, 101, 114
Juvenile Offenders 19
juvenile offenders *see* young offenders
Juvenile Offenders Act 1847 14

Kent Control Unit 135
key performance indicators 154
Kilbrandon Committee 194
King, Joan 117, 133
Kynaston, David 2, 84

Labour Party 106–7, 113, 127, 153–4, 163, 179
Lawbreaker, The 66
Leeson, Cecil 39–41
Liberal Party 24, 127, 185, 191
Lipsey, Mark 161
local control 27, 47, 49, 80, 139, 182–3
London Police Court Mission 52
Longford Report 113

McWilliams, William 3, 70–1, 71–2, 135
magistrates 91, 158
magistrates' courts **82**, **103**, 114–15, 125, 129
Making Punishment Work 169–70
management *see* central control; local control; organisational structure
Mannheim, Hermann 95–6
Marine Society 12
marriage guidance *see* matrimonial work
Martinson, Robert 119–20, 126, 132–3
Marwick, Arthur 106
Massachusetts example 18–20
matrimonial work 91–3, 102, 109, 125
Maxwell Committee 93–4, 112
May Committee 132
Mayhew, Henry 10
media 186
mental health 78, 82, 99, 119
mentally disordered offenders 146
missionaries 31–2, 35, 36, 41–2, 71, 193; *see also* Church of England Temperance Society
missionary work 21, 31–2, 47, 72, 74, 85; *see also* Church of England Temperance Society
modernisation 187–8
Money Payments (Justice Procedure) Act 1935 68
money payment supervision orders 109
Morgan, Rod 167, 172
Morison Reports 107–13, 126
Morrison, W.D. 16, 19

Multi-Agency Public Protection Panels (MAPPPs) 165–6
multi-agency working 142, 154, 165–6, 169, 185

NAPO Members' Action Group (NMAG) 136
National Association of Discharged Prisoners' Aid Societies (NADPAS) 93, 105, 194
National Association of Probation Officers (NAPO) 38, 42, 58–9, 71, 104, 173
National Audit Office (NAO) 148, 176
National Institute of Industrial Psychology 87
National Offender Management Service (NOMS) 1, 173, 176
National Probation Service (NPS) 1, 110,164–5, 159–67; *see also* central control
National Standards 141–2
needs assessments 155, 169
net widening 130
New Choreography, A 166

Offender Assessment System (OASys) 9, 169
Offender Group Reconviction Scale (OFRS) 9, 145, 155
Offender Management Act 2007 175
Offender Management Bill 2006 1
offenders: classification of 6, 9, 12–13; relationship with probation officer 89–90, 179, 179–80
organisational structure 182; *see also* central control; local control; organisation of probation work; structural change
organisation of probation work 36–8; *see also* central control; local control; structural change
overcrowding of prisons 116, 121, 125–6, 132, 176, 178; *see also* prison population

Page, Martin 3–4
parole 117, 118
partnership working 142, 154, 165–6, 169, 185
Pathfinder programmes 162, 167–8
payment by result 166–7
payment of probation officers 26–7, 35, 38, 54, 115; Departmental Committee on